THE RECKONING

THE
RECKONING

FINANCIAL ACCOUNTABILITY
and the RISE *and* FALL *of* NATIONS

JACOB SOLL

BASIC BOOKS
A Member of the Perseus Books Group
New York

Copyright © 2014 Jacob Soll
Published by Basic Books,
A Member of the Perseus Books Group

Books published by Basic Books are available at special discounts for bulk purchases
in the United States by corporations, institutions, and other organizations. For
more information, please contact the Special Markets Department at the Perseus
Books Group, 2300 Chestnut Street, Suite 200, Philadelphia, PA 19103, or call
(800) 810-4145, ext. 5000, or e-mail special.markets@perseusbooks.com.

Designed by Jack Lenzo

A CIP catalog record for this book is available from the Library of Congress.
ISBN: 978-0-465-03152-8
ISBN (e-book): 978-0-465-03663-9

10 9 8 7 6 5 4 3 2 1

I credit this book to Margaret Jacob

Contents

INTRODUCTION

In September 2008, just as I was finishing a book about the French King Louis XIV's famed finance minister, Jean-Baptiste Colbert, I found something remarkable: Colbert commissioned miniature golden calligraphy account books for the Sun King to carry in his coat pockets. Twice a year, starting in 1661, Louis XIV would receive these new accounts of his expenditures, his revenues, and his assets. It was the first time a monarch of his stature had taken such an interest in accounting. Here, then, it seemed, was a starting point of modern politics and accountability: a king who carried his accounts so that at all moments he might have some reckoning of his kingdom.

I was at least as startled to learn next just how short-lived this experiment was. For as soon as Colbert died, in 1683, Louis—consistently in the red due to his predilection for costly wars and palaces like Versailles—discontinued the account books. Rather than tools of administrative success, Louis came to see his account books as illustrations of his failings as a king. He had created a system of accounting and accountability, and now he began breaking up the central administration of his kingdom. This made it impossible to unify the accounts of each ministry into one clear, central register, as Colbert had done, and for any minister to effectively critique, let alone understand, the king's financial management. If good accounting meant facing the truth when the news was bad, Louis, it seemed, now preferred ignorance. Speaking those famous words, "l'État c'est moi," he apparently really meant it. No longer would a functioning state interfere with his personal will.

On his deathbed in 1715, Louis admitted that he had in effect bankrupted France with his spending.

Rather than some relic of a bygone age, the story of Louis's rise and decline seemed to me all too familiar as I digested the parable of the Sun King's golden notebooks. That very week in September, a startling parallel story was taking place during the collapse of Lehman Brothers Bank. A monument of American and world capitalism, Lehman was suddenly exposed now as little more than a mirage. Just as Louis had held onto his power through snuffing out good accounting in his government, so U.S. investment banks had made untold riches, even as they destroyed their own institutions by cooking their books through trading overvalued bundles of worthless subprime mortgages and credit default swaps. A financial system, which had been deemed healthy by accountants and regulators alike, now revealed itself as dysfunctional by design.

If Louis preferred not to know, so, too, it seemed, Wall Street and its regulators had chosen to overlook the rot threatening the entire financial system. The chairman of the New York Federal Reserve, Timothy Geithner, was supposed to have at least an expert knowledge of the financial markets, yet he appeared not to know, or know fully, what was going on just blocks from his office. The Securities and Exchange Commission (SEC)—whose responsibility it is to enforce good corporate accounting—was caught similarly unaware, as were the Big Four accounting firms—Deloitte, Ernst & Young, KPMG, and PricewaterhouseCoopers. No one, it seemed, had effectively audited the bank's books. They missed the barely hidden fact that Lehman Brothers used accounting fraud to manipulate its accounts and appear solvent.[1]

Soon after Lehman Brothers collapsed in September 2008, other American investment banks began failing, and the world financial system was threatened with collapse. In October, the Bush administration stepped in to bail out the banks and buoy the financial system. Thus came to pass the Troubled Asset Relief Program (TARP), which gave massive funds to troubled banks and put the American capitalist economy on a government life support system. By 2009, Barack Obama was president, promoting Geithner to Secretary of the Treasury. Yet, in spite of Obama's claims of a new age of accountability, a sense of impunity pervaded Wall Street. The $350 billion recapitalization of American banks managed to stave off the financial chaos that risked consuming the world economy. Yet, no strings were attached to the money. No audits were ever made to see how the banks spent it. America's economy stumbled, but the bankers, at least, had avoided a reckoning.

Six years later, it is not just banks that are threatened by financial crisis brought on by bad bookkeeping. Leading nations—the United States, European countries, and China—find themselves facing their own larger potential crises of accounting and accountability. From opaque banks and the sovereign debts of Greece, Portugal, Spain, and Italy, to the financing of municipalities worldwide, there seems little certainty in balance sheets and reports on debt levels and pension obligations. Confidence in private auditors and public regulators also lags. At the very moment we most need careful audits to assess balance sheets, the SEC remains woefully underfunded, and government regulation has limited the capacity of the Big Four accounting firms to aggressively audit corporations.

There has been little to no outcry over dangerously feeble financial accountability, private and public alike. One hears complaints about the impunity of banks, on one hand, or some version of indignation over perceived government interference with the freedom of Wall Street, on the other. Yet there has been no serious discussion about what exactly financial accountability is, how it works, where it comes from, and why modern societies find themselves mired in crises of not only financial but also political accountability, as governments and citizens seem either unable or unwilling to hold corporations and themselves accountable.

The Reckoning steps into this breach, looking back seven hundred years into the history of financial accountability, to understand why it is so hard to achieve. Accounting is at the basis of building businesses, states, and empires. It has helped leaders craft their policies and measure their power. However, when practiced poorly or neglected, accounting has contributed to cycles of destruction, as we saw all too clearly in the 2008 financial crisis. From Renaissance Italy, the Spanish Empire, and Louis XIV's France to the Dutch Republic, the British Empire, and the early United States, effective accounting and political accountability have made the difference between a society's rise and fall. Over and over again, good accounting practices have produced the levels of trust necessary to found stable governments and vital capitalist societies, and poor accounting and its attendant lack of accountability have led to financial chaos, economic crimes, civil unrest, and worse. All this is every bit as true in our own day of multitrillion-dollar debts and massive financial scandals as it was in the Florence of the Medici, Holland's Golden Age, the heyday of the British Empire, and, of course, 1929 on Wall Street. Capitalism and government, it seems, have flourished without massive crises only during distinct and even limited periods of time when financial accountability functions. People have known how to do good accounting for nearly a millennium, but many financial institutions and regimes have just chosen not to do it. Those societies that have succeeded are not only those rich in accounting and commercial culture but also the ones that have worked to build a sound moral and cultural framework to manage the fact that humans have a regular habit of ignoring, falsifying, and failing in accounting. This book examines why a lesson so simple has so rarely been learned.

The first successful capitalist societies developed systems of accounting and corresponding financial and political accountability. In 1340, the Republic of Genoa kept a large register in the central government office. It recorded the city-state's finances through double-entry bookkeeping. Accounting brought with it a fundamentally different way of thinking about political legitimacy: Balanced books equaled not just good business but also good government. At any moment, the maritime republic knew the state of its finances and could even make plans for future difficulties. The Genoese, Venetians, Florentines, and other merchant republics, or at least their ruling classes, could expect a certain level of accountability. This was the beginning of modern government as we ideally imagine it: semirational, well ordered, and generally accountable.[2]

And yet, as successful as they were, accountable societies and governments proved to be difficult to maintain. In the sixteenth century, with the decline of the Italian republics and the rise of the great monarchies, the interest in accounting faded. Even as merchants became ever more familiar with the practice of double-entry accounting, it all but disappeared as a political administrative tool outside Switzerland and Holland, bastions of republicanism in a world of monarchies. At the height of the Renaissance and the scientific revolution that emerged from it, between 1480 and 1700, kings did take an interest in accounting. King Edward VII of England, King Philip II of Spain, Elizabeth I, the great Austrian emperors, Louis XIV, and the German, Swedish, and Portuguese kings examined accounts and kept treasurers and account books. Yet none managed or ultimately desired to create the kind of stable, centralized, double-entry state accounting system so carefully controlled by the fourteenth-century Genoese and other northern Italian republics. Indeed, keeping good state ledgers implied that the king answered to the logic of balanced books. Much as they tried to reform their administrations, monarchs, in the end, saw themselves as accountable to God, not to bookkeepers. This inherent conflict between monarchy and financial accountability helped cause centuries of European financial crisis.

Monarchs considered transparent accounting practices dangerous, and, indeed, they could be. In 1781, eight years before the French Revolution, Louis XVI's finance minister, the comte de Vergennes, found his country crippled by debt from the American War of Independence. These debts, he warned, could never be revealed, however, for publicly exposing royal accounts would surely undermine that most critical religion of monarchy: secrecy. In the end, Vergennes knew little about finance—France was, in fact, nearly bankrupt by this point—but he was right about monarchy. Opening up the books opened the floodgates of accountability. When royal accounts and the depth of the crown's financial difficulties were discussed publicly for the first time during political debates in the 1780s, Louis XVI lost part of his regal mystery. For this, and a host of related reasons, he would later lose his head.

Yet even with the emergence of nominally open, elected governments in the nineteenth century, accountability was still often unattainable. During the nineteenth century, as England ruled its empire and was the center of world finance, corruption and unaccountability plagued its financial administration. As nineteenth-century America carefully designed mechanisms of financial accountability, it, too, was mired in the massive financial accounting frauds, scandals, and crises of the robber barons of the Gilded Age. There has never been a perfect model of a constantly accountable state. Financial accountability—both corporate and governmental—still remains elusive even in democratic societies.

Threatened by ongoing financial crisis, as we are just now, it seems altogether timely to examine the history of financial accountability. Oddly, few historians have elected do so. They have examined the financial history of nations while barely acknowledging the central role of accounting and accountability in the rise and fall of great nations. It would seem natural to place double-entry accounting—a true Western invention—at the center of European and American economic history. The study of accounting and accountability allows us to understand how institutions and societies succeed and fail at their most basic levels. We recognize that the Medici Bank, the Dutch dominance of commerce, and the British Empire were successes, yet, of course, they no longer exist. So if each one of these institutions knew massive success, it also knew great decline and fall, and accounting was central to each of these stories. Seen through the lens of the history of financial accountability, then, the history of capitalism is neither simply a history of ascent nor a cycle of booms and busts. Rather, capitalism and modern government have an inherent weakness: At crucial moments, accounting and the mechanics of accountability break down, adding to financial and political crises, if not creating them. The success of a society, at least financially, is, in great part, the mastery of accounting, accountability, and the ensuing struggle to successfully manage them.

Without double-entry accounting, neither modern capitalism nor the modern state could exist, for it is the essential tool in calculating profit and loss, the basis of financial management. Double entry emerged in Tuscany and northern Italy sometime around 1300. Until then, the great ancient and medieval societies persisted without it. Indeed, the advent of double-entry accounting marks the beginning of the history of capitalism and modern politics. So what exactly is double-entry accounting? Single-entry accounting, like balancing a checkbook, tallies only what goes in and out of a single account. Double-entry accounting, by contrast, is a method of exacting control and accurately calculating profit, loss, and the value of assets. It separates credits from debits with a vertical line down the center of the page. For every credit that comes into an account, there must be a debit. One puts income and expenditures into each column and adds them up. Credits must equal debits. For example, each time a goat is sold, the profit goes on the left, and the merchandise sold goes on the right. Then a tally of profit or loss is calculated, or balanced on the spot. Once the balance has been tallied, the transaction is over, and both sides have a line drawn through them. Profit and loss are known at all times.[3]

Double-entry bookkeeping for capitalism can also be understood with what accountants call the fundamental accounting equation: The assets controlled by an organization are always exactly equal to the claims on those assets held by its creditors and owners. This allows businesses and governments to track their assets and obligations, while preventing and deterring theft. These measures of performance—wealth and income and, above all, profit—make double-entry accounting a tool for financial planning, management, and accountability.[4]

The founders of modern economic thought—from Adam Smith to Karl Marx—saw double-entry accounting as essential to the development of successful economies and modern capitalism. In 1923, the pioneering German sociologist and theorist of capitalism Max Weber wrote that the modern firm is bound with accounting, "which determines its income yielding power by calculation according to the methods of modern bookkeeping and striking a balance." Weber saw accounting as one of many cultural elements necessary to the growth of complex capitalism, placing it squarely among the fundamental traits of the Protestant work ethic that he believed allowed early Americans to master capitalist culture.[5]

Even blunter was the influential German economist Werner Sombart: "One cannot imagine what capitalism would be without double-entry bookkeeping: the two phenomena are connected as intimately as form and contents." The Austrian American economist, political scientist, and coiner of the term "creative destruction," Joseph Schumpeter, not only saw accounting as central to capitalism but also lamented that economists had not devoted more attention to it; it was only through a historical understanding of accounting practices, he wrote, that effective economic theory could be formulated.[6]

These thinkers saw accounting as an ingredient to economic success and a key to understanding economic history. What they did not see, however, is how political stability is grounded in cultures of accountability, which rely on double-entry accounting systems. Double entry mattered not only for calculating profit but also because it brought with it a central concept of the balanced book, which could be used to judge and hold accountable a political administration. In medieval Italy, not only did balanced books mirror the divine aspect of God's judgment and a tally of sins but also they came to represent sound business and good government. Of course, it is one thing to have a set of values; the challenge is to uphold them, and maintaining financial accountability was and is a constant struggle. What this book shows is that financial accountability functioned better when accounting was seen not simply as part of a financial transaction but also as part of a moral and cultural framework. From the Middle Ages to the early twentieth century, those societies that managed to harness accounting and long-term traditions of financial accountability and trust did so by full cultural engagement: Republican Italian city-states like Florence and Genoa, Golden Age Holland, and eighteenth- and nineteenth-century Britain and America all integrated accounting into their educational curriculum, religious and moral thought, art, philosophy, and political theory. Accounting became the subject of theological and political works, great paintings, social and scientific theories, and novels, from Dante and the Dutch Masters to Auguste Comte, Thomas Malthus, Charles Dickens, Charles Darwin, Henry David Thoreau, Louisa May Alcott, and Max Weber. In a virtuous circle, the elevation of practical, business-minded mathematics into the spheres of high and humane thinking allowed these societies not only to maximize their use of accounting but also to build complex cultures of accountability and awareness of the difficulties posed by such a culture. With this culture of accountability came capitalism and representative government.

The delicate interplay between accounting and accountability can decide the fate of a company or, indeed, a nation. Financial history, therefore, is not only about cyclical crises or trends in numbers. It is also a story about individuals and societies that become adept at mastering the interplay between accounting and cultural life, yet often lose this capacity and find themselves in unexpected, avoidable, and sometimes cataclysmic financial crises. In this long history, accounting and financial accountability emerge as both mundane and, at the same time, difficult to control. What is remarkable is that the basic lessons of medieval Italian accounting—that it is essential to wealth and political stability but incredibly difficult, frail, and even perilous—are still as pertinent today as they were seven hundred years ago.

CHAPTER 1

A SHORT HISTORY OF EARLY ACCOUNTING, POLITICS, AND ACCOUNTABILITY

[The Domesday Book's] decisions, like those of the Last Judgment, are unalterable.

RICHARD FITZNIGEL, BISHOP OF ELY, 1179

The Emperor Augustus is famous today for his buildings and his statues and as the rather overly modest and fatherly character found in ancient histories and Robert Graves's novel *I Claudius*. He claimed to have found Rome a city of bricks and left it a sparkling city of marble. But the key to Augustus's power can be found in his own account of his reign, the *Res gestae divi Augusti,* "The Great Deeds of the Divine Augustus" (circa CE 14). In it, he describes buildings, armies, and feats. He also includes a lot of numbers. Indeed, he measured his own success by them, bragging that he had paid victorious Roman soldiers 170 million sesterces from his own coffers. Financial numbers, the symbols of Augustus's great achievements, were taken from entries in rudimentary account books. The true founder of the Julio-Claudian dynasty and father of the Roman Empire linked accounting and the transparency of numbers with political legitimacy and achievement.[1]

As is typical in the history of accounting, no one noticed. Augustus the imperial accountant is not a story anyone tells. And of all those princes and kings who followed and emulated the father of the Roman Empire, none ever copied the exact form of the *Res gestae*. Even had they known or understood the numbers from their accounts, few would have published them as measures of their royal potency.

Augustus came from a world in which accounts were accessible and even prevalent and in which a man with Augustus's Roman education as a *pater familias* and patrician felt no shame in showing he knew how to use them. Yet in spite of Augustus's use of accounting as a tool of management and legitimation, it would take around 1,700 years for leaders to legitimate their political power and actions through the publication of financial numbers from account books. What seemed good practice to Augustus and is now standard practice took more than a millennium to take hold. Accounting developed slowly in ancient Mesopotamia, Greece, and Rome until medieval Italians transformed it into double-entry bookkeeping, a powerful tool of profit for capitalist enterprise and government administration.

For thousands of years, the ancient world was steeped in accounts, but there was almost no innovation, and few used the tools at their disposal as Augustus did. Single-entry accounting existed in ancient Mesopotamia, Israel, Egypt, China, Greece, and Rome. The Greeks, Ptolemaic Egyptians, and Arabs reached marvelous heights of civilization and mastered numbers for geometry and astronomy, but they did not manage to create double-entry accounting, so essential for the exact calculation of profit and loss.[2]

Ancient finance was limited to stores accounting, that is, basic inventorying. Max Weber believed that this was due to a separation of business from the home and the lack of a concept of profit and of valuing the total assets of an enterprise over a period, for example, of a year. Yet despite the lack of a modern understanding of capital and profit, a culture and mind-set of accounting did have a prominent place in ancient public life.[3]

In any place where records were kept, tallies, or rudimentary accounts, were made. In Mesopotamia, contracts and warehouse and trade records all made general tallies of accounts, often of the inventory of bakeries. Accounting was for inventorying but also for calculating surpluses of grain, the very dust of civilization that brought with it sedentary villages, farming, and markets. The Sumerians created clay tokens for accounting in 3500 BCE to represent goods shipped or received. Tokens soon gave way to flat clay tablets of written basic inventory accounts, which are common among Assyrian and Sumerian artifacts. The Babylonian legal Code of Hammurabi (circa 1772 BCE) is famous not only for its "eye for an eye, tooth for a tooth" regulation (accounting in its most rudimentary form) but also for basic accounting rules and state auditing regulations for mercantile transactions. Law 105 stipulates that any agent who has not sealed and signed off on the reception of money may not record the transaction in his account book. The state kept an inventory of its currency holdings, which scribes wrote down in the House of Silver of the Treasury, and even kept track of grain and bread stores through basic accounts of inventory.[4]

Once the state became involved in accounting and auditing, numbers and morals mixed with politics. In ancient Athens, accounting was seen as connected to political accountability. From the beginning, a complex system of bookkeeping and public auditing was at the heart of democratic government. The Athenian treasury was considered sacred and kept at Delos under the watchful eyes of its treasurers. Humble citizens and slaves were educated and employed as bookkeepers. For the most part, Athenians preferred public slaves as comptrollers and auditors because they could be tortured on the rack and freemen could not. There were higher officers and book checkers who oversaw public accounts. In contrast to oligarchies—in which the powerful few ruled and there were no systems of financial accountability—democratic Athens had systems of accountability. The accounts of all Athenian public officers were subject to audits in accordance with basic democratic political philosophy. Even members of the senatorial Areopagus (the high court of appeals), as well as priests and priestesses, had to make a full accounting of funds, not just of the accounts of their official business but also of gifts. No citizen of Athens could go abroad, consecrate property to a god, or make a will without a full public reckoning to the state before doing so. The *logistae*—the public accounting officers described by Aristotle in the last book of his study of the Athenian Constitution—audited the books of public officers and city magistrates. Before hearing any case of corruption, these accounting officers made a public audit of the books of the officer in question.[5]

Yet even with this system of account keeping and political accountability, corruption was rife, and Athenians struggled with the concept of accountability. The revered general and statesman Aristides (530–468 BCE) complained that it was considered bad form for *logistae* to make strict audits. A certain level of fraud was expected and tolerated, with aggressive audits seen as threatening the status quo. The historian Polybius noted that even if the state had ten auditors and as many official seals and public witnesses, it still could not ensure someone's honesty. The clever, he implied, could always cook their books.[6]

Honest or not, accounting flourished as the basis of Roman home economics. Aristotle had a concept for the management of public finances, a house or property, which he called *Oikonomia*, the root of the term "economics." *Oikonomia* did not mean financial management with an eye to profit in the modern sense of economics, but rather good stewardship of government and households. The Romans adopted Aristotle's concept, and there accounting began in private homes, where the *pater familias* was charged by the state to keep household books, which could be audited by tax collectors. The head of the household kept a waste book (a daily diary of all receipts), which he would, every month, enter into a register of income and expenditures, often recording future income as well as outstanding loans and debts. Bankers kept the same basic single-entry books. Bankers and sometimes citizens would have to balance their books for audits by a praetor, a city or provincial magistrate.[7]

The Roman Republic and early Roman Empire were managed by a group of auditors called the *quaestores oerarii*, oversight officers of the public coffers. In his *Natural History*, Pliny states that in 49 BCE, the year Caesar crossed the Rubicon, the Roman treasury contained 17,410 pounds of gold, 22,070 pounds of silver, and in coin, 6,135,400 sesterces. Accountants in the treasury communicated with the accountants at the mint and their assistants to ensure that there was enough currency to pay state and most military expenditures.[8]

The quaestors of Rome kept the keys to the public treasury in the Temple of Saturn, now the oldest holy site in Rome, which also contained the tablets of Roman law. Scribes within the treasury also kept monthly registers of incoming and outgoing cash, with the names, dates, and types of each transaction. There were separate registers for debts and for current accounts of the military and provincial quaestors. The central accounting office—the *tabularium*—was overseen by a superintendent and staffed by overseers, scribes, accountants, and cashiers.[9]

As in Athens, state accounting in Rome was haphazard, and fraud was common. In his *Philippics* (44–43 BCE), Cicero complained of bad accounts in his attacks on Mark Antony, known for his debts and shady financial dealings. He claimed Mark Antony had kept bad account books and, in doing so, had "squandered a countless sum of moneys" stolen from Caesar and even forged accounts and signatures. Although Cicero denounced bad books, Vice Consul Mark Antony did not go to jail. Returning to power later that year as part of a triumvirate with Lepidus and Octavius, the future Emperor Augustus, Mark Antony hunted down Cicero and had his head and hands chopped off and displayed in the Forum. This grimly illustrates a constant maxim: The powerful don't respond well to those who call for their books to be opened.[10]

Yet bad accounting has a way of coming back to haunt those who practice it. Augustus in turn killed Marc Antony (whose military organizational skills matched his bookkeeping), took power, became emperor, and brought order to the chaotic empire and to what were now imperial account books. Unlike his rival, Augustus kept good account books—his *rationarium*. Indeed, the Roman historian Tacitus claims that Augustus kept them in his own hand, even once he was emperor (27 BCE–14 CE). They contained a summary of the financial condition of the empire, statistics about the military and building projects, and the amounts of cash in the provincial tax treasuries.[11]

Augustus in turn used data from these personal accounts to write his *Res gestae divi Augusti*, which was etched onto entire walls of public buildings and posted on slabs across the empire. Even with Rome's annual revenues of 500 million sesterces, Augustus was careful to note that most of his achievements—buildings, armies, and most important, personal payments made to soldiers—were paid for out of his own coffers. He also revealed how he accounted for his personal fortune, paying towns for the goods used by his soldiers, and he revealed the sums to advertise his largesse. Thus Augustus thought actively about how to manage the empire, using his own account book as a tool for conceptualizing and planning projects, as well as for propaganda.[12]

It became a tradition to publish data from the imperial account books. Although Emperor Tiberius did not continue the tradition, Caligula, of all people, published a general state of imperial accounts. Nero (37–68 CE), known for his particular interest in gold, named praetorian senators to manage the treasury of the Temple of Saturn. There is ample evidence that Augustus's office of the imperial financial secretary continued working until at least the reign of Diocletian (244–311 CE).[13]

Although this accounting system served as a central tool of imperial management, and even legitimacy, it still had major faults. Books were kept and accounts audited, yet fraud was still expected (and systematically tolerated, especially where leading figures were concerned). At the same time, the economic practices of the Roman Empire did not focus on profit and future earnings, the principal function of double-entry bookkeeping. The Mediterranean Sea sustained the Roman Empire by shipping and trade, yet there was no overarching concept or system by which all the practices of trade were theorized. Loans were instead made on a pawnbrokerage model, stunting the development of a culture of credit. Wealth in palaces and hoarded gold took precedence over the idea of wealth as investment capital for profit. In spite of a slew of practical and theoretical works, no concept of economics for business ever emerged.[14]

The central office of the quaestors changed over time, reflecting the interests of emperors. With the decline of the empire, public accounts came ever more under the personal purview of the emperor, so that, as Edward Gibbon noted, everyone would be inculcated with the notion that all "payment flowed from the bounty of the monarch" rather than from the state. Later emperors considered the treasury sacred, and by the time of Constantine (325 CE) and his new Roman capital on the Bosporus, the chief of the treasury was an aristocratic count rather than a professional bureaucratic officer.[15]

With the fall of Rome in 476 CE, the state was shifting into the personal fiefdom of emperors, kings, and lords, which meant that it could not be audited, as these noble personages supplanted the bureaucratic state and answered only to God. Yet even as the Western Empire crumbled, its heir, the Catholic Church and its massive monasteries, continued to administer land, goods, and payments through basic accounting and auditing. And with the invasion of Goths, Franks, and Vikings, new kings from Charlemagne (742–814 CE) and Emperor Otto (912–973 CE) to William the Conqueror (1028–1087 CE) sought again to establish a rule of law to better to extract wealth and manage their conquered lands. One of the great paradoxes of feudalism—the ever-shifting system of lords, vassals, and serfs that emerged out of the fusion of Germanic kingdoms, counties, and old Roman estate systems—is that the personal holding of public land brought about a slow but steady rise in paperwork and accounting. The backbone of the Middle Ages was not only the Christianity born of the Fathers of the Church and its monastic tradition but also the concept of taxes and property enshrined in Charlemagne's *Capitularies*, his administrative records. Accounting remained a central tool of government, but for wealthy monasteries, Frankish kings, and lords, there would be no Augustan financial revelations.

At the turn of the millennium, as trade increased, so did writing, records, legal transactions, and the importance of accounting. When William the Conqueror invaded England in 1066, he was presented with a novel opportunity. Taking over the whole country in one fell swoop, he could write all feudal documents from scratch, giving himself dominion over the entire country without the inevitable complications of the more conventional feudal model: the dynastic inheritances and marriages that broke up land holdings over time, leaving hodge-podges of disputable territories. The Norman Conquest of England, then, with its opportunity to centralize its own administrative system, brought a proliferation of new feudal land contracts, requiring both secular and ecclesiastical rulers to keep clearer financial records. The *Domesday Book* (1086), William's personal record or account of property rights, legal privileges, obligations, and ecclesiastical rights, also laid out what taxes William could collect under previous royal agreements. Its title, meaning "doomsday," very clearly equated royal audits with the final reckoning of God, claiming no one could escape it.[16]

In the 1200s, with a revival in trade and currency flow, states and landowners began keeping better accounts, and handwritten records proliferated: charters and decrees, certificates, letters, writs, financial accounts, financial surveys and rental contracts, legal records, year-books, chronicles, cartularies (feudal and ecclesiastical deeds), registers (legal or administrative, often held by courts and parliaments), and learned and literary works. All these bits of paperwork were related to the keeping of account books. Law, property, and taxes required ac-countings and records—the basis of any state information network—to be recorded, collected, and stored. In England, the Exchequer, or royal treasurer for revenue, began keeping highly detailed accounts—called pipe rolls because of the rolled shape of parchment—that recorded in-come, spending, and fines. These were used primarily for collecting royal revenue rather than for extracting profit from investment or labor.[17]

State documents were kept not only in chancelleries and town halls but also in legal and parliamentary charterhouses, where they were more open to consultation by lawyers, and in the private collections of magistrates, ministers, and princes. Manor houses, the central points of feudal lordship and the medieval economy, became centers of ac-counting. Although feudal lords had no concept of profit, they ran their fiefdoms to produce a surplus. It was a privilege to keep written ac-counts, for parchment was expensive and, if done on any kind of scale, so was record keeping. Skilled scribes were few and expensive to train. Many accounts were made simply to manage the expenditures of each day and were not preserved as long-term records.[18]

In England, bailiffs, custodians, or legal land managers would learn basic, single-entry accounting, which involved tallying all quittance letters, writing the proper headings for transactions and property (such as horses), and making basic tallies. At the beginning, the bailiff would have to make a statement of past arrears; receipts would have to be en-tered, as well as other forms of wealth. He would then list expenditures on materials not found on the estate and labor costs.[19]

Auditing was central to the work of notaries and sheriffs, who checked the accounts of government officials, especially tax collectors and treasurers. The word "audit" comes from a time when rulers and lords listened to, rather than saw, their accounts. It derives from the word "audience," *auditio*, a listening, in which a sovereign or lord would verify accounts as they were verbally presented. In the thirteenth cen-tury, auditing officials were called the *Auditores comptorum scaccarii*, the

Auditors of the Exchequer Accounts. English state expenditures and tax receipts increasingly came under parliamentary scrutiny. One could go so far as to say that the constitutions of mixed government had practices of auditing built into them, as state finances had to be verified by the different branches of government. However, the king's expenditures and personal revenues, which could be enormous, often remained secret. Although he did present a rudimentary account of his expenditures to Parliament, this was a rare occurrence, and there was no effective auditing system. Edward III (ruled 1327–1377) stated what other kings in Europe would insist on until the nineteenth century: Kings do not render accounts except to God.[20]

All these account books and rolls beg the question: Did they at least work well? Surely a good diligent accountant, keeping daily records, should have been able to ascertain a certain level of mastery over accounts. This was the case in cash and inventory management, but even here, it could not be exact. Without Arab numerals and therefore fractions, there was internal error built in the Roman numeral system. No matter how tenacious an account keeper was, the plethora of *X*s, *L*s, and *I*s made cumbersome numbers such as DCCCXCIII (893) and left no space for fractions. New numbers and a new method of financial accounting were needed if complex trade was to flourish and advance.[21]

By the twelfth century, northern Italy had emerged as the richest and most populous place in Europe, dominated by merchant-run city republics such Florence, Genoa, and Venice. Without kings and with its nobles urbanized and recognizing the authority of city governments, northern Italy became something entirely new: a patchwork of rich city states, ruled by patrician merchants whose wealth came from trade. It was here that multipartner firms, banking, and long-distance trade developed, and with them the concepts of capitalistic profit and double-entry bookkeeping.

Northern Italy was influenced by its contact with Byzantium in the east. With its emperor, its court, its currency (the *nomisma*), and its often luxurious markets in everything from sugary currents and dates to almonds, silk, and scrolls of Greek ancient learning. The Greek vestige of the Roman Empire reminded Italians of their past and tempted them with luxury. Venice, Genoa, Florence, Milan, Lucca, Pisa, and other trading cities sent their ships of goods and built industries in a rich trade network in the eastern Mediterranean. The pope—father, Pontifex Maximus, high priest, and earthly ruler of Rome—from his court of cardinals and princes collected taxes, made law, and directed diplomacy from western Europe to the Byzantine Orthodox Church.

Although nominal subjects of the Holy Roman Emperor (a German or Austrian), Italian cities and communes were jealously independent merchant republics, governed by guilds, councils, senates, and doges. Their officials, often elected, acted like managers of a company and ruled for a fixed time and a salary.[22] In this nexus of merchant cities, great strides in accounting and theories of state management and accountability emerged. Merchants ruled themselves with mercantile methods. Ample evidence of single-entry bookkeeping abounds. In 1202, the Pisan merchant Leonardo Fibonacci (circa 1170–circa 1240) wrote his founding work on calculation, the *Liber abaci*. He had learned the art of the abacus and Arab numerals while trading in the Mediterranean port city of Bougie, Algeria, today Bgayet. A merchant and son of a government official, Fibonacci produced a work that was more than a manual of how to calculate numbers quickly on paper. It was a set of practical instructions on financial problem solving that employed the Muslim invention of algebra to solve complex mathematical problems, such as "How Many Rabbits Will Be Bred in One Year from One Pair (377)." It listed various problems—"Trading Pepper for Ginger," "Three Men Form a Company," or calculating exchange rates—and told how to account for them.[23]

Although Fibonacci was not the first Christian to use Arabic numerals, his work played a major role in introducing them to the merchant community of northern Italy. Only later would abacus come to mean a wooden board in which wooden counters could be moved around within slots or on beaded rods. As noted earlier, it was impossible to calculate fractions or do complex equations with Roman numerals. Arabic numerals brought precision and speed, and the abacus method meant that mathematics could be applied to practical affairs and immediate transactions.[24]

By the end of the thirteenth century, abacus schools were common in Tuscany, and a number of well-known teachers, mostly from Florence, began to spread not only the ideas of Fibonacci's book and Arabic numerals but also how to use the abacus. In 1277, an official Veronese document referred to the presence of a master of abacus accounting in the city, and in 1284 the government appointed a "Maestro Lotto," a communal abacus teacher from Florence. Abacus schools became centers of practical, vernacular schooling for the merchant citizens of Italian republican city-states. They taught applied mathematics and other subjects, such as the alphabet, prose instruction, and the catechism.[25]

The medieval Italian merchants did what the ancient Greeks, Persians, and Romans, the great Asian kingdoms, and the feudal lords could not: Without fanfare or public recognition, they invented double-entry bookkeeping, making the revolutionary leap into the calculation of profit. The only explanation for this is that Italian merchants needed double entry to calculate multipartner firms, equity and profits, and so, in a demand-response process, they developed it. Although we do not know for sure who first did it, Tuscan merchants began developing double-entry bookkeeping. The records are of some debate, but the earliest recognized use of double entry appears in the documents of the ledgers of either the Rinieri Fini brother firm (1296), which traded in fairs across Europe, or the Farolfi merchant house (1299–1300), which traded between Florence and Provence. Rather than a simple ledger, the Farolfi archive exposes something extraordinary and modern: a system of books designed to compute business transactions and holdings in real time. Cross-referencing debits and credits shows that they were indeed offsetting each other. Not only that, the Farolfi ledger records prepaid rent as a deferred expense, thus conceptualizing it in the manner of double entry. Sixteen *livres tournois* were paid for a house four years in advance. At the end of the first year, £4 were written off to the current expense account, and the remaining balance of £12 was left on the books as a deferred charge to be dealt with later.[26]

Aside from these ledgers, there is no single text or moment when double-entry accounting emerges. No single figure seems to have invented it. There are, however, some basic theories as to why it did happen in Italy around 1300. The use of Arab numerals is one reason. Moreover, as trade grew, more capital was needed, and partnerships were formed. The medieval accountant began to see bookkeeping not as a measure of holdings, but as a way to calculate and distribute equity among investing partners. Merchants used accounting not only to keep tallies of income and expenditure but also to unite and calculate the accumulated profits that were claimed by investors. Without double entry, growing shares of profit could not be measured: Only complex accounting could calculate equity in parts over time. The need to both receive and give credit worked the same way: If a debt was paid back over time in installments, double entry could show how much was due at any given moment.[27]

The expansion of trade meant that merchants could no longer always accompany their goods and so relied on agents. As goods left the storehouse, double entry measured that as a loss while awaiting confirmation of income from their sale. Only through the balancing of debits and credits could the action of sending goods out and receiving income for them be tallied.[28]

The earliest double-entry accounts were in paragraph form, and the credit and debit paragraphs were corresponding. Later, these paragraphs became bilateral, meaning written in two side-by-side columns, with pure numbers replacing paragraphs and descriptions. One of the earliest examples of double entry is the 1340 account of the Genovese merchant Jacobus De Bonicha, kept in the state's central ledger for their transactions in the lucrative black pepper trade. This entry is from a ledger that is the earliest known extant major government account book kept in double entry. That it appeared in Genoa should not be surprising, given that city's merchant marine and rich trade with Byzantium. It gives a sense of what early double entries looked like with bilateral form and the matching totals.[29]

Although bankers were far ahead of states in bookkeeping practices, the Genoese figured out how to use double entry to manage and record the city's rich financial transactions, from tax receipts and state expenditures to the loans and debts of the state, along with payments to soldiers and the personal account of the doge. Like a business, Genoa lent money and held trade accounts for which it made investments and recorded not only expenses but, most significantly, a profit-and-loss account. The city's ledgers contain detailed accounts for goods like Chinese silk and pepper, as well as customs receipts. Not only were accounts balanced according to the strict rules of double entry but also state accountants gave actual book references, complete with page num-

STEWARDS OF THE COMMUNE OF GENOA 1340

August 26, 1340	August 26, 1340
Debit Jacobus de Bonicha and, on page 61, credit Anthonio de Marinis for libbre 49, soldi 4.	Credit Jacobus for disbursements made on behalf of the Commune of Genoa in the army of Taxarolii for ships and other necessities, as shown on page 231 of ledger. These were ordered by the Duke and his council, whose decision was written by the notary Lanfranchi de Valle on August 19, 1340.
Item. September 5. Credit Marzocho Pinello, on page 92, for libber 12, soldi 10	
Item. March 6, 1341. Credit his account, on page 100 of the new ledger, for the balance of this account, soldi 16.	Libbre 62, soldi 10.
TOTAL Libbre 62, soldi 10.	

bers, to where each transaction was first recorded before being entered into the main ledger. Every year, the main ledger was closed, and continuing transactions transferred to the new ledger.[30]

The ledgers of the stewards of Genoa were not just for financial calculation and record keeping: They were designed for internal accountability. Fraud in financial statements was a continuing problem. The stewards, therefore, ordered that all transactions had to be recorded with a notary as witness; they allowed no erasures, and all pages of ledgers had to be numbered and verified before any transactions could be put in them. Most important, this system of financial auditing was made official in 1327 by a law called "About Ledgers to Be Kept After the Manner of Banks," which mandated that all business of the commune be recorded by two official accountants and audited annually by the city government.[31]

Students of modern finance and government should marvel at these books. They are clear, their numbers balance, and they have internal checks for fraud. Here was a system of accounting and accountability far beyond what the ancients had developed. Yet, as innovative and effective as this system was, it did not extend beyond Renaissance Italy. The great monarchies of the north would be very slow to adopt the administration of the old mercantile republics. It would take six hundred years before double entry would be used again as a management tool for central state ledgers and audits of combined state finances. Before European governments would effectively use accounting, medieval and Renaissance thinkers would have to strike a balance between the necessity of financial order and the perceived Christian immorality of counting money.

CHAPTER 2

FOR GOD AND PROFIT: THE BOOKS ACCORDING TO SAINT MATTHEW

Deus immensus est ("God is beyond measure").

FULGENTIUS OF RUSPE, 533

O n January 10, 1383, Francesco Datini returned from the papal city of Avignon to his home in Prato, north of Florence. Like many in the growing class of wealthy Tuscan merchants and bankers of his time, Datini had grown rich by trading with the papal court. He dabbled in currency exchange, dealt arms and armor during the Hundred Years' War between the French and English monarchies, and invested in the wool trade, which made fortunes for sharp-eyed merchants from England, Castile, Flanders, Champagne, and Florence. Overcoming the perils of international trade with returns of around 9 percent, Datini managed his affairs so well that, in spite of his modest demeanor, his neighbors knew to call him *il ricco*, "the rich," though the local tax collectors could not find any of it. "We do not know [his wealth]," they said, puzzled, "but God does." Datini was modest, pious, and disciplined. Most of all, he was a good accountant. And yet he was preoccupied by the thought that his very skill in making profit was a sin.[1]

Three years after returning to Florence, in 1386, he declared all his possessions in Prato to be worth 3,000 florins. The tax collectors wisely assumed that the bulk of his great wealth was invested elsewhere, but if they could not find it, they could not tax him. At that time, a pig cost 3 florins and a good riding horse between 16 and 20, a maid's wages were 10 florins a year, a female slave (one of which Datini owned and with whom he had his only recognized child) cost between 50 and 60 florins, and a crimson robe, like the one in which Datini was painted, cost 80. Datini built himself a house in Prato, married, and in 1389, moved to Florence to continue business. He dealt in art and was painted numerous times in his red robes, most notably as one of the "honorable men" in Fra Filippo Lippi's masterpiece, the *Madonna del Ceppo*, which is still housed in Prato's Civic Museum. When he died in 1410, he left a fortune of about 100,000 florins, a king's ransom.[2]

In 1383, as today, it took particular skills to get rich. Less than forty years after the Black Death that carried off half the population of Europe (and both of Datini's parents), and with trade routes plagued by brigands and pirates, there was nonetheless an economic boom, much of it centered in Northern Italy. By the 1340s, the Italians had invented double-entry bookkeeping, the bill of exchange, and marine insurance, and they had perfected payments by book transfer, note, and oral agreement. It was here that money and wool passed, via England, Flanders, and Castile. Florence was the great center of banking, famous not just for literary figures, such as Dante, but also for the florin itself, the city's little "flower." The size of a nickel, with the lily of Florence on one side and John the Baptist on the other (no king's or emperor's head adorned a coin of the republic), the florin was 3.93 ounces of twenty-four-carat gold and then, as today, a valuable coin. To protect it from theft via clipped or shaved edges, florins often circulated and were exchanged in officially sealed leather bags. The florin was so highly valued that Florentine bankers made it the standard currency across Europe.[3]

Datini made his first fortune in Avignon, trading and banking for the papacy there. Much early bank activity took place around the papacy and its court, which received massive tithe and tax funds and needed the money transferred, exchanged, and then deposited. The greatest fortunes of the Middle Ages, those of the Florentine bankers

Peruzzi and Alberti, had been made, in part, by catering to the needs of the papacy. The new tools of credit and exchange allowed members of the papal court to make handsome profits through banking and interest and to transfer their wealth to their families. In Avignon, Datini was a minor merchant, earning with his partner 10,000 florins on an initial investment of 800. What made Datini rich was his capacity to engage not only in banking but also in all sorts of international trade, which flourished around the papal court. Datini sold armor, cloth, slaves, spices, wine, and olive oil. When his daughter Ginevra married in April 1399, the sumptuous wedding dinner included more than fifty dishes for each course of the meal, including pastas, veal, pies, ducks, and pigeons. All were listed, accounted for, in his books.[4]

Datini's archive still exists. At his death, he left 124,549 business letters and 573 account books and ledgers that are still preserved in the Prato Museum, the biggest personal financial archive of the Middle Ages. In minute detail, it reveals medieval Italian life, how complicated business was, and how keeping double-entry books required immense skill. It contains lists of expenditures on household goods such as food, clothing, slaves, dogs, marmosets, and peacocks. All his personal holdings were inventoried, from furniture to an extensive collection of jewelry, right down to the cost of wine (local red wine was one lira a bottle, or twenty silver pieces).[5]

Datini's business sense is surprisingly familiar, considering that he died more than seven hundred years ago. His success came from acquiring investment capital through partnerships. He himself invested little of his own money but was able to attract partners and investors. Only through expert accounting could this be done, for each arm of the business required not only basic accounting but also the calculation at any moment of each partner's and investor's equity and share of profits. Each partner's share and final dividend was proportional to his investment. Some investors received fixed interest rates of 7 or 8 percent.[6]

In Datini's day, double-entry accounting required discipline and mathematical skill, as well as the ability to handle numerous books and to record, analyze, and transfer information between them. To modern eyes, Datini's system is like a giant leather, parchment, paper, and wood computing system. Datini's method would be described by accounting manuals only a century after his death. Later Dutch painters would illustrate the practices described by Datini. Marinus van Reymerswaele's *Two Tax-Gatherers* (circa 1540) shows account books, scraps, rudimentary notebooks, and wooden boxes to hold papers. Many of Datini's books were kept not only by his chief manager, Cambioni, but also by himself, in his own hand, and bore his trademark.[7]

The process of accounting began with writing down the day's transactions—intake and outlay, notes, receipts, and bills—in books called *Qaudernacci di Ricordanze* (memoranda books), which were a mix between scrapbooks and notebooks. Also recorded were the transactions of daily life, such as the purchase of a slave, a good dinner, a cymbal for Datini's daughter, a dog, spectacles, and a mule. Datini would then enter this scrap information into a more orderly, chronological list in books called *Memoriali*. All transactions were then put into double-entry form in handsome leather-bound *libri grandi*, the main ledgers. These sets of books existed for each of his companies, and the first page of each ledger always contained a religious formula: "In the name of the Holy Trinity and of all the Saints and Angels of Paradise" or, more fittingly, "In the Name of God and Profit."[8]

For his companies' daily transactions in petty cash, Datini kept books of debit and credit, as well as accounts for debts. Due to the complexity of all his companies, dealings, and transactions, the integration of all these books was central to managing "the great cash-box" of his company. Other books held his inventories from warehouse stocks, real estate holdings, salaries, and the accounts of his cloth-making industry in Prato. Finally, there were his personal household books, which recorded the expenses of sheets, candles and coal, food and domestic salaries, and Datini's staggering expenditures on fine clothing. The one book that bound them all was his secret book, the *libro segreto*. All medium-size and large-scale merchants kept these secret books, which were part account books, part diary—a safe place of open confession about finance. It was here that Datini recorded the true (and often untaxed) transactions of the business. A *libro segreto* listed all deeds, shares and debits of each partner in a firm, and more personal, diary-like entries recording the birth of children, the lives of ancestors, and daily thoughts. There was no more personal text than this, encompassing the universe of profit and those things that connected one to God. One major set of entries listed Datini's expensive, illuminated prayer books, his very generous gifts to the church, and his alms to the poor. A portion of his profits went to the church, and any time he bought himself a luxury, like herrings, oranges, or wine, he gave a portion to an almshouse or a monastery. The *libro segreto* also contained the final tallies of a company, which might be different from the public tallies of the main ledger.[9]

The scope and number of Datini's books are overwhelming. To keep them was a herculean task requiring personal and managerial discipline. Datini enjoyed his wine, fine clothes, partridges, jewelry, and his slave girl, but he also worked methodically. He wrote to one of his business managers, warning him to think day and night about the work at hand and to constantly take notes and keep books as reminders.[10]

Datini had nightmares about his home falling down and his business ventures collapsing. The pressure, he wrote, was "vexing." To stay on top of his business, he needed good books, but he could not simply order his employees to keep the necessary records. He maintained discipline by punishment. He fined clerks who failed to write the amount in the book before physically accepting money. For each entry error, a clerk was fined one soldo. Datini was convinced that ten soldi in fines would provide a permanent cure to bookkeeping error. This punishment had a religious, penitential aspect. It was, he wrote in his diary, "a blessed rule." Indeed, such techniques seemed to have worked, for all evidence points to Datini's fortune being made not in a single giant deal, but in small increments. The details mattered.[11]

To see all of Datini's books together is to see the birth of modern finance and the information age. Datini's books make him familiar: a businessman of numbers, data, and paperwork. Max Weber is famous for claiming that capitalism grew out of the Protestant work ethic, based on self-discipline and what Sigmund Freud called delayed gratification, the control of the pleasure principle. But Datini shows that, in spite of his taste for slave girls, partridges, and fine clothes, the original capitalist work ethic of Western Europe grew from this disciplined, fearful, saint-loving, Catholic, Italian world of trade, with its connections to Byzantium and the Ottoman Empire. The Italians invented complex multipartner firms, banking, and double-entry bookkeeping, which required an iron work ethic. Datini described the work of one of his partners in Avignon, Boninsegna di Matteo, as doing nothing but read and write in his books, and, Datini assured, he would "not get up from his chair until all is done." The model was simple. One had to enter everything faithfully into account books and keep clear tallies. And one had to worry all the time and be vigilant. In 1395, Datini wrote to his wife that he was so overwhelmed by his business that he worried he was losing his mind. Worry drove Datini to work, and keeping good books kept things in order. One of Datini's managers, complaining that he had not slept an entire night in two years, scoffed at those who told them to "take pleasure lying in a warm bed."[12]

In spite of his own rigor, Datini was always surprised by how few merchants used double-entry accounting. One would assume that many who did business with him saw him keeping his books, for his memorandum book was open and used during transactions. On his return to Prato, Datini complained to his friend Stoldo di Lorenzo that other merchants in his hometown did not keep books, instead trying to remember their affairs. "God knows how they manage!"[13]

Although Datini knew that double entry was the primary tool for accuracy and control, many around him ignored the method. The pharmacist of Prato, Benedetto di Tacco, used a rudimentary bookkeeping system: a ledger and a supplementary book. In his main ledger, he posted receivables and payables, recording debts owed to him by 106 persons. In a smaller book, his *libriciuolo*, he wrote out transactions in detail, such as the sale of sheepskins for one soldo and four denari. Di Tacco then transferred the sum of the transaction to his ledger. He closed accounts by crossing them out. He also mentioned tabulating accounts on an erasable blackboard or, as others did, on loose pieces of paper and in other books, long lost. Di Tacco used accounting, but without double-entry bookkeeping, he could not keep truly accurate tallies, and his calculations were not as accurate or complete as Datini's. He used the method of basic accounting, but he used it haphazardly, as a system of recording. Many merchants did manage to run successful businesses with single entry and accounting by memory. But Datini knew that a large-scale enterprise such as his was impossible to run without the data management tools of his bookkeeping system.[14]

Datini was constantly reminded that his profession and the act of accounting were frowned on. Much of banking went against the canon

laws of the church, which, although very flexible in enforcement, nonetheless condemned money lending. A good Tuscan, he was both pious
in his religion and hard-nosed in his quest for wealth. His motto "For
God and Profit" attempted to marry two concepts—one old, one new—
that did not go well together.

Although it is hard to imagine today, guilt weighed heavily on medieval bankers and merchants. Saint Ambrose (337–397) had warned
that usury—lending at interest—and taking more than one was given
was a sin. The third Lateran Council of 1179 denied Christian burial
to usurers: usury was tied to the capital sin of greed and considered the
same as robbery, lying, violence, and harassment. Dante characterized
moneylenders as thieves who reduced honest folk to poverty. In the
Inferno, he described usurers as obsessed with the money pouches hung
around their necks. Jews were allowed to lend money at interest, but
the Old Testament limited them to lending only to those outside their
community. In any case, they were forced into a profitable yet hated
role.[15]

As always, church moralists looked for ways around the ban. Thomas
Aquinas had made exceptions with the concept of the "just price," which
allowed merchants to charge for damages, whatever those might be.
Words could be defined in so many ways, which was and is the reason to
have a good lawyer. A well-known preacher of Datini's time, Fra Jacopo
Passavanti, complained that money lending was concealed by words like
deposit, saving, purchase, and *sale*. Whatever the commerce of money was
called, Passavanti warned, it was "abominable."[16]

Merchants and often the church found ways of skirting the usury
laws. Datini made money from currency exchange, the basis of medieval banking. A banker would give a note that could be exchanged for
foreign currency in Paris, London, Geneva, or Bruges. The exchange
rate was calculated to be favorable to the lender. In essence, it was lending for interest, which went against canon law. In any case, the church
needed to borrow money, and rich prelates needed sure places to invest
and store their wealth. Cardinals and indeed popes had no problem
giving money to a banker for *discrezione*, which meant that the banker
could give the depositor a discretionary return, or gift—in reality, interest. The sum was decided according to bank profits, and some years
it was not paid, but there was little ambiguity. Bankers, like Datini and

the Medici, had many businesses, and lending for interest was one of them.

Profit was a problem for medieval merchants who sought both wealth and piety. Medieval Italians kept account books while never forgetting that, in the end, no mortal can make the final tally. That is God's work. But one could try to do good works, and to have a sense of where one stood in God's judgment, one could still make a tally of one's sins and good works. Indeed, the church would help them do it. Guilt was intertwined with accounting, to the point where it became essential to its development.

Datini did not believe he was making money for God, and he stated as much in his letters. He tallied both his wealth and his sins, as well as the debt he believed he owed to God. Only at the end of his life did he connect them. Paying back moral debts was called penance, and it involved a kind of accounting. Before double entry emerged, accounting went hand in hand with a culture of keeping moral accounts. It was the very essence of spiritual life. Medieval Christian attitudes toward wealth help explain why, in spite of its force, some kept books, yet others questioned and even rejected doing so.

Religions are based on covenants. Humans must make offerings to the gods or God, and if they forget or neglect to do so, they will be punished in a moment of cosmic reckoning. The prize is not profit, but mortal life and the eternal life of the soul. In polytheistic religions, a lack of offerings could bring down direct punishment, such as the flood of Gilgamesh. For the Hebrews, Abraham made a covenant with God, but so did Moses; in the tablets of the Ten Commandments that Moses brought down from Mount Sinai, God had set out his rules for humankind, and if they did not follow them, they would be punished. The Torah and its complex legal code was a model for moral accounting. Believers would have to identify what God expected of them through moral and spiritual accounting. Talmudic law has a moral debt counterpoint for every action.

Yet it was not clear if good Jews and Christians should strive to keep good books. Could humans keep order in their affairs? Or is it pointless, when God is keeping books for them? In the end, it is God who keeps the book of life with the names of the righteous and a book of death with the adversaries of God.

With a fusion of Hebrew, Greek, and newly Christian traditions, Saint Matthew brought the culture of accounting into Christianity. Yet Matthew's message is not entirely clear, either. He claimed that the righteous should keep good, honest books and not waste money, but he also advocated a rejection of Mammon and its earthly temptations. Matthew (also known as Levi) was a Jewish tax collector for King Herod and the Romans. Jesus invited Matthew to follow him from his tax booth to a feast and a conversion. Jesus defended the conversion, saying that he had come "not to call the righteous, but the sinners" (Mark 2:17). Jesus saw the usefulness of Matthew's training in mathematics and accounting and his knowledge of multiple languages. Matthew had skills other apostles did not have. Matthew became one of the twelve apostles of Jesus, the first evangelist, and the patron saint—to this day—of bankers, tax collectors, accountants, and perfumers (he is supposed to have turned his wooden staff into a perfumed fruit tree).

Medieval and Renaissance artists represented Matthew with the tools of his trade: either his Gospel book or at the counting table. His role was that of a tabulator of money or parables. The images were comparable. Caravaggio's *The Inspiration of St. Matthew* (1602, Church of San Luigi dei Francesi, Rome) shows Matthew writing the Gospel, which also resembles his activity at the counting table. Other artists portrayed him holding an account book or sitting at an accounting table.[17]

Matthew was a reminder that wealth had to be handled honestly, but that it was also earthly and potentially a sin. In his Parable of the Talents, he exhorted the faithful to make profit with money through hard work. Debts should not be forgiven if they are not reinvested well. A man going abroad gave his servants his goods to hold and manage during his trip. His most slothful servant took the talents (gold coins) and buried them. On his return, the man chastised him for not investing them to create more wealth: "Thou shouldst therefore have entrusted my money to the bankers, and on my return I should have got back my own with interest."[18]

Matthew was not clear on whether it is man's duty to create bounty on the earth. He warned, "You cannot serve God and Mammon." Humans were supposed to work hard, make money, but recognize that in the end, it was only Mammon, or sinful greed. Over and over again,

Matthew insisted on the separation between the earthly world of sinners and the true nourishment given only by God: "Not by bread alone does man live, but by every word that comes forth from the mouth of God." Matthew set the dichotomy that Augustine would later develop into an antimaterialist spiritual vision: "Then saith he unto them, Render therefore unto Caesar the things that are Caesar's; and unto God the things that are God's." The lesson is a confusing one. The medieval church may have coveted talents, but it preached against Mammon.

Perhaps Matthew, with his use of accounting parables and metaphors, inspired John of Patmos to write the apocalyptic and graphic Book of Revelation, which discussed in detail the books of life and death. God had account books. He decided who lived and died, and he made the final tally of those who went to heaven and those who were cast into hell:

> And I saw the dead, small and great, stand before God; and the books were opened: and another book was opened, which is the book of life: and the dead were judged out of those things which were written in the books, according to their works. (Rev. 20:12)
>
> And whosoever was not found written in the book of life was cast into the lake of fire. (Rev. 20:15)

The use of accounting metaphors in Christian thought persisted. In the early 400s, Augustine—the prime father of the medieval church—described Christ's redemption of humanity in terms of a balanced account. For Augustine, Christ was a merchant who bought the rebirth and eternal life of humanity: "To pay the price of our ransom he stretched his arms on the Cross."[19]

A former professor of rhetoric, a devotee of wine and brothels, Augustine came to preach a puritanical rejection of the fleshy world he once inhabited. With his Manichaean vision of flesh and earth as evil and only the spiritual as good, he demanded that believers turn away from earthly knowledge and the great science of Aristotle. Instead, it was to the City of God that humanity should turn, and there they should invest themselves and begin paying their outstanding debts for sin and the blood Christ spilled to redeem them.

In the period following the Black Death, in a world steeped in piety, the idea that God did the final reckoning was central, and the images of revelation were not so fantastical. In the *Decameron*, Giovanni Boccaccio described how the plague had swept through Florence in 1348, shattering the well-managed and rich city and leaving its streets piled with the dead. Those who fled, he wrote, hoped that the dead had requited humanity's debt to God. Life, Boccaccio reminded his readers, was fleeting, and death, above all, ever present.[20]

When Datini wrote to his wife about the approaching plague from the east, there was a real sense of helplessness in the face of the wrath of God. Francesco Traini's fresco the *Triumph of Death* (circa 1350) in the Cathedral of Pisa, painted during the period following the Black Death of 1348, illustrates the mind-set that as much as humans try, they cannot escape death. Images like this, along with regular sermons and the great literature of the time, show humans in a helpless state. Especially in Florence, where great writers like Dante and Boccaccio memorialized fleeting life and the price to be paid for human imperfection and sin, all knew that they would have to leave the inferno and climb the mountain of purgatory, suffering for their sins before reaching paradise at the top. The trip had to be made, Dante wrote, for this was part of God's reckoning:

> *But I would*
> *not have you, reader, be deflected from*
> *your good resolve by hearing from me now*
> *how God would have us pay the debt we owe.*
> *Don't dwell upon the form of punishment:*
> *consider what comes after that; at worst*
> *it cannot last beyond the final Judgment.*[21]

By the 1300s, faith, good works, and sin had been placed squarely in an accounting metaphor. The debt "owed," as Dante put it, could be paid, for the church began to devise ways to change the tallies in God's books even before one had begun to climb the mountain of purgatory. True believers had to confess their sins and, once the tally was made, they would have to balance their moral books by penance, paying God's debt either with good works or, paradoxically, as Luther would later

complain, with money. The church was everything—a font of spirituality, a diplomatic organization, and a money machine—but one always
tightly intertwined with spiritual, legal, and ethical concerns. Accountants filled the halls of the papal palaces, where numeracy became a
measure of holiness as true believers paid cash sums for indulgences for
their sins.[22]

Datini paid, too, not only by doing penance but also by leaving
much of his fortune to the poor. In this way, his profit and his system
of tallies fit into this world of moral record keeping. With the plague,
the Hundred Years' War, and the schism of the papacy between Rome
and Avignon, there was a sense among thinkers of the church that
penance could provide solace to the unrelenting terror of death and an
uncertain afterlife. Indulgences—*remissiones, absolutiones,* or *relaxiones*—
translated into lessening the time a person had to spend in penitential
acts or prayers in order to cut time spent in purgatory. The church could
use its powers to intercede on behalf of individuals.[23]

The Christian concept of accounting was more profound than the
simple payment of debts for sin. Christ's blood was seen as a treasure
spilled to save mankind, and as Saint Peter taught in his first epistle,
Christ used this blood to ransom humanity from the evil one. The
French Dominican Cardinal Hugh of St. Cher (1200–1263) believed
that this blood was "stored in a cask in the treasury of the church, the
keys of which belong to the church." Only the church had the keys to
open this treasury and to wash mankind of its sins. The "copious flow
of Christ's blood won for the Church" was an "inexhaustible fund of
merit" on which humans could draw for salvation.[24]

Most Christians came into contact with the concept of accounting
through the idea that Christ's account of blood, along with good works
and penance, could balance out sins in exchange for an afterlife with
limited time in purgatory. Moral credits, debits, and balances were all
necessary for salvation. Praepostinius of Cremona, chancellor of the
University of Paris from 1206 to 1209, went further, claiming that
those who paid money for absolution would receive remittance. The
debt to the treasury of sin could now be paid in silver and gold. While
Protestants would later complain that medieval tradition brought a foreign mercantile element into Christianity, the Old Testament, Matthew, and Augustine show that it was always present. It was based on

the central idea of redemption by payment in Christ's blood and the prayers of the faithful.[25]

As Datini's case shows, the very idea of the debt to God and fears about the final reckoning inspired a consciousness about personal accountability. Indeed, Datini struggled with the conflict between God and profits to the very end. Every day Datini entered his profits into his books, and every day, he believed, they pushed him further from God. By the 1420s, Bernardino of Siena would preach that those who obeyed their parents would be rewarded by wealth from God and that those who didn't would suffer poverty. Yet Datini did not feel that his good management brought him closer to God. His good management was, in part, money lending. Indeed, he admitted he engaged in usury, which he knew to be a sin, and he worried about it.[26]

The fact that his books were so balanced in his favor meant that his debt to God only grew larger. Thus Datini's account books not only measured his profit but also that which he had to pay back to God for his sins. While Datini was not particularly pious, he looked for ways to repay his debt to God. After hearing a Lenten sermon in 1395, he wrote to his wife, "I have sinned in my life as much as a man can sin, for I have ruled myself ill and have not known how to moderate my desires . . . and I pay the penalty gladly." Like others of his time, he feared the last judgment and—inspired by the horrors of the plague, which in 1400 was again approaching Florence and ravaging eastern Europe—he joined the penitential pilgrimages of the Bianchi for ten-day marches and processions, barefoot in white robes with hoods.[27]

Furthermore, monks had urged Datini to leave his fortune to the poor. Against the pleadings of his friends, who warned that all he was doing was making the bishop of Pistoia rich, Datini left his money to the clergy of Prato to pay them to do good works, such as succor the sick, find husbands for poor women, and fight poverty. He insisted that his business friends execute his will so that the money would go only to help the poor. Following his orders, his massive fortune, 100,000 florins, was used to found a hospital for the poor, the Casa del Ceppo dei Poveri di Francesco di Marco. In the Museo Civico of Prato, Fra Filippo Lippi's portrait of Datini in his painting *Madonna del Ceppo* (1452–1453) is still vivid. More than six hundred years later, Datini's children's hospital also exists, and over its old door is an inscription calling

Datini, "The Merchant of Christ's Poor." Today, the city of Prato still holds a mass in honor of his birthday. But in the end, in his dying moments, Datini found it strange that he should have to die. For all his piety and his rich offerings to God, Datini, the devoted accountant, found God's reckoning hard to accept.[28]

CHAPTER 3

MEDICI MAGNIFICENCE:
A CAUTIONARY TALE

It is a good sign if merchants have ink-stained fingers.
—LEON BATTISTA ALBERTI, 1437

Florence is an odd city. In the right light, with dry air in a late afternoon, there is no more beautiful place on earth. The heavy stones give off a rosy hue, and its mixture of humidity and dryness can, on a hazy day, make the city seem like it is floating up to the glorious hills that surround it, to the earthly paradise of Fiesole. But there is another side to Florence, a harder side. It comes in the unrelenting heat of summer, when Florence sits, without a wisp of wind, in the valley, which both cradles and imprisons the city, leaving it fetid and humid. And then it comes for a brief, angry moment in winter, as winds and rains blow down from the hard hills of the Mugello in the northeast, with its dark forests full of wild boars, the birthplace of the Medici. When the weather blows from the Apennines, the stones of Florence turn black and seem to exude the harshness of coal. The cold is wet and unshakable, and the only escape is behind the foreboding stones, near raging fires, where succor is kale and bread stew and Chianti. This duality of beauty and brutality describes the Medici.

To understand the dual nature of accounting—a force for achievement and a possible trap—it is necessary to understand the Medici, their relationship to Florence, and their determining influence on the history of finance and Western culture. It was in Florence that the Medici showed the power of good finance but fell prey to the temptations to ignore accounting. The great masters of the Medici bank used accounting to create a financial machine that allowed them to dominate their age, both culturally and politically, like no family before them. Yet one generation later, they almost lost it all, not simply by bad accounting, but because they no longer considered accounting as an essential branch of knowledge for themselves and their heirs. The greatest irony is that, in the end, the Medici no longer depended on banking for their power. The change was not necessarily by choice. The fact is that the great Medici ran their bank into the ground.

Cosimo de' Medici (1389–1464) was a hard-nosed banker. Known as *il vecchio*, the elder, and, after his death, as *pater patriae*, father of the nation, he was the son of a medieval banker. The Medici were a leading family of Florence, and Cosimo's father, Giovanni di Bicci de' Medici, had held the more-or-less honorary title of *gonfaloniere*, temporary standard-bearer and high magistrate of the republic. Though members of an ancient and important family, they were not Florence's richest or most prestigious citizens. They earned their wealth through shrewdness and, like all successful bankers before them, by doing business with the papacy. Cosimo's father earned a great fortune, leaving more than 113,000 florins at his death, more than Datini's legacy.[1]

If Cosimo's father made the Medici rich, Cosimo made the bank into an international superpower and became the richest man of his age in all of Europe. The Medici's carefully collected riches would be used to pay for the artistic glory of the Florentine Renaissance and the political power of the Medici themselves. Thus the glories of the Renaissance would sit on the mundane foundation of good bookkeeping. Cosimo conceptualized, sponsored, and even inspired the classical Renaissance as its chief defender and patron. But even as he built a new world around himself, he kept many of the habits of his father, the medieval merchant.

Cosimo, too, was born in a golden age, for in many ways Florence at the beginning of the 1400s was the center of Christendom, and in terms of trade, finance, and learning, it was the center of the world.

Chancellor of the Republic Coluccio Salutati (1331–1406) was a recognized Renaissance scholar himself, who declared his age to be golden when he asked, "Ubi Dantes? Ubi Petrarcha? Ubi Boccaccius?" Where else Dante, Petrarch, and Boccaccio? These defining writers of their time not only established Tuscan as the dominant vernacular Italian dialect but also invented modern literature and humanist studies. It was thought that with the study of the past, the Florentines could bring back the glories and riches of ancient Greece and Rome. The classical Renaissance focus on practical knowledge connected humanism to nascent capitalism and industry.[2]

Florence was both a center of banking and commerce and Europe's leading center of education. Tuscany was a highly literate region, and much of this reading and writing was related to mercantile record keeping. Around 8,000 to 10,000 of Florence's 120,000 inhabitants attended schools at any given time, and half of these were abacus schools. There are abundant records showing that even workers and artisans knew how to read, write, and keep accounts. To be a humanist, *umanista*, literally meant to be a Latin scholar and teacher, and Florence was full of artists, poets, and philosophers. Bankers, merchants, artisans, and lawyers learned their trades, but they, too, learned philosophy and the teachings of ancient scholars such as Aristotle and Pythagoras. Although most learned the use of the abacus after 1300, there were also schools dedicated to practical arithmetic. For the elite, there were high schools and academies, and in 1321, the foundation of a university, or *studio*, in which the wisdom of the ancients could be learned. The members of great families, like Coluccio Salutati, formed academies based on the ideals of Plato, in which earthly learning and an understanding of the universe and ethics were seen to bring man closer to God. In negotiating with popes and other cities, Salutati emulated Petrarch and wrote letters in the style of Cicero. Politics, commerce, and learning mingled in the minds of the early humanists. Salutati even brought the Greek Byzantine scholar Manuel Chrysoloras from Constantinople to revive Greek, the language of the ancients that had been forgotten in the West, and to open the works of Plato and Aristotle to a world that had lost their wisdom.[3]

Although Florence was a place where a shrewd merchant could become rich and politically influential, it grew increasingly elitist in comparison with Datini's more republican heyday. Philosophers should be kings, Plato said, and Platonic thought played a central role among Florence's educated elite, who, understandably, increasingly associated their cultural achievements with the moral as well as social authority to lead. Between 1398 and 1406, Roberto de' Rossi—tutor of Cosimo in his youth—opened a free academy for the children of the leading families of the city. With Chrysoloras, he taught Greek and Platonic philosophy to a group of young men who would grow up to lead Florence, among them Cosimo de' Medici, banker and student of Platonic philosophy. It was a heady mix of money and ancient philosophy that, not surprisingly, gave elite Florentines a sense of empowerment.[4]

Thus was the difference between Datini, the self-made man and merchant, and Cosimo, the scion of a banking family, who was steeped not only in the new culture of Renaissance humanism and its worship of Saint Francis and the Virgin Mary but also in the pagan learning of the ancient world. The Medici family was politically tied to the poorer factions of Florence, but Cosimo—famously unostentatious, preferring a mule to a horse—was still a cultural elitist and one of the greatest patrons of culture in history. He often did not attend public gatherings, made way in the street for the old, and even hung back during public processions. Yet this humble citizen was the ruthless ruler of Florence. Machiavelli rightly described Cosimo as prudent and astute in his climb to power. But his use of money would undermine the liberty of the Florentine Republic. This money, said Machiavelli, "brought fear into the state."[5]

The unassuming, quiet, and modestly dressed man, often willing to forgive a debt or an incompetent bank manager, who helped artists and scholars, was also accused of cruelty. At the time, there was no way to hold power in Italy without it. It was a violent place, even if Florence had laws prohibiting the public execution of its citizens. Cosimo was known for taking over the renovations of a church and kicking out other patrons to make the work in his own glory. He exiled disloyal families, split them up, censored their letters, and filled the courts and squares of Italy with paid informers. It was even said that he tortured his enemies.[6]

The master of Florence and of much of Italy, as well as of Europe's finance, Cosimo made his desk the nerve center of a financial and political empire. Letters, packages, coded secret messages, reports, and account books streamed through; he appointed bank managers in London and negotiated cash payments to branches, partners, depositors, and borrowers. He argued over silk quality and the gold content of Swiss coinage. And he managed his personnel, their efficiency, language skills, and even their personal relationships: Some were too handsome, and others had a weakness for fine clothing. In matters of money, personal stability was key, and Cosimo was a keen judge of character and signs of crisis. Realizing its value as an ally, he lent the Republic of Venice 150,000 florins for it to pay to avoid being excommunicated by the pope. The investment sealed a Venetian alliance with the Medici.[7]

As banker to the Catholic Church and master of the exchange routes of foreign trade, Cosimo was the richest man in Europe, and his bank the most influential. Tithes and indulgences needed to cross the difficult routes of Europe back to Rome. The Medici bank made it easy to transfer money by using exchange notes that could be bought in London or Bruges and redeemed in Florence at a rate beneficial to the Medici. In Rome, popes and prelates kept their gold with the Medici. When a cardinal, a statesman, or another merchant wanted to borrow money, say, five hundred florins, he could approach a banker like Cosimo, who would write out a bill of foreign currency exchange. The purchaser of the note promised to pay the sum back to the Medici. The Medici would then draw up a bill of exchange for the same sum and send it to London or Bruges and exchange it at a profit. Dealing in such exchanges, the Medici earned annual profits between 13 and 26 percent. The purchaser paid back the original sum, and the Medici kept the other profits—all legally in the eyes of the church. Along with exchange, the Medici lent money to states and its own city government, often collecting state taxes in Florence and Tuscany as repayment. They also maintained deposit accounts for wealthy figures (popes and cardinals among them), invested in farms and cloth production, and traded in everything from almonds to unicorn tusks.[8]

The Medici accumulated great wealth between 1380 and 1464. In 1427, two years before Giovanni di Bicci de' Medici, Cosimo's father, died and left him in control, the full assets of the Medici bank or *tavola* (trading table) equaled 100,047 florins. In 1451, the profits of the bank alone exceeded 75,000 florins, although this amount had to be divided among partners. In 1460, the Milan branch of the bank had assets of 589,298 florins.[9]

Cosimo used his money to expand Florence's power in Tuscany and even to buy peace for the warring city-states of northern Italy. He also caused a brutal and unpopular war to subjugate the neighboring city of Lucca. Ultimately, however, he weakened the republic by replacing Florence's army with mercenaries under his own hire. In 1433, his enemies had him imprisoned in the cell at the very top of the tower of the Palazzo della Signoria (called the *Alberghetino*, the "little hotel") in the main square in Florence and condemned him to death. However, during the three weeks while his execution was being deliberated and a parliamentary session of the *balia* was called by the tocsin of the bells, he was busy writing promissory notes to, and forgiving the debts of, the leaders of the city government. A thousand florins here and there did the trick. Cosimo was surprised at how little it cost, later admitting he would have paid ten times more, if his captors had only known to ask. He also paid mercenaries to mass outside Florence. By the time he was done spreading around florins, the *balia* changed his sentence to exile. He was allowed to flee to Padua and then Venice, his well-paid ally, where, through his bank branches, he worked for one year in exile and became even richer, eventually buying out all his enemies and giving massive donations to the church and to his influential humanist scholar and artist friends. In the end, he bought out and undermined his enemies and reentered Florence as its undisputed master.[10]

Cosimo's own fortune, often synonymous with that of his family and bank, was enormous and can only be estimated. Following the law of 1427, every Florentine landholder or merchant had to keep double-entry books for the state tax audit, the *catasto*, the records of which still exist. Every good merchant kept two sets of books, with a *libro segreto*, a secret book for their eyes only, and plausible public books for state audits. When Cosimo's brother died in 1440, their joint fortune was audited by the *catasto* at 235,137 florins, but this was not the full measure of his wealth, which was ever growing. The *catasto* did not include his collections of gems, art, and books, nor did it include all his holdings. In his memoirs, Lorenzo the Magnificent—Cosimo's grandson and later the leader of Florence—claims that between 1434 and 1471, 663,755 florins were spent on alms and taxes for public buildings, 400,000 of this during the time of Cosimo. At that time, a respectable city palace cost about 1,000 florins, and most of the population of the city was too poor to pay even a florin of tax. Cosimo could pay a king's ransom, for he had more money than most kings and entire nations.[11]

Cosimo funded the great artistic projects of Florence. As a civic humanist, he used his money to erect buildings with artists like Brunelleschi, who built the Basilica of San Lorenzo, the most modern large-scale building project of its time, and to sponsor public art and scholarships. This brought him goodwill, power, and prestige. Artists and humanists loved him, as did many of the citizens of Florence, for Cosimo was not only a truly cultured man but also very generous, with a knack for forgiving loans. As humanist advisers and court artists became the envy of the princes of Europe, their approval of Cosimo brought him international hard power and more influence at home.

Money was power for Cosimo, he was good at earning it, and that was due in great part to his knowing how to manage it. Not only did Cosimo benefit from the finest humanist education of his time but also he trained in the Rome branch of his father's bank, which handled papal accounts, and was familiar with all aspects of the business. The statutes of numerous artisan guilds required their members to keep double-entry books, which were also mandated by the state for the *catasto* tax. Ledgers were also seen as legal contracts in financial disputes. Florentine judges had the habit of scouring books to decide financial rights. Bad books did not help make a good case.[12]

A merchant's education was rooted in bookkeeping, and leaders like Cosimo learned to master it from an early age. In any family business, younger members apprenticed in their family's shops or in branches abroad. Real bookkeeping could only be learned by experience, which is why Florence, with its trade and bookkeeping laws, produced such a rich tradition of accounting. It was ingrained in both culture and law. Merchants learned by rote all the basics of the shop, from copying and writing out letters of exchange to keeping books.

Although later he delegated duties to his managers, Cosimo was a practical overseer, and central to this was his early mastery of accounting. The Florentine archives show that Cosimo himself kept books and often managed his own farms. A 1448 notebook shows Cosimo doing the basic accounting to run his farm in the Mugello, using simple double-entry and bilinear (parallel) credit and debit columns on the same page. Accounting was an intimate tool for ordering everything from Cosimo's personal production of olive oil to running his massive machine of finance. Without it, the activities of a shop or branch could never be managed or understood. But Cosimo had to learn it in real time, in live business transactions and office management. Real business could be learned only on the shop floor, and double entry was a real-time record-keeping method.[13]

Double entry became a necessity of banking because no other practice could have guaranteed that so many complex transactions could be calculated for profit and recorded in real time. As the practice of offsetting (a deposit guaranteeing the writing of a check) became common, only double entry could keep track of money moving through various accounts. This was an alternative to simple currency exchange but obviously harder to calculate and record. Many businesses held numerous debts, credits, and transfers, which meant that wealth was constantly in flux and had to be calculated daily. Printers, vintners, tailors, cloth merchants, silversmiths, cheese makers, butchers, stationers, hostelers, grocers, international traders and bankers, and finally the state and its own financial institutions were all bound in a web of transactions and account ledgers.[14]

Unlike Datini's business, the Medici bank was not a centralized entity. Each branch was a firm unto itself, with a partner as manager, but the major partner was always a Medici. That meant that if one branch failed or was sued for a breach of contract, it did not necessarily affect the others. When Tommaso Portinari was sued over the defective packing of nine bales of wool, he argued successfully that the bales had been packed by the London branch and that the Bruges branch was therefore not responsible.[15]

Cosimo was the senior partner in eleven different enterprises, from the main bank in Florence to wool and silk manufacturers and various Medici branches in Europe. What grounded his power was his role as

chief investor and chief auditor. The 1455 Articles of Association forming the partnership of the Medici Bruges bank make this clear. The
Medici gave their managing partners latitude in making business decisions, but they also exerted discipline. Article 7 forbade Agnolo Tani
to play cards or dice and entertain women in his chambers. Article 8
stipulated that he could be summoned to Florence at any time to render accounts and that once a year, on March 24, or more often if
requested, the manager was expected to balance the books and send
the accounts to Cosimo and his head bookkeeper, who would verify
them in Florence.[16]

Giovanni di Amerigo Benci was Cosimo's most trusted manager
and accountant, beginning his training at age fifteen as an office boy for
the Medici bank in Rome before moving on to a successful stint at the
Geneva branch from 1424 to 1435. With this experience under his belt,
Benci returned to Florence in 1435 as Cosimo's principal collaborator,
manager, and bookkeeper. At twenty, he had mastered double-entry
accounting, which made him a valuable employee and confidant. He
wrote all of the bank's bills of exchange, tallied the books, audited, and
even kept the *libro segreto*: The third extant *libro segreto*, spanning the
years 1435–1455, is in Benci's hand. This was the period of the bank's
greatest success. Although Benci made large bequests to the church
and had Leonardo da Vinci paint a portrait of his daughter, Ginevra,
he was always disciplined: he kept all the books, no entries were
missing, and Cosimo, the great overseer, knew this and rested easier.
Two years after Benci's death, the *catasto* revealed that his own family
fortune was second only to that of the Medici.[17]

With Benci, Cosimo developed a system of audit and executive
control. Every year, the senior partner of each branch would prepare its
books and send them to Benci for audit. Although partners owned part
of the firm, Cosimo maintained executive control. He often audited
the books with Benci, and it is certain that he verified the final ledgers
and accounts of the *libro segreto*. Many books in the Medici archives
show verification marks of the final audit. If the year-end ledger
showed losses or irregularities, the head of the branch was called to
Florence for a personal audit. In the later years, figures like the Bruges
branch director, Tommaso Portinari, were called to the imposing
Palazzo Medici Riccardi to stand in front of Cosimo and Benci while

they conducted a line-by-line audit, questioning the partner on each transaction.

Cosimo was a man of two worlds, for he had one foot in the Middle Ages and the other in the Renaissance, which he helped invent. Although some Neo-Platonists saw all formal knowledge as an element of holiness, others believed that some learning was inferior and beneath the interest of the noble, Platonic elite. Merchant and noble values began to clash. Plato's allegory of the cave, which described a lower cave people being ruled by an intellectual elite who through the wisdom of their souls sought the good of the republic, was a model not only for secular education and culture but also for political elitism.[18]

The Neo-Platonic ideal of human glory based on artistic, cultural, and political achievement did not always leave a place for the gritty practical matters of business. Cosimo did not want his sons to share in the vulgar world of medieval business, and the noble blood sport of Renaissance politics would be their preserve. Accounting, the very tool that helped Cosimo fund the Renaissance, began to be seen as a lower and even immoral discipline.[19]

The Renaissance was in direct opposition to the teachings of the medieval church, in which Augustine had expressly demanded that the faithful turn away from earthly learning and the hope of perfecting themselves. Faith alone was to succor humanity. Yet under Cosimo's patronage, humanists studied Plato and Aristotle and other previously forgotten Greek texts brought by the Byzantine scholar Manuel Chrysoloras—who first translated Plato's *Republic* from Greek into Latin—and others who came to Florence in the early 1400s. Plato's works appealed to these Florentine men of the world in that they connected human learning and cultural achievement with perfection and godliness. If God was the creator, then Platonic man became closer to God by imitating or searching for his wisdom.

In his quest for power and prestige, Cosimo turned not only to banking and politics; he also used artistic and religious patronage to cement his power. He funded the Council of Florence in 1439, in which the Eastern and Western churches sought to unite. Cosimo hosted Pope Eugenius IV and the delegation from Byzantium, which included not just churchmen but also Greek scholars eager to reintroduce the lost language of Aristotle and Plato and their unknown texts. Georgius Gemistus Pletho and Manuel Chrysoloras came to Florence bearing works by Plato previously unknown in the West, and with Cosimo's help, they taught Greek. For the first time, Plato's works could be read in their original by humanist scholars. Pletho and Chrysoloras's leading Florentine student was a member of Cosimo's household: Marsilio Ficino was the son of Cosimo's physician, and when he died, Cosimo took in Ficino. Now the leading Greek scholar of Italy, Ficino set up a Platonic Academy in Careggi, Cosimo's favorite country house.

And so began the most influential philosophical movement of the Renaissance, one that would transform Christianity by bringing to it an ideal of human, earthly achievement. Ficino called for spiritual contemplation, but he believed that this contemplation, mixed with learning, could bring both human perfection and happiness on earth, as well as in the afterlife. Unlike Augustine, he called for a truce between pagan learning and Christian piety. If the Romans felt that life was guided by the winds of fortune, those with intellect could try to guide life on earth. Ficino wrote that things foreseen by prudence could be controlled by humans. Augustine had commanded the faithful to do away with their books of Aristotle, but here Ficino referenced his *Nichomachean Ethics*: To control nature, God's creation, it was necessary to reduce it to "an intellectual foundation." Quoting John 19:11, Ficino linked Greek philosophy to Christianity, claiming that man's intellectual power over fortune could only be God-given and was, therefore, a virtue.[20]

Neo-Platonism meant not simply a contemplative quest for wisdom to become closer to God but also a quest to mimic creation itself through art. Donatello and Botticelli painted classical themes and earthly portraits. The more realistic and beautiful their works, the more godly they were. And Cosimo supported and admired them for this very reason. These materialist patricians were still pious like Datini, but ancient philosophy opened avenues for the rich and brilliant to become closer to God, an appealing idea to those who enjoyed the fruits of Florentine commerce and the pleasures of its high culture. This was a new vision of man's relationship to God that put them on an equal stage, sharing the spark of creation.

But there was a conflict. Ficino's follower Pico della Mirandola (1463–1494) was from a noble family from the Emilia-Romagna near

Modena and had no sympathies for mercantile ethics. He was of Lorenzo's generation and never knew the period when the great bankers brought glory to Florence through their practical skills. Pico was influenced both by his own sense of nobility and by Ficino's Platonic writings. He met both Lorenzo and Ficino in 1484, and both became protectors of the brilliant young scholar. Pico's *Oration on the Dignity of Man* (1486) is in many ways the manifesto of the high Renaissance, for it defined man as a noble creation of God who could, in his own right, create. "Oh great and wonderful happiness of man! It is given to him to have that which he chooses and to be that which he wills." Pico lauded human intellect and held up mathematics as a divine science of understanding nature. However, for Pico, numbers had to remain pure, beyond the impure earthly interests of business. One should not confuse "divine arithmetic," he warned, "with the arithmetic of merchants." This antimercantile view was a cultural shift. The aristocratic philosophy of Neo-Platonism began to eclipse merchant values.[21]

Cosimo always kept his books, but they were not part of the noble world of philosophy and artistic creation that now permeated his spiritual Christian world. If Datini's dilemma was God and profit, Cosimo had inadvertently set up a tension between merchant and divine knowledge, between the base activity of financial management and the higher pursuits of the Platonic elite. It was a dilemma that would have serious ramifications for Cosimo's family, his associates, and the bank.

Understandably, Cosimo had high ambitions for his sons. He saw the Medici as rulers of Florence. Perhaps because of his immersion in Neo-Platonic philosophy, perhaps simply as a sign of his ambition to found a princely family, or maybe as a moment of hubris, Cosimo did not teach accounting to all of his sons. This choice would not only undermine the Medici bank but also helped destabilize Florence itself.

Cosimo had two legitimate sons. The eldest, Piero, had a sense of business but no hard training. He followed the humanist curriculum of teachers like Angelo Poliziano, who focused training on Latin and Greek oratory. Piero would rule the republic. Cosimo's second son, Giovanni, did receive rigorous business training. His role was to rule the bank, and for that he learned like his father did and knew how to keep books and make audits. The problem was that Giovanni enjoyed the pleasures of the good life. He knew how to keep books, but he lacked the discipline to keep them well. He died in 1463 at the age of thirty-four. Piero, known as "the Gouty," was competent but sickly. He ruled from Cosimo's death in 1464 to 1469, and during this period, he attempted to continue the prudent banking strategies of his father. The Medici bank had a head in Piero, but no manager. There was no ultimate auditor, and without one, the bank could not function.[22]

For modern tourists, one of the emblematic faces of Renaissance Florence is that of Cosimo's grandson—the eldest son of Piero—Lorenzo de' Medici (1449–1492), the leader of Florence during its golden age of art. He was considered remarkably ugly in his own time (Machiavelli compared him to a deformed prostitute), but his portrait and busts are unmistakable symbols of the golden age of Florentine art and its fascination with sensuality and force. Botticelli, Bronzino, Verrocchio, and Vasari immortalized Lorenzo's long jointed nose, auburn mane, and fierce expression. He was a poet, a student of Neo-Platonic philosophy, and a friend and patron to Botticelli, Leonardo da Vinci, Michelangelo, and Ghirlandaio. He was also an autocrat, an arbiter of power in Europe and traded with the Ottoman Turks, the new masters of Constantinople. He was also a bad accountant. He trampled Florentine republican liberty, emptied the coffers of the city, and, with this wealth, bought the power of the papacy for his family. The Medici helped build Florence, but now, under Lorenzo, they sapped it of its financial stability and republican freedoms.

Lorenzo is known as the Magnificent, and indeed he represented Florence at its zenith and most dramatic. He comes as close as most political figures ever do to having achieved a level of immortality through fame and art. Historically, *magnifico* is an odd word in Italian, for it has several meanings. Today it is associated with Lorenzo's defiant face, power, and artistic patronage, but in the 1400s the term was actually a technical title of respect for the head of a banking firm: *magnifico major mio*, "my magnificent boss." Rather than a princely title, it was an administrative title within the firm. But following the Medici family, it evolved into a de facto princely status. Lorenzo's title was stretched to *la Magnificenza Vostra*, a more formal title, that, as its holder became princely, it did, too. It should have been a reminder that Lorenzo was still the head of the Medici bank, but quite the opposite happened.[23]

By the time Lorenzo took over the bank at the age of twenty, the managerial transformation was complete. Lorenzo was only the nominal head, not the true manager. He was a master of politics—he survived the early tough challenges to his control of the city, rose through his own skill to rule it, and took over the papacy for his family. But he had neither training in accounting to manage the bank nor the rigorous standards necessary to oversee balancing the books of the city. Although he still had to pose as a citizen of the Florentine Republic, he was educated as a modern prince. It was for this reason that the republican Machiavelli watched him closely.[24]

Lorenzo's capacities and fine education were recognized by his contemporaries. The humanist Alamanno Rinuccini denounced Lorenzo as a tyrant but admitted that he had a "versatile mind" and was able to dance, shoot arrows, sing, ride, play games and musical instruments, and write poetry. To foreign princes, he was a model, and he even sent out his own teachers to train kings and rulers. And he was still head of the Medici bank. But he didn't have the skills or, indeed, the will to run it—Machiavelli said of him that he was an able prince but a poor banker. As a result, Lorenzo resorted to plundering Florentine state coffers to keep the bank afloat. Adam Smith drew the conclusion from this reflection that princes and the state should leave finance to professional financiers.[25]

And so he needed a good and trusted accountant to take not only the role of Benci but also that of his grandfather Cosimo, who had been the ultimate auditor. With the death of financially competent family members, the Medici turned to Francesco Sassetti (1421–1490), the most successful and trustworthy of the great branch managers, who now made all essential decisions for the bank. He oversaw the firm's account books and did all the final audits. It was Sassetti who managed the bank, not as a partner, but in Lorenzo's words, as "our minister." The language was no longer of a firm, but of the court of a prince. Sassetti had not profited from Cosimo's elite education; he had grown up more in the mold of Datini—a competent bookkeeper, bank manager, and merchant who grew rich by disciplined service to the Medici financial system. Sassetti had earned the Medici family's trust by his able handling of the Geneva branch of the firm. An accountant by training, he began to take an interest in Neo-Platonism and the patrician patronage that supported the arts of Renaissance Florence. Unlike Cosimo, who could mix business and culture, Sassetti's cultural interests distracted him from his books.

When Sassetti returned to Florence from Geneva in 1458, he came back to a new life. He was no longer a branch partner but the senior (and rich) manager of the entire Medici bank. He was trusted implicitly. However, being a leading member of the Medici entourage in the 1470s, long after the death of Cosimo, was far different from the life Benci led. Sassetti increasingly spent time not pouring over his accounts, but rather studying with the leading humanist teacher of his day, Angelo Poliziano, and was close friends with Ficino.

Sassetti became involved with civic life and was soon embroiled in a fight with the Church of Santa Maria di Novella, which, for reasons of family prestige and precedence, wanted to deny Sassetti the right to a crypt. Forced to give up this place of honor in one of Florence's most important churches, Sassetti decided to build his own chapel in an area where he owned numerous houses. Here he could showcase his influence, wealth, piety, and sophistication; he worked closely with the great painter Ghirlandaio and became his principal patron.

Conceiving the Sassetti Chapel became Francesco's consuming passion, and it is one for which posterity is grateful. The chapel is one of Ghirlandaio's masterpieces. Its famous frescoes include *Zacharias in the Temple* (1486–1490), which contains portraits of not only the painter himself but also the Neo-Platonists Ficino, Christoforo Landino, Poliziano, and Demetrios Chalkondyles (Demetrius the Greek). The conception of the Sassetti Chapel was a collaboration between the painter and the accountant. Their goals were to make a pious, Christian painting but one that honored Neo-Platonic values and Sassetti's place in the civic hierarchy of Florence. In his *Lives of the Artists*, Vasari says that Ghirlandaio painted the Neo-Platonists in the most lifelike form possible, to show the greatness and central importance of the most learned men in Florence. In one scene, Ghirlandaio painted Sassetti, Lorenzo, Poliziano, and Saint Francis receiving the stigmata. In another, Ghirlandaio drew kneeling portraits of Francesco Sassetti and his wife. Along with these are the *Tiburtine Sibyl Moving the Emperor Octavius to Adore Christ* and a Nativity scene. Ficino complimented Sassetti on his chapel as the very embodiment of the Neo-Platonist ideal.[26]

Ficino, however, knew more about philosophy than he did about business. By the time Sassetti's chapel was finished in 1485, its patron was facing financial difficulties. In his 1488 *Testament to His Sons*, he was frank that the "grievous and dangerous consequences" of poor branch management in Lyon threatened the Sassetti family's fortune and their famous Palazzo de Montui, which he recommended donating to trusted friends in the church so that it would not be confiscated or lost to the family. In spite of his motto, "My fate be kind to me" (*Mitta Fata Mihi*), and his good works and culture, fate had turned on Sassetti, and he worried if he would survive at all.[27]

He blamed the Lyon branch manager, Lionetto de' Rossi, for "bad and neglectful government" of the branch. But Sassetti was technically the managing partner in the branch and therefore responsible. He was the final auditor, and he had let things go. Sassetti had not only allowed branch managers to take risks; he had also stopped keeping rigorous accounts, which was the very essence of his job. Remarkably, one of his personal secret account books survives, his *libro segreto* from the key years 1462 to 1472, and it shows Sassetti's failure. He kept the accounts of the bank in double entry, and in the first years, he kept them assiduously, as he was supposed to. He kept records of the great wealth of his own estate (52,047 florins in 1466) and of the bank's branches, such as that in Avignon. All were in good double-entry form. But beginning in 1472, Sassetti's entries became sporadic. Whole entries went missing. Sassetti, who had trained in the old school of accounting discipline, no longer maintained it. Furthermore, he was not keeping strict control of the branches. He gave more leeway to the branch managers to audit themselves, which effectively meant giving up the reins of management. Branch managers began lending money to foreign princes, a practice Cosimo had forbidden in his day. In 1469, disaster first struck the London branch, when Edward IV did not pay back his debts incurred during the War of the Roses. But it was in 1479 that the Medici bank was brought to its knees.[28]

Already Lorenzo had allowed the ill-fated Bruges branch manager, Tommaso Portinari, to make enormous loans to Charles the Bold, Duke of Burgundy, a man famous for not honoring his debts. Cosimo had thought little of Portinari but nonetheless allowed him to move into a higher partnership level. Portinari owned only about a 13.5 percent stake in the branch, and the Medici owned more than 60 percent. Yet Sassetti gave him free rein. And Portinari enjoyed his place in the court of the duke, where he was received on a footing of royal familiarity. It was not that Portinari was a poor manager himself. The branch's bookkeeper, Carlo Cavalcanti, spent his days bending over the huge ledgers and working the abacus. It was the loan to the Duke of Burgundy, which both Sassetti and Lorenzo surely approved because of political considerations. The great French historian and statesman Philippe de Commines (who had a long conflict with the bank over interest not paid) was stunned at how much cash Portinari apparently had on hand. Portinari extended the duke more than 6,000 Flemish groats of credit, twice the capital of the entire partnership. If the duke did not repay, the loss would be enormous. But Lorenzo's interest may have been securing the duke's support for Medici alum mine interests in Burgundian territory.[29]

Whatever the reason, it went against bank policy, as the loan unbalanced the books. Charles of Burgundy did not repay the loan. When he died in 1477, he owed the bank more than 9,500 groats, three times the capital of the Bruges bank. Further loans were made, but the court could not even meet interest payments. Although the exchange rate fluctuated, the resulting losses for the branch were a staggering 70,000 florins (consider that Cosimo's fortune was assessed at more than 120,000 florins at his death).

In 1478, Lorenzo sent an emissary to make Portinari an offer he could not refuse: He had to liquidate the Medici share and pay back the family. From being a master of finance and politics in Europe, Portinari became destitute. In another example of artistic irony, Portinari had been involved in a long lawsuit to recover a Hans Memling painting of the Last Judgment, commissioned by the Bruges branch between 1467 and 1471, which had been hijacked off a boat by Polish pirates. He now had to give up his claim on the picture. In it, Saint Michael the Archangel holds a scale on which he weighs souls and decides which go to hell. It was a final reckoning in which the life of an accountant had imitated art, for the man depicted on the scale was none other than Tommaso Portinari.

Lyon was not simply another debacle for the Medici bank. This time Sassetti himself was a partner and risked losing all his wealth. As a long-experienced manager and accountant, he must have recognized the danger so evident in his account books. Between 1462 and 1468, returns at the Lyon branch ranged from 70 to 105 percent. Average bank returns were 8 to 10 percent, and a good Medici branch could hope for 15 to 30 percent, based on favorable relationships and high-interest loans to the wealthy and powerful. But returns of 105 percent showed that there were anomalies. Clearly, doubtful credits were allowed to stand on the books for long periods of time, giving a false impression of profit. The auditor's job was to identify these bad credits and revalue them. Sassetti never called the manager to an audit, and he instituted no system of traveling auditors. Because of what Sassetti called the "wicked and negligent mismanagement" of the once incredibly wealthy Lyon branch, and of Sassetti himself, at the age of sixty-eight he was now, in 1488, forced to travel to France to make an audit.[30]

Ghirlandaio, who had once painted masterpieces to celebrate Sassetti's leading place in the Medici bank and Florentine cultural life, now painted the farewell portrait of the failed accountant. A masterpiece by Ghirlandaio, the portrait *Francesco Sassetti and His Son Teodoro* (circa 1488) hangs in the New York Metropolitan Museum of Art, a peaceful portrait of a man and his young son with a rural Tuscan backdrop. The museum's description of the painting notes that Sassetti, "general manager of the Medici banking empire," appears younger in the painting than his late sixties. All evidence suggests that Ghirlandaio painted this work in Sassetti's absence. Indeed, by 1488, Sassetti had left Florence to deal with a crisis at the Lyon branch of the firm. He was so concerned that he would never return that he left this painting as a last legacy, along with a will.

When he returned from Lyon in 1488, Sassetti had lost his fortune and his family's leading place in Florentine affairs. The Medici bank was no longer a power. As Adam Smith noted, princes make poor bankers, for the temptation to put personal glory over sound business sense is ever present. Lorenzo lost much of his banking fortune, but he could still use public funds to finance his family's projects. After the Medici were expelled from Florence in 1494 and the republic was restored under the chancellorship of Machiavelli (who knew how to keep double-entry books), the Medici used their wealth to hire mercenaries and take back the city. Lorenzo's grandson, Lorenzo di Piero de' Medici, would come back to topple the republic and rule from 1513 to 1519. He imprisoned and tortured Machiavelli. Lorenzo's second son, Giovanni de' Medici, would be named Pope Leo X in 1513; one great-grandson would come back to rule a considerably less influential Florence as the grand duke Cosimo I of Tuscany; and another would become Pope Leo XI in 1605 (albeit for twenty-six days until his death). But Lorenzo's poor management had reduced the bank to almost nothing, and his politics had hobbled the once-powerful republic. The only trace of how much Medici hubris cost Florence is in the account books now in the archives of the defunct republic.

Cosimo de' Medici spent part of his fortune sponsoring the philosophy of Neo-Platonism and his own quest for earthly glory. To the extent his family remained powerful, he succeeded. Medici became popes, grand dukes of Tuscany, and progenitors of the kings of France. The story of the Medici and their hapless accountant, Sassetti, shows that a tradition as old and ingrained as Florentine bookkeeping could quickly evaporate. Cosimo, the greatest banker of his age, could never have imagined that his fascination with the philosophy of Plato would help undermine the culture of accounting and accountability for hundreds of years. Indeed, it was one of his most potent and lasting legacies.

CHAPTER 4

The Mathematician, the Courtier, and the Emperor of the World

I do not wish to break my brains trying to comprehend
something which I do not understand now, nor have I
ever understood in all my days.

—PHILIP II, KING OF SPAIN, 1574

I t is ironic that the first printed manual on double-entry bookkeeping appeared at the moment Italian power in Europe began to collapse. The Dominican friar, humanist, and mathematician Luca
Pacioli (1445–1517) published his *Summa de Arithmetica, Geometria,
Proportioni, et Proportionalita (Treatise on Arithmetic, Geometry and Proportion)* in 1494, the same year that the first invasions of Italy brought
down republican regimes and installed French and Spanish royal power
on the peninsula. Double-entry accounting had existed for around 200
years, yet only now, as the rule of the Renaissance merchants waned,
were its methods printed in an accessible manual. Pacioli's story is, at
least at its beginning, the story of the first published manual on accounting. It is also the story of how this manual languished for almost
a hundred years, ignored by merchants and thinkers alike. In the great
monarchies of the sixteenth century, ruled by sometimes chivalrous and

Neo-Platonic princes, accounting became scorned as a low merchant art, even as kings and princes struggled to find good accountants to administer their finances. This prejudice against accounting would have grave ramifications for the continually bankrupt Spanish Empire.

Pacioli is considered the father of accounting, and his manual is its founding work. All major manuals on accounting, from the Renaissance to the modern age, are based in part on Pacioli's publication, making him the central author in the history of accounting. Yet as Francesco Datini's use of double-entry bookkeeping shows, Pacioli's treatise came late in the game, when accounting and its culture were losing prestige. It did not become one of the great books of the Renaissance, with a hallowed place in humanism. Few great scholars and thinkers, and fewer still political leaders of the 1500s, even knew the book, and fewer still used it for government administration.

A Tuscan Franciscan friar, an expert in geometry and algebra, and a student of Neo-Platonism, Pacioli came from the same world as Cosimo de' Medici, in which business was the basis of political power. He believed that accounting was tightly linked to civic humanism: the mix of business, classical learning, and urban cultural patronage that made cities such as Florence wealthy showcases of commerce, learning, art, and architecture. As a churchman and a mathematician, Pacioli believed that this great chain of being was held together by God's language: mathematics. Double-entry bookkeeping was a very earthly but necessary mathematical method and philosophy for regulating daily financial life.[1]

Pacioli's life followed a remarkable professional trajectory. Skilled in mathematics, he had trained to be a merchant in an abacus school in his Tuscan hometown of Borgo Sansepolcro, near Arezzo. He found a place in the workshop of the great painter and famed mathematician Piero della Francesca, who had helped revive Euclid's works on geometry and whose paintings, such as *The Flagellation of Christ* (circa 1455), are brilliant but imperfect studies in perspective and proportion. Despite never being an original thinker but rather a good explainer, Pacioli had a knack for making friends with great artists of the time. Della Francesca took a great interest in Pacioli and brought him to Milan, where he introduced him to one of the leading humanists of his time, the famed engineer, architect, and philosopher Leon Battista

Alberti, who, like earlier humanists, liked to combine practical, artisanal knowledge with formal philosophy. Indeed, in his *On the Family* (1434), a treatise on the philosophy of the household and family life in Florence, Alberti stressed the importance of accounting and home economics. Alberti brought Pacioli to Rome, where he become a churchman and a famous university teacher, interacting with such artists as Gentile Bellini and Giovanni Bellini, Botticelli, Ghirlandaio, Pietro Perugino, Luca Signorelli, and perhaps even Dürer.[2]

The most famous painting of an accountant is that of Pacioli attributed to Jacopo di Barbari (1495). It shows the master of algebra and proportion with his student, Guidobaldo da Montefeltro (1472–1508), the Duke of Urbino. In this work, Pacioli is shown working on a problem of algebra, but at the lower right-hand corner of the work there appears a ledger. In 1474, Pacioli became tutor to the Duke of Urbino's son, an eminent post in one of the great humanist centers in Italy. Here was the height of Italian humanism: a Franciscan monk, with a prince, calculating the way to understand and represent human proportion through mathematics. Urbino was the most refined court in Italy, yet it still had a foot in the medieval merchant past that linked guild masters and city patricians to nobles. Indeed, the duke himself encouraged Pacioli's teaching of accounting, for Urbino, like all small Italian city-states, depended on trade for its wealth.

Most notably, Pacioli was a close friend to Leonardo da Vinci. Leonardo sketched a dodecahedron, which was earlier seen in di Barbari's portrait of Pacioli, a study for proportional painting and geometry. Leonardo also made drawings of Plato's five regular bodies (earth, water, air, fire, and sky), both solid and hollow. Pacioli described his friend as a "prince among mortals." Leonardo had long conversations with Pacioli about three-dimensional painting and, indeed, painted *The Last Supper* (1495–1498) in close consultation with Pacioli on the use of perspective and proportion.[3]

Pacioli lived in a world in which classical humanists and political leaders valued double-entry bookkeeping as an essential form of knowledge. Quoting Virgil, Saint Paul, Saint Matthew, and Dante, Pacioli assured the reader that God will take care of the vigilant, charitable hard worker who knows how to count. The balance of account books represented the moral equilibrium of God. Where Datini gave advice to his employees, Pacioli sketched a worldview. Hard work, accounting, and profits were holy virtues. The *Summa*'s chapter on accounting, "On Computing" (*De computis* in Latin), was a founding work for later political economy, for it spelled out the fundaments of finance and explained why they were essential in the maintenance of republics. Commerce, industry, and profit, implied Pacioli, were the basis of healthy states and public financial administration. Here, conceived with the tools of the Italian Middle Ages and Renaissance, was a book for the modern age.[4]

The basics of accounting have changed little since Pacioli printed his *Summa* more than 500 years ago. The Tuscan monk did not claim to do anything new. But he recognized that there was no systematic guide to "accounts and their keeping" in an "orderly way." Pacioli felt that accounting would help the duke's subjects be good merchants, and in doing such, he promised the duke in his dedication of the book, credit and business would flourish in his realm. If transactions were kept faithfully, that would not only help merchants but also put them in good stead with God, for they would be "trustworthy" and "upright." The road to trust and goodness was through the clarity of mathematics and how data were recorded in books. The Venetian system, as Pacioli called it, provided measures of profit and loss based on the balance of credits and debits, and this helped bring godly order to the human world.[5]

Pacioli's accounting manual offered the merchant the basic and essential tool of capitalism: the capacity to calculate at all times his assets and liabilities. The first step in good accounting was to make an inventory of assets—from houses, land, and jewelry to currency and silverware, linens, beds, spices, skins, and other merchandise. Assets were the capital from which debits and credits were made. Then books had to be kept, recording spending and income as related to capital holding. Four books were necessary: the inventory of assets, the memorandum (*memoriale*), the journal (*giornale*), and the ledger (*quaderno*).[6]

In the memorandum, the merchant wrote down or pasted receipts from the day's transactions, "hour by hour," detailing "everything he sells or buys." The memorandum was necessary not just for real-time recording of data but also for recording all the different monetary transactions that could take place in a number of different currencies—they would have to be calculated into a single currency value. At the end of each day, the merchant would have to systematically transfer notes, receipts, and summaries of transactions in the memorandum into the journal as debits and credits.[7]

The journal was a chronological record of all pertinent information for each transaction, noting the dates, the agents, the merchandise, and the currency. All would be noted under *per* ("for"), to be debited, or *avere* ("to have"), to be credited. These chronological debits and credits would then be transferred to the ledger. Each time a transaction was transferred to the ledger, a letter (*A*, *B*, or *C*) was written to mark where the transaction could be found in the corresponding book. Then a red line was drawn through the transaction to show that the credit had been transferred, and a second red line was drawn when it was balanced with a corresponding debit. The ledger was systematically organized under headings for specific products, such as "Ginger," or for specific businesses or ventures.[8]

Going beyond explaining what double entry was, Pacioli gave concrete examples of types of transactions. Readers could see exactly how to keep certain forms of accounts. He explained how to manage a household, a business trip, a multipartner venture, and a municipal public account, as well as how to account for a loan for a drug store. Providing sample entries from existing firms, he insisted on the rule the Medici had broken: Proprietors had to audit their managers.

Pacioli hoped that accounting would make his society better: "Businessmen maintain republics," and he claimed that accountants needed more skill and discipline than lawyers. Indeed, for Pacioli, the merchant was the key figure in a republic, for merchants could count, calculate, and manage abundance and war, famine and pestilence. Republics needed well-educated, disciplined, and moral merchants, for they were disciplined and vigilant managers of both business and government. Pacioli did admit that accounting was not for everyone. Laziness, he warned, could bring catastrophe.[9]

The discipline of accounting was central to republican accountability. Pacioli insisted that a good merchant kept good books so that they could be easily audited by city officials. A good merchant or clerk kept accounts so there would be no suspicion that they were false. The identity of all handwriting must be verified by notes or personal presentation to officials. Pacioli also explained how to handle accounting when dealing with tax or excise officials and how to present one's accounts to them. He lamented that public accounting officials were often poorly trained and mixed up their books. "Woe to you if you have anything to do with these people." The businessman must "keep his head in his store" and bring clearly kept books to any tax transaction or audit. Even more, tax officials, too, had a responsibility to be impeccable accountants. Venice, he noted, is glorious for punishing tax clerks who misbehave or keep bad books.[10]

A practical man, Pacioli recognized that not everyone was fit to keep books. Discipline was essential, for nothing, Pacioli warned, could be omitted from the records. Even business conversations should be written down alongside transaction accounts. "The merchant," he noted, "can never be too plain." Pacioli also recognized that cheating was a problem. It was always possible to keep two sets of books. "Unfortunately, there are many who keep their books in duplicate, showing one to the buyer and one to the seller. What is worse, they swear and perjure themselves on them." Even accountants often, and indeed systematically, kept secret books to hide their business from tax collectors and competitors. Datini did it, and so did Cosimo. Pacioli recommended that all bookkeepers invoke the name of Jesus, "in whose name all business should be transacted," by writing a cross on each account book. Datini and Cosimo did that, too, on their secret books. In reality, "For God and Profit" depended on an odd mix of clarity and deceit. Pacioli hoped that early training, based on sound religious ideas, would produce a form of accounting that was both ordered and moral.[11]

Here, for the first time, was Datini and Cosimo's method, explained for all to see—and to copy. It was more than a model for merchants; it also outlined the basic methods and ethical controls necessary for good public finance. A practical Italian reader might have seen it as the perfect handbook for the management of a prosperous republic. What had been common but mostly private Italian knowledge was now potentially open to all. The secrets of the counting house were demystified and soon internationalized. Potentially any city or prince could, with Pacioli's book, establish accounting schools and train the kind of administrative elite described by Pacioli.

Commerce now had a rhetoric, a mode of argument and proof. Humanists were obsessed with the Roman lawyer Cicero, who claimed that the rhetoric of making arguments and providing proof was a great civic virtue. Good citizens expressed themselves publicly and proved their points. It was a civic duty to do so. An account book was like an argument with a moral end. Its data were laid out and tallied, and its final sum was an argument for success or failure. Although the calculations might be complex, the final tally could be seen as an unimpeachable claim. That had authority in finance and law. It also had the numerical force of the sciences. Potentially, Pacioli's printed manual could teach mathematics, the theory of proportion, and accounting to all who read and mastered it. Pacioli had high hopes for the success of his book.[12]

And yet the book did not catch on. Pacioli's *Summa* itself was not a particularly successful book by Renaissance standards. There was the edition of 1494, which is extremely rare and must have been printed in a quite limited edition, and the second edition of 1524. The aristocracy and high nobility still had a foot in the recent mercantile past, but they were not necessarily in the market to buy an accounting manual. Medici popes were the grandsons of Medici bankers. Figures like the powerful Chigi family of Rome were still merchants but also humanists and men of the church. Pacioli's work would have made sense to them, for, in their lives, commerce, mathematics, and algebra all crossed in a quest for wealth, art, and wisdom. But among Italian merchants and even wealthy landowners, it was believed that accounting had to be learned by experience at home, in an office, or in an accounting academy.[13]

In any case, in Italy, homemade accounting manuals were easily accessible. There is ample evidence that Pacioli's chapter on accounting was a printed version of a commonly circulated Venetian manuscript accounting manual of the time. This might explain why there were few Italian translations of Pacioli's book. In great humanist tradition, the book was used as a basis for others' works that never directly credited him. The first person to reproduce large sections of *De computis* was Domenico Manzoni in his *Double Entry Books and Their Journal (1540)*. Manzoni was a Venetian abacus master who had trained with the famous accounting teacher Antonio Mariafior. Manzoni's book included large passages verbatim from Pacioli. He also tried to clarify a number of questions, such as which items should be debits or credits and how to value live things (always tricky even with today's statistical probability), and he included an illustrative set of account books with three hundred sample entries. A merchant could thus consult Manzoni on how to transform a transaction into a journal entry.[14]

What is most striking about the fifty years following the first publication of the *Summa* and *De computis* is how few reproductions of the work there were. Accounting knowledge flowed mostly out of Venice but not with any clear trajectory. Books about currency exchanges, markets, tides, ports, exchange paperwork, and taxes had long been written by hand or printed and circulated as business manuals. There was a long manuscript tradition of homemade merchant manuals and books that traveled in boats and carts and were always kept near desks and accounting and exchange tables. These books were called the *ars mercatoria*, the business arts. Mostly, merchants made them by hand as part of their series of account books.[15]

Pacioli's lack of success in spreading the theory of double entry was not entirely his fault. At the very moment his book was being published, his Italian merchant world was literally under attack by the Spanish and French monarchies. In 1494—the year the *Summa* was published—France, followed by Spain, invaded the peninsula and turned the richest parts of Italy into a bloody battlefield for more than sixty years. It has been said that the age of the Italian republic gave way to the age of chivalry, but the transition was brutal as civic, mercantile humanism also gave way to the aristocratic, even imperial ideal by the force of arms. In this new era of ascendant kingdoms and empires, Pacioli's old dictum about healthy republics and good merchants had little echo. The ethics of business, banking, and the balance book befitted neither the divine right monarch, the soldier, nor the courtier in the same way it had the merchant managers of Italy.

Duke Guidobaldo of Urbino strikes a noble pose in his portrait with Pacioli. It is telling, though, that di Barbari's painting is remembered for the accountant and not the duke. Guidobaldo had good taste in humanists, but he was a woeful ruler, sexually impotent, sickly, and unlucky in war. He was driven from his court by Cesare Borgia, the brutal son of Pope Alexander VI, but in spite of the continued domination of Italy by its Spanish masters, Guidobaldo was lucky to return to power in 1504. Serving him on his return was a young soldier from Mantua, Baldassare Castiglione, in command of fifty men-at-arms. Castiglione is not remembered as a soldier or even as the papal nuncio he was at his death in Toledo in 1529. Instead, he is remembered as one of the greatest authors of the Renaissance whose book *The Courtier* (1528) became one of the defining works of Western literature. It also undermined the values of accounting by describing the ideal noble as someone who did not dabble in the intricacies of finance.[16]

Castiglione described the perfect courtier as one who had "no shortcomings whatsoever." This was not Christian humility, but rather a knightly form of Neo-Platonism. Castiglione's flower of chivalric and humanist Christendom would be expert in personal discipline, self-control, and all the knowledge required by the courts of the pope, the king of France, and the Holy Roman Emperor. A great courtier would have to be pious and know how to serve, converse, sing, dance, love, fight, and write sonnets. Like the legendary knight Amadis de Gaul, he would be a courteous, virtuous knight. Above all, he would have to be prudent—that ancient ethic of Aristotle, Seneca, Tacitus, Plato, and Cicero—and he would have to hide his emotions and motives, weigh his options, and navigate a world of courtly servility and power. Even more, Castiglione's book preached the idea of *sprezzatura*, je ne sais quoi, or the aristocratic illusion of effortless achievement. It was in stark contrast with the ethic of meticulous bookkeeping in accounting and the revelatory practice of both calculating and auditing. There could be no *sprezzatura* in the cold numbers and relentless record keeping of accounting.[17]

What is interesting here is that Castiglione never mentions the kind of administrative expertise harnessed by Cosimo and explicated by Pacioli. He never mentions finances, let alone accounting and the idea of being able to keep or audit books—an elemental practice of statecraft. It was *The Courtier*—a book without numbers that shunned merchant culture—that was, in the end, embraced by noble and even merchant readers. A nobleman, Castiglione was at first hesitant to publish his book, so the manuscript circulated instead. But demand was such that he eventually asked the great Venetian printing house of Aldus Manutius to publish it. In 1528, a first print run of 1,030 copies appeared. In all, around fifty editions of the work appeared in the sixteenth century, making it one of the great best sellers of its time, in stark contrast to Pacioli's two editions. There is evidence that *The Courtier* was read by even the Holy Roman Emperor himself, Charles V (1500–1558), ruler of Spain, the Hapsburg lands in Austria and Hungary, the Netherlands, Burgundy, Milan, southern Italy, and an overseas empire on which the sun never set. When Castiglione died in 1529, the emperor remarked, "I tell you one of the finest gentlemen in the world is dead." It was high praise from the ruler of half the world.[18]

Neo-Platonism discredited accounting not just for Castiglione but also among influential humanists by feeding into old prejudices against business and earning money through trade. When the most famous of all Neo-Platonist philosophers, Pico della Mirandola, scorned merchant knowledge, it was his school of aristocratic humanism that appealed to the elites of Europe and its empires. The humanist curriculums of giants of the late fifteenth and early sixteenth centuries, like famed scholar Erasmus of Rotterdam and Ignatius Loyola, founder of the Jesuits, stressed discipline, note taking, and record keeping, but not for financial gain. In Erasmus's *Education of a Christian Prince* (1516), finance is never mentioned. Founded in 1534, the Jesuit order stressed mathematics in its curriculum, but not for trade. Indeed, Jesuits kept accounts themselves. To run their monastic order, Italian Jesuits taught themselves accounting for the household and financial management of their enormous undertakings. They also created elaborate systems of moral accounting in which sins and good deeds were tallied in "spiritual account books." The Jesuits were famous for teaching applied geometry, navigation, astronomy, and even military engineering, yet their official curriculum did not include accounting. They would become the teachers of kings, but kings could do no reckoning on their own kingdoms. There was a cultural taboo on commercial accounting.[19]

Scholastic thinkers had long condemned money lending. Quoting Saint Jerome, the great twelfth-century legal thinker Gratian had clearly stated: "The merchant cannot please God." This medieval view persisted in the Renaissance. Rabelais noted that a truly "noble prince never has a *sou*" and that to "save money is truly a villain thing." In his

Essays, even Montaigne explained how the profit of one man damages another. Noblemen fought, prayed, lived in luxury, and even administered. But they did not count money.[20]

Accounting, or at least bad accounting, was associated with avarice and sin. The evolution of Quentin Matsys's painting *The Banker (or Moneylender) and His Wife* gives a sense of this persistent discomfort with counting and accounting for money. Painted in 1514, and now in the Louvre, it shows a banker weighing coins, as others lie on the table. His wife, beside him, holds a page of a book of hours. The art historian Erwin Panofsky describes how Matsys mixed a religious, devotional scene with a realistic portrait of Renaissance office life. Rather than a critique of money handling, the banker seems to portray the seriousness of a careful merchant and his pious wife. It was reported at the time that the picture's frame contained a passage from Leviticus 19:36: "Just balances, just weight, . . . shall ye have."[21]

Matsys's image of money handling and piety would inspire a popular series of eight paintings begun in 1519 by Marinus van Reymerswaele with the same title, but very importantly, the book of hours in the wife's hand was replaced with an account book. This substitution had major significance. The banker and his wife had lost the book with the image of the Virgin and Child. Now they had only a book of monetary numbers. Without the religious book, the scene was now purely mercantile, showing only material temptation and not pious management. These paintings were stark warnings to a profession that, van Reymerswaele suggested, had no morals.[22]

A Catholic who had attended the University of Leuven, Van Reymerswaele went further. He apparently copied another painting by Matsys, now lost, of two customs collectors, transforming it into the first popular anti-accounting image. His *Two Tax Gatherers* (1540, National Gallery, London) is not only an outright attack on the covetousness of moneylenders, but also on official tax collectors, taxes, and the tricks of accounting. It is exceptional in showing the tools of accounting: Books, receipts, exchange slips, and file boxes litter the room. The accountant dutifully makes readable entries into a finely bound account book. The second figure in the painting, twisted and grimacing, appears to be a client making a verbal order. The account book is in the center of the painting, and the second figure points to it, smirking and grimacing, to give a clear sense that the transaction being recorded is dishonest. Whether depicting business or tax collection, the painting connects financial management and bookkeeping to immorality, trickery, and unchristian behavior.[23] Pacioli's manual was tainted by this critical view of business.

The moral conundrum was that kings needed bankers and merchants to raise revenues for their armies, navies, palaces, and courts. The sometimes vile act of accounting was an ever more necessary administrative tool. Kings needed it, but they most often did not have the knowledge or skilled administrators so common to merchant republics. The lack of an accounting culture would strain the financial administration of many states and even the Spanish Empire.

By the late 1530s, the Holy Roman Emperor, Charles V, had every reason to see himself as the first among gentlemen in the world. Ruler of the Spanish and Hapsburg empires, he had defeated the French, taken over the papacy, and ruled Italy through the Kingdom of Naples, outward to Milan and Urbino and down to Sicily. He had secured his New World holdings and set out his Hapsburg administration across South America. The fabled wealth of the Peruvian (now Bolivian) silver mines of Potosí was now in the hands of Castile. Charles's grandparents, Ferdinand and Isabella, had captured that most exotic but familiar of jewels: The caliphate of Granada capitulated in 1492, and with it the wealth of Al-Ándalus, today Andalusia, fell into the hands of the Spanish who had lived next door for seven hundred years. But even more than the riches of the Alhambra or Peruvian silver, Charles owned the most valuable jewel of all. For all his tropical and Mediterranean might, Charles was born in Ghent, and at the basis of his Burgundian inheritance were the old lands of the Charolais—Belgium and Holland. With their unending supply of international trade, the Netherlands was becoming the richest place in the world. Fewer than a million good Dutch burghers produced 40 percent of the tax receipts of the Spanish Empire, whose population numbered tens of millions of souls.[24]

Charles needed not only good courtiers; he also needed a good accountant, and while he knew it, he did not know how to transform this knowledge into effective policy. The problem of empire is that it is a source of unimaginable wealth, but good accounts often show that it costs more than it earns to hold regions, ports, and colonies across the globe. This was Charles's problem, and it would be the enduring legacy of the great imperial dynasty he founded. Before Charles was ever rich, he was in debt. The Spanish nobility had conquered and stood to administer so much territory that it needed financial managers to handle its massive income and staggering expenditures. The emperor had to get his cut of everything, and being a good Burgundian, he relied on the massive legal apparatus of his empire to require that all transactions be calculated and that everyone pay their *alcabala* (5 to 14 percent sales tax) to the emperor.

Bankers were in short supply in Spain. So Charles put his fate in the hands of bankers from Germany, Italy, Holland, and Spain, and he set out to reorganize Spanish financial administration. Not surprisingly, in a merchant empire with holdings in Italy and Holland, bankers in Genoa and Augsburg, and its massive fleet bringing gold, silver, spice, rare woods, plants, and the profits from its slave monopoly and sugar and tobacco farms into Seville, account books were everywhere. Yet the old imperial knight did not know how to use them.[25]

The concepts of accounting and auditing existed in some parts of the Spanish administration and the Spanish merchant community, especially in Seville. Founded by their Catholic Majesties Ferdinand and Isabella in 1503, the Casa de la Contratación, or House of Trade, was a giant record house and center of administration for Spanish trade with the Americas. It was managed by Sevillian merchants who, having traded across the globe and worked closely with Italians, were sometimes fluent in double entry. Basic accounts, the *Libros de cargo y data* ("charge and discharge books"), were kept in double entry. The bylaws of the institution stipulated that the Casa was to constitute a warehouse for moving merchandise to and from the Indies, and as such, it would act as a customs house. The crown appointed three chief administrators: a factor, a treasurer, and an accountant. The *Libros de cargo y data* were to have distinctive bindings, and the accountant was to record in detail all the treasurer had received and spent. As in Genoa, there was a system to limit fraud: All operations had to be recorded in a central book, and each entry had to be signed by three officials.[26]

The complex operations of a sixteenth-century empire and colonization were, at least theoretically, financially managed. For example, the belongings of those deceased in the New World were transferred to the Casa in coffers. Careful accounts were made of the contents of each coffer (often precious metals and jewels), and if they were not reclaimed by heirs, the contents were accounted for as income, indeed, important income for the crown. Double entry was useful in accounting for this floating wealth that could be disbursed either straight to an heir or as state income spent on salaries and crown expenses.[27]

Charles needed to make the financial system of the Casa de la Contratación that of his own administration. The challenge, however, proved elusive. In 1523, Charles V centralized the Real Hacienda by bringing state administration and tax collection under one account. In the Pragmatic Sanction of 1552, the emperor decreed that all account books for merchants and administrators be kept in double entry or at least in books that recorded receipts and expenditures. In 1556, the emperor created the position of Factor General of the Kings of Spain, an expert in double entry, who was responsible for keeping the *Libros de cargo y data* for the whole empire.[28]

This did not make Charles a financial manager, nor did it mean he had the skilled administrators to carry out his policy. Although Charles wanted good administrative accounting, he never implemented the reforms. In what was to become an ongoing tradition for the great monarchs of Europe, Charles and his ministers simply juggled his income with his outsize imperial debts. Because of his aristocratic ethic, account books were of no interest to him. By the time of his abdication in 1556, the empire was running a 36 million ducat debt and a million a year deficit, and 68 percent of total revenue went to pay previous loans to foreign bankers.[29]

When Charles's son Philip came to the throne, he was not Holy Roman Emperor (his uncle Ferdinand inherited that title); rather he was king of Spain, Portugal, and ruler of the Spanish empire. Philip II was the first grand-scale, hands-on bureaucrat king, yet he, too, refused to do accounting. His information system was so vast, so intricate, and in some cases so efficient that even the Venetian ambassador sent his reports back to Venice via Spanish royal messenger posts. This king, on whose empire the sun never set, was not a traveler, but rather inhabited his own virtual world, enclosed in the halls of his immense monastery palace, the Escorial, which he filled with mountains of dispatches and reports (he was known as "the king of paperwork"). The Escorial was a cavernous center of power from which the king worked at his desk, trying to read and respond to every report written from his international network of agents. More than 100,000 documents crossed his desk each year—far more than he could effectively manage. He maintained massive archives, most notably in the walled castle of Simancas, as well as in the rapidly expanding imperial trade and industry archives in the Casa de la Contratación. In the end, however, Philip's information system was as cumbersome as the empire it tried to manage. His dominion was so large that it sometimes took seven years for him to respond to correspondence from such far-flung posts as the Philippines. Studies of Spanish administration show the frustration engendered by one man's control of too much minutiae. Philip managed to keep general control over his system, but there were many issues and projects to which he could not give his attention, and accounts were primary among them.[30]

One would have expected a man so obsessed with data and control to take a keen interest in accounting. Indeed, Pacioli's Christian accounting might have appealed to Philip. Like Charles V, Philip spent a great deal of time worrying about money. He dressed in black, like a sober merchant or, as he said, like a monk. He studied Saint Thomas to understand the concept of "just price" rather than profit. Although he maintained the identity of a monk-king, he was a much more hands-on administrator than his father. Yet Philip admitted his "ignorance as to financial affairs" and that he knew nothing of accounting: "I cannot tell a good account book or financial report on the subject from a bad one. And I do not wish to break my brains trying to comprehend something which I do not understand now, nor have I ever understood in all my days." Philip felt only frustration and disdain for finance. Even with his obsessive habits of micromanagement, he had no intention of trying to understand the books of his empire. He would leave the absolutely essential task of managing the state's books in someone else's hands.[31]

Philip had to pay for the Holy League, a Mediterranean fleet that defeated the Ottoman Turks in 1571 at the Battle of Lepanto. It was glory indeed for his Catholic Majesty, but it came at a staggering price. Even after the battle, maintenance of the fleet cost 7 million escudos between 1571 and 1573. At the same time, Spain was fighting a rebellion in the Netherlands. Not only were almost half the tax receipts of the empire threatened but also maintaining troops who were waging savage warfare even on civilian populations cost 11 million ducats between 1572 and 1575. Balance this against the 5 to 6 million ducats the crown received in income from both American and Castilian holdings, and it is clear Philip's position was untenable. Bankruptcy loomed, and Philip needed to act.[32]

In 1573, Philip appointed Juan de Ovando (1515–1575) to oversee a new Council of Finance and implement reforms to avoid bankruptcy. An inquisitor at the Sevillian Tribunal of the Holy Office, Ovando was a powerful member of the great governing bodies of Spain's empire: the Council of the Spanish Empire and Presidency of the Council of the Indies. Inquisitors were not simply crushers of heresy but also highly trained administrators. They oversaw church religious doctrine, law, and finance. Ovando's job was to reorganize state finance. He recognized that the king had given him a difficult job, pointing out that "finance was an object of especial terror [to most in government] since so few seemed to grasp what was involved."[33]

Ovando studied the effectiveness of state financial reporting and auditing. What he found was that the three principal financial institutions of the crown failed to share essential information. The Contaduría de Hacienda concerned itself with the day-to-day running of the treasury and the collecting (farming) of taxes. The Contaduría de Cuentas checked the accounts and presented its findings to the crown. The Consejo de Hacienda developed financial policy with an eye to raising more royal income. Without intercommunication, these three institutions often replicated each other's functions. Ovando saw a "multi-headed hydra" that was constantly in dissonance and often misinformed. Financial information was not accurate. He complained that the heads of his own administration were "so busy . . . nobody considers [financial] affairs as his own."[34]

Ovando did not know double entry, but he understood its centralizing and balancing principle. His office would need a building of its own and trained, dedicated administrators to attend meetings in which all Council of Finance decisions would be made with a quorum of four. Ovando evoked as a model the Spanish viceroyalty of the Kingdom of

Naples and its Royal Council of Finance, of whose members it was said "there is not one who does not understand it (accounting and finance) as if it were his own domestic budget." Naples not only had abacus and double-entry schools; Pacioli himself had taught there for a time and had probably helped train accounting masters. As in other Italian cities, double entry was a prized form of knowledge, even among the governing class. The Spanish viceroy, don Pedro de Toledo, collected taxes through the established Neapolitan system, and although this system was chaotic, the state financial records were at least centralized and its managers highly trained in accounting techniques.[35]

Ovando's correspondence makes it clear that this was not the case in Spain. The council, he warned, needed not "priests and lawyers," but trained "clerks and accountants" who could be promoted as auditors. Only in this way could the Spanish government create complete account books. One internal memo noted that the officials in charge of international taxation and finance did not have the financial tools to effectively negotiate with Genoese and German bankers. Finally, Ovando made an essential and, by this time, revolutionary point: This central council would need the direct support and attention of the king. Only he could be the final auditor. Without this, Ovando's concept of an inquisitor of state accounts would not have effective authority.[36]

On April 11, 1574, Ovando produced a giant balance sheet of Philip's finances. Although it was based on faulty financial reporting and primitive accounting, the report was a remarkable achievement, and its numbers were unarguably dire. The crown had an estimated income of 5,642,304 ducats. It had a debt of well over 73,908,171 ducats. Essential annual expenditure was around 3 million ducats. Even without any expenditures, it would take the crown fifteen years of full income to pay off its debts.[37]

Ovando and the king had a global financial crisis on their hands. With the Netherlands burning and all corners of the empire calling out for funds, Ovando felt the crown needed to raise taxes. But to collect more tax revenue, the state needed better accountants and financial administration. Here was Philip's moment to modernize and centralize the Spanish government. At Philip's behest, Ovando had proposed centralized accounting as the necessary administrative tool. Yet, as Philip himself admitted, double entry is a very threatening tool. He knew that whoever mastered his books would have, in some ways, more power than he did. Ovando lamented in a letter that "his majesty did not trust me or the (other ministers) of finance," so financial matters were often decided by Philip's smaller council of high ministers, which Ovando considered financially ignorant.[38]

Threatened by Ovando, these powerful members of the government fought back. One of Philip's counselors, Antonio de Padilla y Meneses, questioned whether Ovando, already an old man, knew anything of financial matters. He had neither able ministers nor formal training. Padilla questioned if anyone at an advanced age could truly learn finance from scratch. It was a science and true profession, he said, like being a doctor or lawyer. Padilla admitted that he himself could never learn it. He knew that good accountants had to be trained at a young age to gain fluent mastery of numbers and the discipline of keeping daily, complex books. But the crown would not train accountants to fill its own administrative needs.[39]

By refusing to fully implement Ovando's reforms, Philip made the government's financial woes worse. Perhaps this fulfilled Philip's personal obsession with maintaining control over his government. Rather than creating and centralizing state accounts, Philip went on a financial witch hunt and in 1575 made a series of audits of his own administration, bogging it down at the very moment Ovando believed it needed to be mobilized to manage the state bankruptcy. He obsessed about paperwork and administration, but there was a deep voyeuristic quality to his interest. He loved confidential memoranda from informants and was most inspired by Ovando's claims that ministers were embezzling royal funds. Yet this was a distraction, and the king now had even more trouble raising revenue to master his empire, the richest part of which was tearing away in the Dutch Revolt. More than ever, the crisis of the Spanish monarchy seemed a crisis of accounting and accountability.[40]

Philip, for all his faults, realized that one can fire one's accountant, but the problems do not go away. And he realized that Padilla was right: He needed a trained accountant to master his finances. Merchants had been part of the empire's administrative apparatus, and they most often hailed from Seville, the merchant entrepôt of the empire. Those who learned to mix trade with state administration passed through the Casa de la Contratación and could be effective administrative experts. Philip's attention was drawn to Pedro Luis de Torregrosa (1522–1607), a man who had the practical merchant experience Juan de Ovando lacked and was less of an administrative threat to the jealous king.

From 1559 to 1562, Torregrosa had worked for the Casa de la Contratación—the state imperial house of trade—one of the few parts of the government that kept double-entry accounts. Benefiting from his superior administration and the wealth of precious metals from the New World, Torregrosa made a welcome profit for the crown. By 1573, Torregrosa had begun administering the sales tax. Trusted by Philip II, he was a state auditor and helped manage the royal mint. By 1580, Philip clearly understood that Ovando's recommendations needed to be followed. He asked Torregrosa to create a central state account book in double entry. This required other state officials to give Torregrosa their own books, and there was so much resistance to the reform that the emperor himself complained of "those who opposed the creation of this account book."[41]

Again, Philip's interest in administration was outweighed by his grander ambitions and follies. In 1588, he launched the most disastrous naval expedition Europe had ever known: the Armada. It had deep roots in accounting, for building a fleet, maintaining ships, and keeping their logs all necessitated skilled accounting. The facts of the debacle are well-known—the captain of the fleet was inexperienced, and the weather played against the Spanish. The English small boats decimated the larger open-sea Spanish vessels. Dozens of ships were lost, and tens of thousands of men died or were taken prisoner. Added to this was the ongoing revolt of the Dutch provinces and the loss of their massive tax revenues. The Armada was a financial disaster that Philip, as part of his personal penance, now had to work to fix. The direness of Spain's situation—which Philip considered a punishment by God—perhaps explains why he acquiesced and backed major accounting reform.

Torregrosa understood that to survive these disasters, the Spanish state needed a functioning accounting system. Without a Spanish manual on double entry, it would be impossible to explain the necessary reforms, let alone train the accountants Ovando had insisted were

so clearly needed. Torregrosa worked with his godson Bartolomé Salvador de Solórzano, an international merchant from Seville, to publish the first Spanish treatise on double-entry bookkeeping. Solórzano had traveled the Indies as a merchant. He had worked for the Italian merchant Giovanni Antonio Corzo Vicentelo de Leca, who had become a wealthy citizen of Seville and who had clearly taught Solórzano double entry. Ninety-six years after Pacioli's *Summa*, and three imperial bankruptcies later, Solórzano published his *Cash-Book and Accounting Manual for Merchants and Other People*.[42]

Pacioli's influence is clear in the manual, but Torregrosa was the mastermind behind a larger project to use this book to reform society and politics. Torregrosa went further than Pacioli in his dedicatory preface to Philip II, in which he explained that double entry was a method necessary not only for commerce but also for the statecraft of "kings, princes, and great lords." The manual, he boasted, was particularly suited for kings who wanted to rule justly. It was a remarkable claim and a pioneering vision of what kings and princes did. In Torregrosa's eyes, they were the arbiters of business, profit, and financial administration, and as such, they needed the tools of calculations and audits. Even more, he explained how to bind and count ledger pages to prevent fraud. Here was perhaps an appeal to Philip's inquisitorial instincts.[43]

In the 1580s, Torregrosa began putting his theory into practice. The king had allowed him to create the office of the General Book of Royal Finances. He kept double-entry accounts for all state receipts and expenditures, "ordinary and extraordinary," in four large account books and a number of journals. In order to keep his central ledger, Torregrosa kept more than a dozen books for various branches of financial administration. He even had a stock of specially made paper with special punched binding holes to guarantee that no outside pages could be surreptitiously introduced. By the early 1600s, Torregrosa kept two central state ledgers that contained the royal accounts for moneys distributed and received for royal services.[44]

Although initially successful, Torregrosa's reforms met with fierce opposition. Members of the Grand Chamber of Accounts, a medieval body, sent the king a list of twenty-five objections against Torregrosa. The keepers of the books of expenditure and revenue did not like being audited. Even businessmen felt that Torregrosa had become too effective and were apprehensive about having their profits exposed to the insatiable state. Philip died in 1598 and Torregrosa in 1607. The monarchy was still in financial disarray and again declared bankruptcy. There was only so much a good accountant could do. The Duke of Lerma, the favorite minister of the new king Philip III (reigned 1598–1621), kept a central state ledger but did so poorly, and it was not balanced. Torregrosa's reforms had failed. He had never found a competent staff to man his department, and few administrators had been trained in double entry. There was still a shortage of accountants, and his reforms worked only where he could keep the books. Spain had no effective accounting training centers. Pacioli's manual and all the work of the accounting reformers had had little influence in Spain and its empire.

By the reign of Philip's grandson Philip IV in 1621, Spain was still in debt and deep into the Thirty Years' War that would ravage Europe. With little will, Torregrosa's accounting office had simply stopped functioning, and the monarchy disbanded it that same year. Spanish writers like Cervantes considered the monarchy jaded and lazy. Reform languished, and American gold and silver had begun drying up, with bullion shipments declining by five times from a high in the mid-sixteenth century.

In 1628, north of Cuba, the Dutch admiral Piet Hein, along with the Dutch Jewish pirate Moses Cohen Henriques, seized a Spanish treasure fleet containing more than 11 million guilders in gold and silver, enough to fund the Dutch army for eight months and enrich the coffers of the shareholders of the Dutch East India Company. Not surprisingly, this was a monetary disaster for Spain. The state had no more income. In *Don Quixote*, Cervantes described the ragged and miserable poverty of Spanish nobles, soldiers, students, and professionals who could squeeze no more income out of the parched Castilian earth or out of the government, which rarely paid its pensions. The state was so corrupt that it was common knowledge that the wealthy noble grandees were now starving the population and holding the monarchy ransom with prohibitive loans. Philip's historic accounting reforms disappeared silently into the hot dust of Castile and from the memory of history. It was remarkable that with so few trained administrators and in the face of prejudices against accounting, the reforms happened at all. More than a missed opportunity, it represented how difficult powerful kings would find it to implement financial reforms that led to political accountability. Pacioli's book would eventually find a receptive audience not under a king or emperor, but ultimately in Holland, among the sympathetic citizens of a merchant republic opposed to absolute monarchy.[45]

CHAPTER 5

THE DUTCH AUDIT

Everything has remained obscure and they haven't come up with anything but procrastination and excuses instead of the accounts book (*rekenboeck*), which, as we suspect, they had smeared with bacon and which was eaten by the dogs.

—DUTCH EAST INDIA COMPANY SHAREHOLDER
COMPLAINT, 1622

B y the early sixteenth century, the Netherlands—the richest European province of the Hapsburg Spanish Empire—had replaced Northern Italy as the center of the international economy. In 1567, a Florentine trader described the staggering wealth of Antwerp's rich merchants, their beautiful shops, fine tapestries, grand houses, forty-two churches, stock exchange, and Hanseatic Trade House. It was, the Florentine noted, the richest and most beautiful city in the world. Portuguese ships laden with spice and Spanish silver ships made port in the second biggest city in northern Europe. It also became the center of accounting in Europe. It was here that Pacioli's work on accounting would finally be put to use and diffused on a large scale. It was these Dutch accounting books that sparked an international interest in accounting. Yet even as the Dutch mastered, popularized, and used accounting for state administration, they, too, struggled not only with the rigorous demands of double-entry book-keeping but also with the challenges of maintaining financial and political accountability. This might be the very lesson of the Dutch Golden Age: Those who wanted accountability had to struggle to learn accounting and to defend its legitimacy. The story of Holland shows not simply how the Dutch invented accountable government and finance but also how hard they were to maintain.[1]

For all its riches, the Netherlands in 1567 was not a free state, but instead ruled by King Philip II of Spain as part of his father's original dominions. Although Flemish and Dutch subjects of the Hapsburg king prospered with international banking and trade (as well as whale oil, fishing, and cheese making), they also had to survive Spanish taxation, as oppressive imperial auditors sought to make the Dutch pay for the continually bankrupt Spanish Empire. The Dutch came up with multiple schemes to sate the needs of the Spanish crown. Like other states in need of bond money (a publicly financed loan), they devised ways to raise public monies through the forced sale of life annuities (annual payments maturing into life insurance or pension-like benefits) to wealthy citizens. With this income, the Dutch paid off the Spanish.[2]

Interest-bearing annuities were nothing new. Italian city states, France, and Britain had also tried them. What made Holland different was that it had an effective provincial tax collection system, the trusted Kantoor van de Financie van Holland. The Dutch trusted the state to pay interest. European interest rates (between 4 and 5 percent) were pegged to Dutch bonds precisely because provincial tax receipts were considered reliable. Tax receipts were sometimes managed in double entry, but even more, they were legally subject to public scrutiny. Not only liquidity but the very possibility of accountability engendered trust. Yet no one ever called for an audit of the provincial tax collectors, or for a central state account register, because the tax collectors apparently did their jobs so well.[3]

As the Dutch economy grew, accounting schools sprang up, primarily in Antwerp. Because the Hapsburg dominions had once been part of the ancient kingdom of Burgundy, Dutch tax law was written in French, and thus Dutch accounting schools were called "French schools." Dutch subjects learned French and double-entry accounting to pay taxes to the Spanish Holy Roman Emperor.

All that changed with the Dutch Revolt (1568–1648), during which the seventeen Protestant provinces of the northern Netherlands revolted and ultimately broke away from their repressive Hapsburg overlords to become a de facto republic in 1581. The immediate loss of Dutch tax revenues caused yet another Spanish bankruptcy. But Philip II not only wanted taxes from his richest subjects but also tried to force them to remain Catholic; he believed that no subject should ever have a religion different from his king. "And so I would rather lose all my kingdoms," Philip remarked, "than consent to this." The emperor got part of his wish. Philip, who faced a war with the Ottoman Turks in the Mediterranean, uprisings in Italy, and the challenges of managing his worldwide empire, could not pacify the Dutch on their home soil. With less than a million inhabitants, this little federated Protestant nation, of which 20 percent of its landmass was below sea level and another 40 percent was exposed to tides and flooding, had taken on the mighty Catholic Spanish emperor and, with military victories in the 1570s, finally beaten him in war and declared independence in 1581.[4]

In 1585, the massive Spanish Imperial Army laid violent siege to the southern city of Antwerp. When the city fell, its Protestant residents fled to the free north. Once with a teeming population of 100,000, Antwerp was reduced to 40,000 inhabitants when its rich artisans and merchants headed for Amsterdam, which, in turn, became the republic's leading city and the center of world trade.[5]

Amsterdam also became the world center of accounting expertise. One poet later wrote that double-entry bookkeeping was the secret to Dutch wealth:

> *This was the fam'd and quick invention, which*
> *Made Venice, Genoa and Florence rich:*
> *The Low-Countries (in all senses such)*
> *By this Art now speaks high and mighty Dutch.*

By the mid-seventeenth century, Amsterdam's burgomasters had founded the Wisselbank, which guaranteed currency for invesment.

Adam Smith would later note that balanced accounts made the bank run smoothly. The Dutch Republic was also home to the world's primary stock exchange. Dutch banks offered loans that could be directly invested in merchandise futures. With the proliferation of business to every level of Dutch society, there was a general consensus that double-entry accounting was necessary knowledge. From street vendors and even prostitutes, to merchants and nobles, the Dutch needed to know double-entry accounting to navigate their little oasis of commerce and tolerance. With the complexity of the stock exchange, Dutch merchants' knowledge of finance became more sophisticated than that of their Italian predecessors or German neighbors.[6]

With publicly traded, multipartner firms organizing worldwide seaborne commerce, Holland's riches became legendary. The Dutch East India Company managed a merchant empire that brought in cargoes of Brazilian wood, Asian plants, and Arctic whale oil. Many of these riches came from the Spanish Empire, which Holland exploited more profitably than the Spanish themselves. The marketplace in Amsterdam was flush with the treasures of its trade: fish and fruit from the four corners of the globe; round and long pepper; several sorts of nutmeg, some covered in skin, others flowering; batons of cinnamon piled high in cross stacks; packets of cloves; shining borax crystals. There were stalks of rhubarb and sugarcane, piles of gunpowder and saltpeter, wax, gum, and ginger. The odors of styrax flowers, spicewood, frankincense, and myrrh wafted across what was, to visiting foreigners, an overwhelming display of commercial marvels.[7]

Along with products, other things flowed in from around the world, including reports, accounts, logbooks, and works of science and natural history, assessing political climates, trading routes, and fluctuations in commodities prices. Dutch consuls sent reports from Dutch whale oil factories in the Arctic, plantations in the West Indies, and trading posts in Europe, Brazil, Surinam, Manhattan, and Aden. Dutch trading posts could be found anywhere in the streets of the world, even in their own backyard, in cities of their hated neighbors the French, such as Nantes and La Rochelle.[8]

Accounting became a central element of Dutch education. Dutch elites formed a small, tight-knit group. They had a sense of the importance of both literacy and financial fluency. Literacy was at the center of both Dutch Calvinist and Catholic religions—reading and understanding the Bible oneself was part of the individual's relationship with God and salvation. By the seventeenth century, Holland was the most literate place in Europe and the most literate in accounting.[9]

Dutch accounting schools proliferated in the 1500s, often alongside the Latin schools, where even prestigious scholars and educators like Isaac Beeckman, founder of the influential Dordrecht Latin School, had detailed knowledge of accounting practices. On April 26, 1503, Jacob van Schoonhoven from Bruges received a license from the burgomasters of Amsterdam to teach reading, writing, arithmetic, and French to "anyone who might be interested." Van Schoonhoven was given the legal right to "teach all that was useful for merchants." This included weights, measures, tolls, and exchange rates. As early as 1509, Amsterdam saw the introduction of a "French school" that taught double entry. The public demanded that city governments sponsor bookkeeping schools. From the late fifteenth century onward, merchant schools could be found in Leiden, Delft, Gouda, Rotterdam, Middelburg, Deventer, Nijmegen, Utrecht, and Bergen-op-Zoom.[10]

Accounting manuals also proliferated. The Flemish Yan Ympyn de Christoffels (1485–1540) first adapted Pacioli's work into a Dutch accounting manual. A cloth trader from Anvers, he traveled extensively, visiting Portugal and residing in Venice for more than a decade. Only after Ympyn's death, his wife, Anna, published *New Instruction and Proof of the Praiseworthy Arts of Account Books* (1543) in Antwerp. It differed from Pacioli's manual in that it did not include a chapter on inventory, but it did give a full sample set of books, examples of exchange bills, and introductions on how to account for them. Ympyn's work did not always improve on Pacioli's model. It failed to systematize balance sheets of profit and loss and recommended that books be closed when they were full and not at regular intervals (which allowed for more systematic management control). Nonetheless, Ympyn's manual became an important conduit of double-entry bookkeeping in Dutch, English, French, and German.[11]

Other influential mathematicians, such as Valantijn Mennher and Claes Pietersz, also followed Pacioli in combining the teaching of formal mathematics with merchant bookkeeping, which, in Holland, was seen to be the finishing touch on a good education. Mennher was a Bavarian who moved to Antwerp and became a citizen in 1549. He became famous for teaching mathematics and double entry, rising to the head of his guild. He published four works on bookkeeping between 1550 and 1564. He promised his readers the calculation of profit through making audits for all branches of a business periodically, on the same day. From the 1570s until his death in 1606, Claes Pietersz not only taught private courses in arithmetic in Amsterdam but also, in 1576, published two manuals in Amsterdam on Italian bookkeeping, calling the practice "very profitable for merchants." One manual was translated into English under the title, *The Pathway to Knowledge* (1596).[12]

The notion that the Netherlands was the center of world commerce and that this dominance was founded on the mastery of double-entry bookkeeping is suggested by the famous German woodcut, *Allegory to Commerce* (first published in 1585) by the German printer, calligrapher, and accounting teacher Johann Neudörfer the Elder and Jost Amman, a Swiss artist and engraver. The large woodcut is remarkable not only for its fine detail but also for showing a public consciousness that commercial success depended on double entry. Even more, the woodcut explained how to keep books. There are three sections of the woodcut: At the top, the patron deity of commerce, Mercury, holds a scale in his right hand. Each of the two pans of the scale holds a book, and they are connected by two cords marked "debitor" and "creditor." Under the scale, the goddess of Fortune stands on a large book marked "Journal," which stands atop a pillar. All of commerce rests on fortune, but it rewards moderation and deliberation, which are the products of accounting.[13]

The two bottom thirds of the woodcut are earthly. The central part of the engraving shows the worldly center of commerce, represented by Antwerp and ships upon the River Scheldt. Commerce and accounting had a place now, and it was not Venice or Florence. The message is even clearer in the lower third of the image. We not only see merchants in their storerooms and accounting houses but also see them keeping double-entry books, and the basic practice is explained. In the center of the workshop is a tabernacle containing a book entitled *Secretorum Liber*, the "secret book." Underneath are three set of images describing how to keep double-entry books. At the top is a memorandum that shows live transactions being kept. Below it is an accountant putting entries into a journal with inscriptions on how to keep each book: "Every day I write in my Journal." Under the scene depicting the keeping of the final ledger is the basic lesson of double-entry: "The Debit to the left-hand side / The credit belongs to the right." The *Allegory*'s message is clear. Commerce depended on mastering double entry. Yet it also makes clear the limits of this earthly science and the medieval warnings against financial hubris. A skull and a vase emitting smoke represent the transitory nature of both life and business. Next to them is "Be devout, fear God and repent."

As pious as many of the Dutch were, they also took massive risks, invested in stocks, outfitted ships, and made enormous fortunes. Although Holland espoused religious tolerance and a more egalitarian society than its neighbors (peasants owned land, got rich making cheese, and could buy stock), it was part of the early modern world, and as such, it was a potentially violent place. It was ravaged during the revolt by Spanish soldiers of the Duke of Alba who put babies on pikes and hung peasants on trees like dead game. In 1584 in Delft, a French Catholic supporter of Philip II assassinated the Protestant William the Silent, the first prince of Orange-Nassau, the leading house of the County of Holland, with a pistol shot to the prince's chest as he descended from his dinner table. The prince's dying words asked for God's mercy on his soul and on his people. The burgomasters of Delft were less merciful and had the assassin's hand cut off and his body disemboweled and drawn and quartered.

William's son, Prince Maurice, became the stadtholder—the head of state—of the Netherlands and duly went off to universities in Heidelberg and Leiden, becoming one of the most learned princes of his time. He mastered the classics, mathematics, and engineering to make war on the Spanish, which he did with great skill. And he took a course in double-entry accounting, which he learned and later used.

Maurice struggled for power with the de facto prime minister of Holland, Johan van Oldenbarnevelt, a soldier and primary leader of Holland for thirty-two years of its rebellion. In 1617, during internal religious conflict that pitted him against Prince Maurice, Oldenbarnevelt demanded that the Protestant northern States of Holland (the *Staten* after which Staten Island is named) declare independence from the southern, mostly Catholic States of the Spanish Netherlands. During the struggle, he and his supporters, including the father of international law, Hugo Grotius, were captured. Oldenbarnevelt's head was chopped off in the public square after the old leader asked his executioner to "make it short." Like a seventeenth-century Dutch still life painting, the Netherlands gave the impression of stolid peace, but moments of political crisis brought blood and gutted corpses.

Amid the political chaos and violence, the Dutch continued to succeed in business, and with religious discipline, they immersed themselves in bookkeeping. While at the University of Leiden, Prince Maurice met Simon Stevin (1548–1620), one of Holland's leading humanists and an admirer of the practical tradition of Alberti and Pacioli. He ignored the noble Neo-Platonic warnings of Pico della Mirandola and mixed high learning with the merchant arts. That a prince and a lowborn (indeed, bastard) engineer would meet at a university and become friends was already a European anomaly. That Stevin would teach the prince double-entry bookkeeping was another.[14]

Stevin excelled in linguistics, cosmography, perspective, algebra, the study of decimal fractions, the theory of numbers, physics, navigation, and astronomy. He also made a careful study of double-entry bookkeeping. Stevin was a civic humanist whose achievements far surpassed those of Pacioli. His learning had practical applications, especially in the management of water, and he was given the most sensitive positions in civil administration. He became the inspector of dikes and the chief administrator of the Dutch army.[15]

Stevin was attuned to the connection between mathematics and government. His manual of accounting, *Accounting for Princes* (Amsterdam, 1604) went through several editions. The book was innovative in recognizing the difference between the capital of the enterprise and that of the owner, and it explained how to minimize entries by compounding various transactions into larger numbers. Confident in the world of numbers, Stevin did not mention God in his treatise. In true scientific fashion, he called his balance sheet his "proof statement." Stevin's manual was revolutionary in recommending accounting for civic financial management. Double entry was not simply good for governments; it was essential for princes and leaders. Stevin condemned those who argued against the usefulness of double entry for municipal administrations. Why, he asked, do government clerks and bailiffs become rich yet leave their offices in debt and financial chaos? Unaccountable management, he insisted, made governments fail. A prince versed in double entry could read treasury books himself and not simply rely on the treasurer's word. Merchants, he assured the prince, would make better treasurers than the bureaucrats and taxmen presently in the prince's employ. Prince Maurice was stunned by these ideas. Although he admitted he found bookkeeping difficult to grasp, he claimed he would study it further. Maurice not only had his personal accountant keep double-entry books for his personal affairs but also applied double entry in his administrations. Holland had achieved what Spain never could. It was the first time a prince—albeit a republican one—learned double-entry accounting and used it for political administration.[16]

On September 1, 1638, Marie de' Medici, former queen regent of France and mother of King Louis XIII, made a triumphal four-day royal visit to Amsterdam. Much had changed in the fifty years since Philip II launched his ill-fated repression in the Netherlands. Philip's Armada fiasco had sealed the decline of Spain, and the Dutch Golden Age had begun. The Medici French queen had come to Amsterdam not to see the riches of its culture, but, rather, the wonders of its great company, the United Dutch East India Company (*de Vereenigde Oost-Indische Compagnie,* or VOC). By the beginning of the seventeenth century, the VOC boasted double the tonnage of goods shipped of the English East India Company and ten times the capital investment, as well as unparalleled profits. It set the prices for most internationally traded goods from Amsterdam, Brazil, and Manhattan to China. It built warships and forts and fielded armies. Privately financed, it was the international arm of the Dutch government, and for almost a hundred years, it made little Holland the center of world trade.

There was great symbolism, then, in this Medici queen (although exiled by Cardinal Richelieu) visiting the rich market city on the Amstel, with its policy of religious tolerance and relative political freedom, its canals full of ships overflowing with goods, and its banks and stock exchange humming with the activity of entrepreneurs. In hindsight, Marie de' Medici appeared to be visiting the future (a little more than a month later, the first Dutch settler would install himself in the Bronx). Amsterdam was a city of wonder, in which the exotic goods of the world could be seen for the first time by European eyes.

In a description of the queen's visit, the Dutch humanist Caspar Barlaeus claimed that the grandeur of monarchy would come face-to-face with the opposing grandeur of "industry" and "international trade." Far from Florence, the burgomasters of Amsterdam were showing the "daughter of Cosimo" (in truth, she was a distant relation, from another branch of the family) the greatest trading city. Most important, Marie visited the House of the East India Company. If the very idea of monarchy was based in its military prowess, here was a new force that had gutted Spain and its empire. This great "company," bragged Barlaeus, is like "a prince": It raised armies to fight wars across the globe and despoiled the king of Spain of his empire. This was not simple pageantry, but ideology, too. "Our Republic," said Barlaeus, clearly echoing the claims of Spain, spreads its empire "as far as the sun shines." Monarchy had met its match in "commerce," "work," and "industry." All this, the Dutch knew, depended on good accounting.[17]

The VOC had been created thirty-six years earlier by Johan van Oldenbarnevelt, who was concerned that too much competition among the Dutch would undermine trade. He designed a single federated company to represent all the regions of Holland—the United Dutch East India Company. The charter of the company showed the mixture of private capital and state interests that Oldenbarnevelt felt would best serve the republic. The company was charged not only with a trade monopoly but also to uphold the interests of the Netherlands.[18]

The charter also stipulated that any Dutch citizen could buy shares in the company and that "there shall be a distribution of dividends as soon as 5% of the proceeds from the return of the cargo have been cashed." The company was directed by the *Heren Seventien* and the *Bewindhebbers*: seventeen principal stockholders and the next sixty or so largest investors. The stock was traded on the Amsterdam Stock Exchange, making the VOC the first publicly traded limited liability company in history, a milestone in the history of capitalism. Dutch citizens could freely invest in and divest out of the company by simply buying or selling shares, not by removing their capital investment directly from the company. Confidence in the company was to be based on internal accounting. The charter stipulated that the company hire professional bookkeepers and that the board of the company would regularly audit the accounts of all boats and warehouses. In the Dutch spirit of open government, the charter mandated that every six years the company would publish a public audit that would make a general account of all the costs of the company, as well as its profits and losses. Any manager failing to present his accounts would be subject to punishment.[19]

The Dutch fondness for accounting did not derive only from a merchant ethic. It also came from an older tradition in Dutch culture: water management. If the dikes broke and the water came in, Holland would be lost. Good municipal management, therefore, became a matter of life and death, and this provides one reason the Dutch took accounting and accountability so seriously. The Netherlands could not survive without its system of dikes, dunes, drainage systems, and canals, which were administered by local *Waterschappen* ("water boards"). Like the different regional chambers of the VOC, the water board directors were directly accountable to their local populations. They had to be. If funds and public works were mismanaged, regions would simply be swallowed by water, and many would die.

A Dutch saying goes, "Wie het water deert, die het water keert" ("Whom water harms stops the water"). This might have been why Stevin, Holland's finest engineer and a master of double entry, was chief inspector. It might also explain why municipal accounting had to be good and relatively transparent. Local audits, or *schouw*, were communally recognized as part of a "pragmatic consensus," necessary to guarantee good municipal administration and dry land.[20]

Trust developed from consistently good civic financial management was one reason the Dutch had the faith to buy shares and were able to create the first publicly traded company. But this trust was soon tested by the internal workings of the VOC, which caused the first modern company to have the first shareholders' revolt. The biggest investor in the VOC was Isaac Le Maire (1558–1624), a Flemish merchant settled in Amsterdam who, like Francesco Datini, had his hands in numerous business interests, from selling merchandise and handling bills of exchange to selling marine insurance and equipping Eastern trade voyages. He had a history of dodgy accounting practices and predatory commercial ventures. Despite being a swindler himself, La Maire called for corporate accountability. In 1602, he bought 85,000 guilders' worth of shares in the VOC. But Le Maire was no simple investor. He not only wanted returns; when he did not get them, he secretly organized competing trade expeditions while hedging against VOC stocks by a futures share-selling scheme. He was accused of embezzling from the VOC, whose board then sued him. Le Maire vowed revenge against the company and not only continued to support competing (and failing) ventures but also corrupted the VOC's chief accountant, Barent Lampe, and had him put false shares into the books to favor Le Maire's schemes. In 1609, Le Maire wrote a letter of complaint to Oldenbarnevelt demanding public audits. Between 1607 and 1609, stock values dropped from 212 percent to 126 percent.[21]

Le Maire's schemes failed, but stockholder fears were real. To dispel them, the VOC's board of seventeen directors—the *Heren Seventien*—declared that they would issue more dividends but that they could not submit to a public audit of accounts, which would play into the hands of the Spanish and threaten the interests of the state. The VOC was the military imperial arm of the Dutch state, which could not afford such a loss. Accountability posed risks to all involved. The directors successfully pushed this argument and garnered shareholder and public trust during the first twenty years of the VOC to avoid a true public audit. Perhaps this explains why, in its early years, the VOC did not keep a central double-entry ledger, which would have facilitated audits.

By 1620, no external audits had been made and no dividends paid, and there were accusations of insider trading—profits made by sweetheart deals within the company itself and a manipulation of accounts by not including share capital on balance sheets, thus making assets appear larger than they were. The VOC rates of return dropped to 6.4 percent from the historical average of 18 percent. Public opinion began to turn against the *Heren Seventien* and other leading shareholders, the *Bewindhebbers*. Stocks were now being bought and sold not on the basis of financial data, but on rumors in the marketplace. Secrecy was undermining the first modern capitalist venture.[22]

Finally, in 1622, disgruntled stockholders published a pamphlet, *The Necessary Discourse*, attacking the *Heren Seventien* and *Bewindhebbers*. In it, they rejected the logic of state secrecy on the grounds of national security and insisted that the company be run transparently. They complained that there had been no audits and that instead of producing a *rekenboeck*, or accounts book, they graphically claimed that the *Bewindhebbers* had "smeared it with bacon" so it would be "eaten by dogs" to hide their illicit earnings. The stockholders sarcastically complained that the directors would conduct a general audit only once everyone was dead. They further accused the *Bewindhebbers* of not behaving like serious merchants.[23]

The complaining stockholders argued that what they wanted was a proper financial audit, a *reeckeninge*. Then followed specific accusations of corruption, such as directors' sale of indigo at below-market prices for a personal profit. Directors were accused of having made personal profits from manipulating stock prices and taking a cut of every part of the massive industrial and commercial project. The theft was said to be shameless. One director, while inspecting a ship's cargo, saw a golden crucifix, stole it, and put it in his pocket. But due to its size and weight, it broke through and could be seen hanging out of his half-opened trousers. When another director noted that the thief was "not able to bear his own cross," the man unabashedly grabbed the crucifix from his pants and walked away with it. This was truly an embarrassment of riches.[24]

In the end, Prince Maurice's administrators found a solution. Although he used double entry in his own administration, the student of Stevin rejected the language of accounting and accountability and instead embraced reason of state, but in a Dutch style. There would be no public reckoning, but the state would audit the company in secret.

Although Holland was the European leader in accounting and political accountability, maintaining transparent government and finance was a constant struggle. As Johannes Hudde (1628–1704) found fifty years later, there was still no central ledger for calculating the total balances for the company. Hudde was a mathematician and mayor of Amsterdam and, in 1672, was named governor of the VOC, head of the *Heren Seventien*. He epitomized the governing elite, being not only fluent in mathematics and bookkeeping but also willing to use them for government and for internal audits. His management of water levels is still famous, as he established a system of stone markers, Hudde

Stones, that marked high-water points throughout the city. He studied mathematics at Leiden, was a follower of the French philosopher Descartes, and corresponded with famed skeptical philosophers and mathematicians Spinoza, Huygens, and Newton. Hudde worked with Leibniz to develop infinitesimal calculus, establishing Hudde's Rule: two polynomial equations, or two different equations, that come up with the same sum. It was a fitting discovery for a man who set as a task trying to balance the books of the VOC.[25]

Hudde sought to create a balance sheet for the VOC but realized that the central bookkeeping of the company made this difficult. One reason was that the company did not account for liabilities. He set about separating assets from liabilities. Assets included all goods at sea (merchandise and cash), ships, equipment, war materials and forts, food, property, and ammunition. To measure liabilities, he took into account debts with or without interest, unpaid wages, and share capital (the cash value of a share upon its sale), as well as risks such as losses at sea and shipwrecks. The loss of a ship could ruin a merchant or an entire firm. Hudde also sought to take account of all the heterogeneous currencies used in world trade, no easy task, and to apply risk values to merchandise according to local contingencies. He tried to tally statistics over ten-year periods, something only someone who was both a mathematician and a merchant accountant could do. This was one of the pioneering moments in the use of probability statistics in merchant accounting. He realized that the cost of maintaining merchandise surpluses often outweighed their value and therefore recommended, for example, destroying certain stocks of spices that ended up costing more than they were worth after duties and shipment costs. He figured that rather than amassing stock, he needed to create more demand to spur sales. This was profit thinking based on liability accounting and careful trade and probable price statistics.[26]

To make his point, Hudde wrote philosophical principles and sample problems for the VOC managers, essentially outlining early principles of cost accounting: "A merchant has a stock of 100 pounds of cloves. The annual sale is 50 pounds and the annual production 50 pounds. What is the value of the 100 pounds stored?" The answer, he stated, was "Nothing, on the contrary, they involve losses, as they cost warehouse rent and other expenses." His quest for the right valuation was absolutely necessary for keeping books and making profits. He also tried to balance the recording of expected profits with real profits, something we struggle mightily with today. To do this, he devised a statistical calculation to predict profits over twenty-five-year periods. This was the only way to calculate trade values of commodities thousands of miles away, whose sale value would not be established for years to come. Hudde's principle was that no transaction could be recorded without assigning a value and loss to it through a credit and debit entry for each item.[27]

There is not enough evidence to conclude that Hudde actually succeeded in drawing up effective balance sheets for the VOC. As director of the *Heren Seventien* and mayor of Amsterdam, he was a busy man. But he did appoint a number of internal bookkeepers to continue his work. One died in a shipwreck, and another, Daniël Braams, was appointed in 1690 to keep accounts for the whole company, taking into account valuation principles. However, he died right after making the first drafts of his accounts. The *Heren Seventien* appointed another bookkeeper, but the order was never carried through. If the directors of the company failed to keep good books, they nonetheless took Hudde's lessons to heart and were very prudent about predicting profits and costs. The spirit then, if not the practice, of good accounting took hold within the VOC's administration.[28]

The lesson from the VOC is thus complex. The greatest capitalist enterprise predating the 1800s never instituted double entry in spite of an awareness of the practice and a rich number of experts who could have done the job. Nonetheless, the spirit of accounting weighed over the company, inspiring internal audits, attempts to make calculations, and great prudence in calculating value, profits, and loss. Stevin's general idea held.

Figures like Hudde—fluent in humanist learning, the sciences, and commercial mathematics—ruled Holland by the second half of the seventeenth century and applied their skills to state management. In 1662, the free-market republican theorist Pieter de la Court (1618–1685) wrote *True Interest and Political Maxims of the Republic of Holland*, a virulent attack against monarchy and a detailed outline of how economic management through accounting and free markets spurred the

Dutch economy. To effectively forge economic and political policy, de la Court believed he had to master political theory, ethics, history, mathematics, accounting, and an expert knowledge of commerce and trade.

De la Court saw Dutch freedoms and political accountability as the response to monarchical tyranny. The inhabitants of Holland, he expounded, can "receive no greater mischief in their polity, than to be governed by a monarch or supreme lord." He recognized that this tradition came from the Italian republics. Before John Locke wrote his *Treatises* on representative government, de la Court claimed that industry, commerce, free trade, and political liberty could trump monarchical might. De la Court's writings were a victory call of merchants over princes in a battle that raged as both Spain and France invaded Holland, trying in vain to wipe out the threatening republican political system. Indeed, de la Court's message was an open challenge to oppressive, absolute monarchy: Successful industry and commerce were not possible, de la Court claimed, without political and economic freedom and accountability, as well as religious tolerance.[29]

De la Court successfully sought the protection of Johan de Witt, the Grand Pensionary of Holland (leader of the government when there was no effective stadtholder). De Witt not only paid for the publication of de la Court's work and allowed his name to be added as a coauthor but also may have added some of his own writings. He was both a sophisticated philosopher and a skilled merchant administrator who worked to develop republican political theory as well as economic policy. With de la Court, de Witt represents the Dutch ruling elite, which saw both republican ethics and mathematics as a tool for good government. As Grand Pensionary of Holland from 1652 to 1672, de Witt oversaw a particularly rich period of the Dutch Golden Age during which, in spite of the hostility of Spain, Sweden, England, and France, Holland flourished as a center of trade and tolerance and also art, science, philosophy, and theology, as well as political debate, printing, and international communication.[30]

De Witt was a product of the classical education of the Dordrecht Latin school and also of Cartesian mathematics, on which he published. He trained as a lawyer and traveled through France and England. He was a classical statesman in his knowledge of courtly government and diplomacy, but he was also a mercantile manager and a trained mathematician, and his lasting achievement was to develop mathematical principles for life annuities in his *Treatise on Life Annuities* (1671), one of the first practical applications of the theory of probability on economics. Working off Descartes's theories of geometry, in 1659 he published a book about the calculations of lines and curves, which was useful not only for applied physics but also for ballistics.[31]

By the seventeenth century, Holland's wealth and freedoms were both celebrated and feared throughout the world. Yet peace did not come to the Netherlands. After the death of the Stadtholder William II of Orange in 1650, Johan de Witt had led the Netherlands for more than twenty years. Yet as Holland's wealth grew, so did the envy of its powerful neighbors, France and England. In the 1650s and 1660s, the English and Dutch fought numerous battles over the English Channel, trade routes, and even colonies. The English captured the Dutch colony of New Netherland and its capital Manhattan in 1664. In 1672, Louis XIV's troops raided and plundered Holland. De la Court and de Witt could calculate, account, and call for republican government, but even with all their wealth, 1 million Dutchmen could not resist 23 million Frenchmen with a hostile, absolute Sun King and his giant army bent on bringing the arrogant, lowborn merchants to their knees to beg for mercy from Catholic France. The Princes of Orange, with their long and violent political tradition, sensed an opportunity to seize power from de Witt and regain their authority as heredity stadtholders. They deposed him and organized a mob to gut and lynch him and his brother Cornelis (the de Witts' fingers and toes were cut off, and members of the mob ate their internal organs). A silversmith exhibited Cornelis's heart in his shop for years. Tolerance, mathematics, and free trade could not trump the rabid government of violent men and mobs.

Accounting had come of age, but it had not imposed reason yet. Indeed, many saw just how powerful double entry could be, and like de la Court, they understood that it could threaten absolute power and entrenched interests. From now on, politics and accounting would be admired and emulated, but also feared. The bloody end of the de Witt brothers presaged a long struggle to bring mathematical clarity and accountability to politics.

CHAPTER 6

THE ACCOUNTANT AND THE SUN KING

I have already begun to taste the pleasures to be found
in working on finances myself . . . no one should doubt
that I will continue.

—LOUIS XIV TO HIS MOTHER, ANNE OF AUSTRIA, 1661

I n March 1661, Louis XIV of France came of age and took posses-
sion of the largest kingdom in Europe and possibly the richest in
the world. It was a time of great hope. After a near century of war,
revolt, and violence, France had a brilliant young king, a man of culture, with an affinity for great artists and love affairs. We rightly think
of Louis XIV, with his enormous powdered wig, dancing ballets and
attending fireworks and plays by Molière. Like his great-grandfather,
Philip II of Spain, Louis believed in his absolute, divine right. God
gave him his power, and, in his mind, he was accountable only to this
high authority. But Louis lived with a paradox. Although he hated the
smug wealth of the Protestant Dutch burgomasters, he was fascinated
by their tool of commerce: accounting. The problem was that he saw
not only its uses for administration but, later, its threat as a tool of
accountability.

The man who would become the master of Versailles and the greatest artistic patron of his age, and who would wage war on all of Europe,

began his reign under the watchful eye of his trusted accountant. His godfather and de facto prime minister, the wily old Italian Cardinal Jules Mazarin, on his deathbed left the young king not only part of his fortune (including the priceless Mazarin diamonds) but also his personal accountant who built it: Jean-Baptiste Colbert (1619–1683). Mazarin assured Louis that there was no more useful man in the entire kingdom. The monarchy was managed by a top accountant, a man versed in the practices of double entry. Thus Louis's story is tightly intertwined with the history of accounting. Louis's brilliance was not only in valuing artists and culture and using them for propaganda. He also understood that he needed a good accountant and that to audit his own accounts, he, too, would have to learn accounting to oversee his fortune and administration.

Louis came to the throne of a country impoverished for a king of his stature. The crown had suffered from the Fronde (1648–1653), the civil war that followed the death of his father, Louis XIII, and shook the regency (1643–1651) of his mother, granddaughter of Philip II of Spain, Anne of Austria, and her chief adviser and minister, Cardinal Mazarin. Indeed, Louis's own fortune was next to nothing, and he depended on Mazarin to run and finance the kingdom. He needed to build a fortune that would allow him to master not only France but also the world.

Louis immediately asked Colbert to initiate him into the secrets of accounting, which Colbert had used so effectively to support the crown during the Fronde. Louis later described to his son how he and Colbert set out to make accounting reforms. Louis understood that one of the central pillars of his administration was the main register of royal accounts. Louis wrote that he gave Colbert control over state finances, not only because he was "diligent" and trustworthy but also because Louis knew Colbert could keep books.[1]

Louis was very lucky that Mazarin had found Colbert, for in another time and place the Colberts might have been patricians, in the mold of the Medicis. In any case, they not only shared the merchant knowledge of the old Italian bankers but also were directly related to them. Jean-Baptiste Colbert came from a merchant banking family from Reims, the great cathedral and cloth town and capital of the Champagne region. Seventeenth-century France, however, was not Renaissance Italy, and bourgeois patricians did not become the princes of their cities. In a culture dominated by wealthy nobles and increasingly by a centralized monarchy in the tradition of Philip II, the primary avenue of social ascension for an ambitious financier or merchant was through service to a great aristocrat or, inevitably after the failed noble rebellion of the Fronde, to the crown.[2]

Colbert's father began his career not as a simple cloth merchant, as the cliché goes, but as a *négociant*: an international wholesale merchant and financier. The Florentine tradition was never far from Reims and Lyon, which had been connected through trade and banking since the Middle Ages. The Colbert family was linked to the Particelli, the influential Franco-Italian banking family into which Colbert's sister married.[3]

Colbert attended the Jesuit school in Reims. Aside from grammar, humanities, and rhetoric, Jesuit pedagogy had a special curriculum designed for merchants that did away with theology and classical culture and focused instead on geography, natural science (with possibly some engineering), reading comprehension, note taking, filing, and the formal organization of one's reading and lecture notes into notebooks.[4]

In his mid-teens, Colbert trained to be an accountant. Unlike Italy or Holland, France had no official accounting schools, so Colbert apprenticed in firms with strong ties to his family. He first worked in the Lyon office of the Italian banking family Mascranni, where he learned international banking and basic accounting and exchange practices, as well as some Italian. He then went on to take a clerkship at the Parisian accounting house "l'étude Chappelain" and later at the law firm of Biterne, where he learned financial law, a basis of state administration.[5]

Working in merchant houses and accounting firms provided specific sorts of training. An apprentice would learn the *ars mercatoria*, the mechanics of running a firm, involving diligent record keeping at all levels. For actual trading, it required a mastery not only of merchandise—from cloth, metals, plants, and spices to slaves—but also of its evaluation and measurement. As they had since the Middle Ages, merchants still carried with them reference books, but many made personal notebooks of currency exchanges; customs forms and rules; the translation of basic financial terms in major European languages; a schedule of tides, sunsets, and sunrises; merchandise descriptions; maps; navigation information; and city descriptions. Colbert was particularly skilled in paperwork handling, the laws and procedures of exchange and trade, and administrative archiving. Finally, apprenticeship offered Colbert real-time training in accounting. He was now ready to apply his skills to the French job market.[6]

Colbert's initial training led in 1639 to his purchase of a position in the French army. This was his first position in royal administration; as a financial administrator and accountant, he traveled across France, writing administrative reports on troop numbers and supplies and managing regimental finance. Decades earlier, this might have been the end of the story: Colbert would have remained a wealthy bourgeois financier or simply a bureaucrat. But his mastery of accounting and clear report writing brought him to the attention of his superiors, and soon Colbert was named personal intendant, or administrator, to Cardinal Mazarin himself.[7]

The meeting of Colbert and Mazarin brought together two complementary spirits. Mazarin had amassed a colossal fortune, larger than that of the crown, but he did not have the expertise to manage it. Colbert, on the other hand, had spent his entire youth training to manage large fortunes, but he did not have one. He was now close to the largest fortune in France. The cardinal's cellars were filled with treasures—a massive collection of artwork, antiquities, and jewels. But Mazarin's real wealth was contained in enormous and unorganized piles of feudal contracts and deeds for various sorts of landholdings, industries, and dubious financial schemes. Mazarin stated frankly that he had no idea how much wealth he actually had or how much he could raise to fund his armies. In any case, as the Fronde drew on, Mazarin needed ever more funds. Thus he needed a good accountant not only to put his finances in order but also to raise money quickly for the war effort.[8]

Colbert's persistence was boundless, and he began the hard job of ingratiating himself to the cardinal and rendering his services indispensable to the de facto ruler of France. Colbert began examining Mazarin's archives, pouring over mounds of paperwork and feudal deeds, and finding untapped revenue and unpaid debts. He also began managing industrial projects and various sources of income, along with

Mazarin's massive ecclesiastical landholdings. During the years 1650 to 1653, a detailed correspondence between the two men reveals the extent of Colbert's management of Mazarin's affairs. In a report on the cardinal's finances dated September 31, 1651, Colbert informed his master that he indeed had received "all the papers" and that he was working to "terminate the difficulties" in bringing order to the cardinal's finances. In 1652, working with the queen's treasurer, the parliamentary President Jacques Tubeuf, Colbert was still trying to obtain all Mazarin's papers and bring to term the cardinal's various business ventures. Colbert the auditor was at work, studying the cardinal's papers, "clearing up" errors, and saving "his Eminence" hundreds of thousands of livres of income. "I beg you to believe," he wrote the surely grateful Mazarin, "that I have not made any notable errors."[9]

Although Mazarin initially found Colbert vulgar and presumptuous, within a year he declared him simply "indispensable." Colbert's work bore fruit, and any personal faults an accountant or financial adviser might have are easily overlooked when money starts flowing in. In 1658, after the Fronde, Mazarin had 8 million livres in cash. By the time of the cardinal's death in 1661, Colbert had turned this sum into 35 million livres, a great part of which would be Mazarin's legacy to Louis XIV.[10]

As much as Colbert succeeded in building and managing Mazarin's fortune in the 1650s, he nonetheless remained a household servant. As an accountant, he was close to the center of the new royal state, but he was not yet a part of it. Indeed, the idea of an accountant rising higher was unheard of in France. However, Colbert's services were so important, and his counsel deemed so valuable, that on his deathbed Mazarin recommended him to Louis, and Louis wisely took Colbert as his accountant and personal confidant. When Louis took power in 1661, he and Colbert were already at work.[11]

Jean-Baptiste Colbert is famous for his theory of mercantilism: that there was only so much gold and wealth in the world and that France had to create industry so that this limited supply of wealth would flow away from Holland and Britain to France. To do this, he set up state-sponsored monopolies and organized France's empire in the New World (with its estuary in Louisiana, the Mississippi was then called the Colbert River). Whether Colbert's industrial project worked is the subject of fierce debate. What is less debatable is how innovative Colbert was as a financial manager. Adam Smith warned against state interference in financial matters, but he admired Colbert, foremost for his skill as a financial manager, tax collector, and accountant. Smith lauded Colbert's knowledge of industry and state accounts, as well as his success in "introducing method and good order into the collection and expenditure of the publick revenue."[12]

Accounting was not simply about good administration. It was also a tool of power and repression. On taking the office of Controller General of Finance, Colbert immediately began raising revenues and auditing the king's perceived political foes. Colbert was particularly involved with bringing down his own nemesis, Nicolas Fouquet (1615–1680). Fouquet was Mazarin's and Louis XIV's early superintendent of finances. By all accounts, he was brilliant, dashing, greedy, and paranoid. A writer and keen political observer of the time, Madame de Sevigné, painted Fouquet as the victim of Colbert's ambition and Louis XIV's dictatorial tendencies. But Fouquet was undeniably presumptuous. He made the infamous mistake of assuming that he would be Louis XIV's prime minister and that he could dictate polity to the young king.[13]

In August 1661, at the moment Louis had taken personal rule after the death of Mazarin, Fouquet threw an ostentatious party at his chateau in Vaux-le-Vicomte, south of Paris. Louis was humiliated by his minister's sophisticated opulence and patronage of high society and culture. Vaux was grander than any abode Louis possessed. Like all intendants of finance before him, Fouquet pilfered money from royal funds; this was an understood advantage of the position. Not only did Fouquet steal, however, but also he managed royal funds badly, and he made the error of using them to outshine the king, whose personal finances after the Fronde were still shaky. Had Fouquet spent his money on only culture and parties, perhaps Louis might not have been so bent on destroying him. Louis had Colbert place a spy dressed as a fisherman off the coast of Belle-Île, Fouquet's island off the southern coast of Brittany. Colbert's agent provided a detailed map of the island, as well as a report that detailed Fouquet's 1,500 laborers, 200 garrisoned soldiers, and 400 cannons on the island, as well as munitions and supplies for 6,000 men. The great engineer Vauban was building fortifications on the island's coast. Even more, Colbert's agents reported that Fouquet had made plans to take over the Caribbean island of Martinique and to use his own coastal island to receive all the goods produced there. In short, Fouquet was building a miniature kingdom and a small empire. As an independent and wealthy noble, with an army and fort held outside royal authority, he was a threat to Louis.[14]

In September 1661, Louis and Colbert moved to arrest Fouquet and exile his family and friends. Colbert wrote out several detailed plans for the arrest. All Fouquet's offices would be sealed, and state lawyers would invest the premises and confiscate all papers. Colbert wanted not just Fouquet's secret plans and letters; he also wanted Fouquet's accounts, which, to him, were the strongest proof of treason. Colbert insisted that royal tax lawyers be present not only to seal documents but also to rush them back to his own office. Colbert knew that an effective audit was based on control of all financial papers. As the chief of the king's musketeers, Captain Charles d'Artagnan—who would be immortalized by Alexandre Dumas in *The Three Musketeers*—led the arrest of Fouquet and the ensuing search and ransack of his house. In Fouquet's office, behind the armoire, they found a massive, bound folio notebook, called the *Cassette*. Colbert ordered the papers sealed and speedily sent to him by courier. D'Artagnan was ordered to arrest all Fouquet's assistants and search them for hidden papers.[15]

Unprepared and outmaneuvered, Fouquet was stunned by Colbert's raid, which also unearthed Fouquet's massive correspondence with various ladies who served as lovers and informants, as well as accounts pertaining to payments, gifts, and bribes. The *Cassette* listed all of Fouquet's various agents and spies, many in the royal court and administration. The detailed accounts revealed his financial dealings as well as his plans and finances for building his fortress on Belle-Île.[16]

When Fouquet was put on trial for treason, the public rightfully perceived Colbert as pulling the strings behind the scenes, giving new meaning to his family crest's symbol, a climbing snake. Even if the trial did not convince the public of Fouquet's guilt, it made clear the intention of the crown to act above the law. It also revealed something essential about Colbert: He was willing to use accounting as a political weapon. Colbert rightly saw the keys to overthrowing an enemy in his account books, which revealed his network, his finances, and his plans. It was a political move worthy of the Medici, but the stakes were higher. With France's population of 23 million, the largest army in the world, an expanding seaborne empire, and the aid of a very good accountant, Louis hoped to become master of Europe.[17]

Immoral and ultimately cruel though he was, Colbert still made notable innovations as Louis's de facto prime minister. In his *Historical Memoirs on French Financial Affairs* (1663), Colbert explained how he and Louis integrated accounting into statecraft. He described not only how he taught Louis the basics of "the Italian method" of accounting but also how the king then used it in daily royal administration. There is only one copy of this text, written in Colbert's hand. Unfinished, it is Colbert's longest and most detailed single work. It was meant to inform Louis of the financial precedents of past kings.[18]

Its detailing of royal accounts suggests that Colbert's *Historical Memoirs* were meant for Louis alone. The text explains how much previous kings taxed, how much revenue they earned, and which officials managed the funds. But Colbert warned that in the past, kings only *confirmed* financial policy: Auditing and control were done solely by their ministers. Kings could not actually confirm the books themselves, and this led to graft and mismanagement. With accounting, Colbert argued, he could produce up-to-date figures on royal finances, taxes, manufacturing, and seaborne trade. Colbert included past financial accounts from the time of Fouquet, which conveniently showed the fallen minister's errors and "dissipation."[19]

Most important, Colbert described how the king should preside over the Council of Finance and how Colbert himself should organize it and the state account book. Colbert would be the chief accountant and Louis the chief auditor. Colbert recommended that "an exact register be kept of the entire receipts of expenditure of the State for each year" and that those of past years be verified.[20]

To be the auditor in chief, Colbert explained Louis needed to understand the basic methods of bookkeeping, straight out of Pacioli. What is new in Colbert's text is that the word *firm* or *company* is replaced by *the State*. Colbert innovated, recasting double entry as an art for kings. And state account books, Colbert noted, would be classified.

"By this clear and easy method, "Colbert assured Louis, "His Majesty has placed in himself all his own security, and has reduced his reliance on those who have the honor to serve him in this function." Except, of course, Colbert, who throughout his life kept the books.[21]

Louis understood and liked bookkeeping, at least in complex single-entry form. Louis wrote to his mother, "I have already begun to taste the pleasures to be found in working on finances myself, having, in the little attention I have given it, noted important matters that I could hardly make out at all, but no one should doubt that I will continue." Twice a day for more than two hours, Louis went over dispatches from his ministers and agents concerning all topics of government, often examining financial reports in detail. At the same time, Louis never became a true accountant at the level of Cosimo de' Medici. The king competently followed Colbert's bookkeeping. Louis and Colbert corresponded constantly on questions of finance, with Colbert sending the king requests for expenditures to be authorized. The king's chief reporter was Colbert, who presented his summaries to the king more than twice a week but most importantly on Friday, when he presented an overview of all the information he had collected and the royal accounts. Colbert would leave half the page of his reports blank so that the king could respond in the margins. At first, Louis liked the numbers, writing to Colbert that it was "very agreeable" to hear him speak of finances. And at first, Louis uncharacteristically deferred to his accountant, writing in the margins of account books: "It is for you to judge what is best."[22]

Colbert collected vast amounts of information, and he then had to find a way to present it to the king. Colbert kept state account books and one hundred thematic administrative scrapbook folios. Louis sometimes wanted to see Colbert's various compendia, but more often, he wanted the final report. As a good accountant, Colbert kept vast inventories containing the scrapbooks, journals, and ledgers for each head tax collector and for most offices of government. He maintained ledgers of state accounts, which Louis could verify himself. Above all, the account books were clear, easy to read, and easy to annotate. Louis did not have time for messy paperwork, and Colbert made sure never to give him any, often berating accountants and agents for poor bookkeeping or inaccurate memos.[23]

Due to the vast and still medieval administration of much of the government, Colbert was unable to systematically establish the use of double entry for general government business. Colbert was expert in double entry, but few administrators were trained in this merchant art. Nonetheless, Colbert developed a sophisticated form of state accounting that worked according to a number of the principles of double entry. Louis, Colbert, and other ministers of the Council of Finances signed off on the tallied account books. If these final accounts were tallied in the presence of the king and his council, the more complex preliminary bookkeeping and verification was done by Colbert for Louis, who set up the books so that they would be easy to verify. These account books represent an ideal of kingly financial information handling that Colbert used to exhort Louis to become an accountant king, which, to a certain extent, Louis did, at least for a time.

Clearly trying to make his reforms permanent, Colbert was the first to successfully introduce accounting into the educational curriculum of French kings. In 1665, Colbert wrote manuscript instructions for Louis's heir that contained information pertaining to finances. In them, he discussed the need to master finance through handling and keeping account books. Colbert recommended to the young prince that he should note by hand all state accounts every year. He should learn to audit state financial registers, so as to verify everything from state savings to expenditures and receipts. He should never stop doing this work, warned Colbert, for it is so delicate that it can be left to no one else. In short, Colbert felt the young prince needed to learn the basics of accounting and inventory management in order to be king.[24]

More than that, Colbert imbued Louis's government with a merchant's sense of financial secrecy. In 1661, as the king and his leading minister worked to form their first government, Colbert wrote a memo to Louis on how to organize and manage the Royal Council, mandating that all ministers and members of government take oaths of secrecy and that anyone breaking the oath be expelled from government. Secrecy meant not only the discretion of ministers and secretaries but also keeping state financial information under tight control.[25]

This state secrecy contrasted with Colbert's public accounting policies. He championed a number of works on economics and accounting. He ordered Jacques Savary, the author of many of Colbert's trade laws, to write the *The Perfect Merchant* (1670), featuring a section on double-entry bookkeeping for business—part of Colbert's Law of Commerce of 1673, which required businesses to keep double books to be regularly verified by the government. In this case, Colbert's public rules for accounting not only set standards but also were a form of policing, for merchants rightly feared the heavy arm of taxation to follow public royal audits. The crown was now sponsoring accounting at all levels of society and the state.

Colbert also created something unique for the king: pocket account books for Louis, which were state ledgers and explanations of how accounts worked. These portable accounts are the most dramatic example of how Colbert turned accounting into a personal tool of government for Louis XIV. The French National Library has twenty notebooks under the heading "Notebooks of Louis XIV." During or after each fiscal year, one or two of these carnets were made for Louis, summing up various accounts and giving the final budget tally for the year. They are bound in red maroquin leather, with gold titles, and held closed by two gold pop clasps. They measure about six inches by two-and-a-half inches, made to be kept in Louis's pocket for easy reference. In the first edition from 1661, the manuscript is written on paper. However, it is clear that such simple ledgers were beneath Louis's sense of personal grandeur. If Louis was going to carry account ledgers on him, he was going to do so in a manner befitting the Sun King. Colbert appears to have sought the aid of Nicolas Jarry—France's famed manuscript illuminator—and his workshop in creating new vellum notebooks with illuminations. Starting in 1669, the notebooks contain richly adorned illuminated frontispieces. One 1670 notebook has fleurs-de-lis on the spine of the binding. By the late 1670s, even after Jarry's death in 1674, the notebooks were illuminated, and even simple accounts were written out in gold and colored paint and decorated with flowers. Using his own account books, Colbert created ledgers that were treasures fit for the Sun King, which Louis kept in his pocket and probably consulted during meetings with counselors and secretaries, as well as while going through state dispatches and intendant reports.[26]

The royal ledgers were simplified, listing only expenditures and earnings, as well as comparing the income from each tax farmer. They gave final single-entry tallies of spending as compared with cash on hand. They gave comparisons, such as tax farmer income between 1661 and 1665, so Louis could see change over time. For example, the *Abrégé* of 1680 compares state revenue between 1661 and 1680. The ledgers listed all state tax revenue and all the names of the local accountants who produced accounts in a given regional capital.[27]

Humanists kept commonplace books of religious or political maxims, but Louis kept in his pocket Colbert's ledgers with their golden, illuminated calligraphy. What is significant here is that the notebook and archiving culture of accounting moved ever closer to the central practices of royal statecraft. Louis mixed his traditional, late humanist education with the practical and legal knowledge that Colbert and his house scholars, intendants, and agents provided him. Humanist education was clearly useful, but it was not enough to run a state effectively. For the first time, in the administrative project of Louis XIV and Jean-Baptiste Colbert, accounting and traditional learning were used together to manage a large government.

Jean-Baptiste Colbert fell ill, with great pain and a fever, on August 20, 1683, and died on September 6. Despite a rumor that a partial disgrace had led to his illness, his autopsy revealed a "giant stone" in his kidney, blocking his ureters. No one had expected him to disappear from the scene so suddenly. Although Louis was clearly upset to lose an old friend and his closest political confidant, he had become increasingly irritated with this harbinger of bad news and his all-too-clear accounting updates on the state of French politics, finance, and industry. For almost a decade, Colbert had complained to Louis about his expensive palaces and even more expensive wars against neighboring countries like Holland, which bankrupted the fiscal state that Colbert had built. Louis had grown tired of Colbert's nagging and the unbalanced figures in the notebooks in his pocket.[28]

Louis chose not to replace his chief informer, and the notebooks duly stopped appearing. He broke up Colbert's power base centered in the Ministry of Finance and the Royal Library. With this move, Louis stopped the possibility for a true state apparatus to emerge beyond his personal control. "L'État c'est moi" was quite literal and in stark contrast with Max Weber's ideal of the impersonal centralized state. Louis clearly saw a well-oiled state bureaucracy and central archive as a threat to his personal power monopoly. More than wanting to be informed, Louis wanted to have the sense that he was in control. By closing down Colbert's central office within the state and the information state that supported it, Louis could divide and rule his ministers.

After Colbert's death, no minister under Louis XIV would again have as much power and as much information. Even more, Louis began playing the great ministerial families of Colbert and his rival Le Tellier against each other, and they began hoarding financial information to retain power. The limits of absolutist government were, in part, the limits Louis imposed himself. Indeed, Louis XIV did not leave his heirs a centralized state, but a very messy set of strong, competing ministries, with no single administrative core. By breaking Colbert's system, Louis hobbled the French state in the long run. Without a central and powerful figure like Colbert, skilled in bookkeeping, at the head of each ministry, no serious audits or central accounting was possible. The minister's heirs now used the family financial archive as a defensive weapon. The great memorialist of Louis XIV's court, Duke de Saint-Simon, recounts that the Colbert family made a formal policy of keeping state financial information out of the hands of the hostile Louvois family, which held competing government ministries. Colbert's brother, Édouard François Colbert, Count de Maulévrier, recommended that all requests for even official state financial information be met with "good grace" but ignored. Claude Le Peletier, who became Controller-General of Finance on Colbert's death in 1683, in turn complained to Louis XIV that he was unable to understand the state's financial workings, for Colbert had kept them secret—"enclosed in his very self," Le Peletier perceptively noted. He said Colbert's family was not forthcoming with information, and the papers of the Royal Treasury did not add up without Colbert's personal account books.[29]

Without financial data going to a central state register, France continued in the tradition of the Middle Ages: A minister's financial records were seen as a valuable piece of private property, and not that of the state. The endless failures of eighteenth-century French governments were due not only to the secrecy and folly of royal fiat and terrible financial management but also to Louis's splintering of the state apparatus. Its accounting capacity remained limited and in the hands of a few ministers and their families. It helps explain why, with all its possibilities, genius, and might, France stalled and began to crumble. By Louis XIV's death in 1715, France was bankrupt, with no effective accounting system. Seventy-five years of financial crisis and a great reckoning awaited the French.

CHAPTER 7

THE FIRST BAILOUT

I can calculate the orbit of heavenly bodies, not the
madness of people.

—SIR ISAAC NEWTON, 1721

Like the French, the English in the seventeenth century struggled with government accounting reform. Even in the country
of constitutional monarchy and parliamentary oversight, financial accountability came slowly, met fierce resistance, and remained a
fragile political tradition. The whole idea of a constitutional monarchy
was accountability to Parliament, yet it would take the English more
than 150 years to establish oversight of royal finance.[1]

As early as 1644, following public calls for inquiry into the management of state revenue, Parliament established a Commission of
Accounts. Led by William Prynne—a Presbyterian leader deeply
concerned with the public accountability of the state, and whose political pamphlets critiquing royal power caused Charles I to chop off
Prynne's ears in 1634—the commission never gained political traction.
The powerful Earl of Clarendon, an ally of the crown, worried that the
commission allowed Parliament to exceed its jurisdiction. There would
be no end to the inquisitorial powers of such a body, which, Clarendon
worried, had no financial expertise. Although the monarchy fell in
1649 during the Civil War and was restored under Charles II in 1660,

no effective system of financial accountability was established. In 1675, in response to parliamentary demands for full accounts of royal revenue and expenditure, the crown responded: "Tis not usual for this House to inspect the King's Treasury."[2]

The lack of qualified accountants within the state was a concern of both members of Parliament and crown ministers. Chief Secretary to the Admiralty Samuel Pepys (1633–1703) bemoaned the lack of accounting expertise in Charles II's government. In his famous *Diary*, Pepys regularly discussed accounting for the state, and for himself, "striking" his "tallies" at the Exchequer office, and then later, at home, settling more accounts with another official, which he found "very troublesome," before bed. Pepys worried that neither his superior, the Commissioner of the Admiralty, the Earl of Sandwich, who was responsible for the British Navy, nor King Charles himself understood basic accounting. Even worse, Pepys considered the Lord Treasurer of the Navy, Sir George Carteret, a "madman" for not knowing how to keep accounts and for not knowing someone who did. The navy was without a financial rudder.[3]

Nonetheless, Charles II came to understand that reforming state accounting could be to his advantage. In 1667, he founded an accounting office in the royal treasury. Although Pepys doubted it would work, this new financial administration managed to hire competent secretaries of the Treasury, who kept good books. However, members of Parliament in turn worried that the Treasury would give Charles too much power by the simple fact that its good accounting practices and sound financial management gave him access to more revenue. Thus both the monarchy and Parliament tried to use accounting and calls for accountability to their respective political advantage.[4]

In 1688, by request of Parliament, the former Dutch Stadtholder King William of Orange-Nassau and his joint monarch, Queen Mary II, ousted Charles's brother and heir, the Catholic James II, in a bloodless coup known as the Glorious Revolution. William and Mary ruled under a parliamentary constitution that enshrined religious tolerance, protected Protestant and commercial interests, and subjected all major royal decisions to Parliament's approval. In many cases, supporters of the new monarchy were Whigs with merchant backgrounds from the cities. In turn, the crown depended on this new urban elite to counter the landed Tories, who often held sympathy for the absolutist-leaning Stuarts.

The 1689 Bill of Rights stipulated that the monarch could not tax without approval of Parliament and, ideally, that both the crown and Parliament would be financially accountable. Spurred in part by John Locke's writings on political liberty, relative freedom of the press began to emerge as Parliament eased restrictions on publishing. Yet even with new political openness, it remained difficult to hold the government financially accountable. In 1698, the economist critic, excise tax collector, and Tory Member of Parliament Charles Davenant (1656–1714) tried to calculate public tax revenues, but, in his *Discourses on the Publick Revenues*, he complained that he "met with extream Difficulty and Opposition in Procuring the sight of Accompts relating to the Revenue." The state account books had been shut to him, and all his inquiries had been rebuffed. Davenant believed that public accounting of state funds was a necessary part of governing a successful commercial society, for secret reckoning was untrustworthy and undermined competent governance and trade.[5]

By the reign of Queen Anne in 1702, full-fledged party politics were taking place on the floor of Parliament, pitting liberal city Whigs against traditionalist country Tories in a battle of pamphlets and arguments about the nature of the new monarchy. As debates raged about public debts, trade balances with France, and the finances of union with Scotland, the Tory newspaper *The Mercator* exhorted its own critics to "search the Books" to prove their arguments. The scene was ripe for a savvy politician, fluent in accounting, who could tap into public dissatisfaction with state finance.[6]

Robert Walpole (1676–1745) stepped into this role. Walpole would go on to be First Lord of the Treasury, Chancellor of the Exchequer, and Britain's first Prime Minister, holding power a record twenty-one years. He understood the power of accounting in government, and he harnessed it. But like Louis XIV, Walpole would find political accountability an unwelcome by-product of good state accounting.

Walpole grew up in a uniquely British world in which accounting and mathematical calculation had become part of political life. Francis

Bacon (1561–1626), an influential politician and the inventor of the empirical method, had founded a tradition of scientific thinking and merchant methods in political administration. Bacon pioneered the idea that looking into nature and its management, and into commerce, was part of the act of researching God's presence in the material world through observation. Both Bacon and the political philosopher Thomas Hobbes saw accounting as a tool not just for commercial management but also for thinking about politics. In his *Leviathan* (1651), Hobbes ascribed the very birth of logical reasoning to accounting. Without addition and subtraction, Hobbes claimed, it was impossible to find the morally correct thing to do in politics. No one had ever so emphatically made the connection among accounting, ethics, and politics.[7]

Walpole was educated in the climate created by these political philosophers. Although his ethics were frequently questioned, he was reputed to be a brilliant accountant. Educated at Cambridge—and with a father who was an avowed follower of Baconian philosophy and an active manager of his estates—Walpole came from a background steeped in accounting culture. He represented a new breed of English politician, one highly versed in applied financial mathematics, in the style of the Dutch leader de Witt. But arguments about the numbers were not always accurate. Audits, or claims of audits, were thrown around in the political arena, most often with no factual basis. Walpole took office as Treasurer of the Navy in 1710, only to be dismissed by Robert Harley's new Tory ministry one year later in a hail of accusations of corruption in the Duke of Marlborough's military administration. Walpole fought back, defending Marlborough by drafting the financial calculations for Arthur Maynwaring's pamphlet, *A Letter to a Friend Concerning the Publick Debts, particularly that of the Navy* (1711), in which he calculated the costs of the Navy in relation to the public debt and claimed that costs had not particularly risen during his administration despite to the added expense of the long and costly War of Spanish Succession fought against France. Walpole's wartime calculations allowed Maynwaring to lay the blame of debt at the feet of Walpole's predecessors.[8]

In April 1711, England and France were locked in war. Both countries amassed enormous debts in the conflict. In Britain, there was fear that the government could not pay back the £50 million the state had borrowed. The debt took 60 percent of the British national income to service. Many believed that it would undermine the nation and lead to financial and political catastrophe. There was public outcry and calls for parliamentary action.

Edmund Harley, the Auditor of the Imprests—responsible for verifying the expenditures of state ministers—accused Walpole of being responsible for much of the debt by not having accounted for £30 million in naval funds. This time, Walpole defended himself with a pamphlet titled *A State of the Five and Thirty Millions mention'd in the Report of a Committee of the House of Commons* (1712). It gave a detailed explanation of how state accounting worked and of how the money that seemed to be missing from state accounts had not yet been posted because of the time it took for many accountants to pass accounts in front of a state auditor. Walpole blamed missing numbers in his own accounts on the process of keeping state books. Accounts were not official until the "Charge" and "Discharge" columns were "balanced and signed off on by the Auditors of the Imprests." If his foes in the Country Party—a political faction of the landed gentry opposed to the financiers of the city and the rising power of the Prime Minister—had understood "common addition," he complained, they would have understood the House of Commons report. It was a remarkable moment: a leading government minister defending himself by accusing his foes of not understanding the basic methods of double-entry accounting.[9]

In his pamphlet, Walpole issued a public demand to reform how state accountants worked. The outdated rules of the Exchequer would need to be reformed so that checks and limitations would force state accountants to keep clear and timely books. But the Tories' accusations of "notorious corruption" stuck, and Walpole was convicted by the new Tory government and sent to the Tower of London for seven months. But his reputation as a wily master of state finance was now established. He was called "'Lynn Bob,' the 'Norfolk Robin,' alias 'Robin Hood,' alias the 'Norfolk Gamester,' alias the 'Norfolk Punch,' the 'Norfolk Sting,' the 'Quaker' or the 'Jew' of Norfolk," all epithets of scorn, but also measures of his prowess and appetite.[10]

In the midst of arguments about the national debt, Walpole came back to power again, a month after the death of Louis XIV, in October 1715. This time he had real power as the First Lord of the Treasury. The national debt was now within his personal purview. At George I's accession on August 1, 1714, the debt had stood at more than £40 million, with annual interest payments of more than £2 million. This was the point of political contention: How could this debt be lowered, while still maintaining a defensive military footing against France? Walpole set to work studying the debt and making a plan to present to Parliament on how to reduce the 6 percent interest payments on the debt.[11]

In 1717, Walpole passed a plan through Parliament to lower debt interest to 5 percent. The savings from this would then be placed into a sinking fund, a sophisticated way to pay off debt. The sinking fund was based on the idea of stopping compound interest by paying off the debt's principal and thus preventing the spiraling of future interest payments. This meant that the government would both pay interest on the debt and dedicate a fund to pay off the capital on the debt. Further savings on interest would again be reinvested in the fund. Through his knowledge of finance, Walpole had managed to find an effective way to cut the debt, but not fully pay it down.[12]

What appeared to be the solution to the debt crisis came in the form of an investment scheme. In 1720, the Tory First Lord of the Treasury and Chancellor of the Exchequer Robert Harley created a stock company whose proceeds could be used to pay public debt. He modeled his plan on the French Mississippi scheme, which, by 1719, was reaping massive returns for investors across Europe. With rumors that Spain had given up its trade rights in South America and old stories about Drake and Raleigh finding an El Dorado in the New World catching the imagination of both the public and the political classes, Harley, together with John Blunt—director of another stock company and bank—created the South Sea Company. The crown would give the company a trade monopoly for the east coast of South America from the Orinoco River to the Terra del Fuego and for the entire west coast. In return, the company would offer all holders of government debt shares in the company. In other words, using creative accounting, government debt was magically turned into shares of the South Sea Company. The company agreed to assume around £31 million of government debt for a payment from the government of 4 percent interest and £1 million in cash for liquidity (cash so that it could operate). Once stocks were sold, the company would pay the government £4 million outright for monopoly rights. In exchange for a trading monopoly, the government had found a way to service its debt using private investors. It was a miracle of modern finance.[13]

But there was a catch. When anticipated income failed to materialize in early 1720, the company relied on false profit statements to lead a speculative boom. In what now amounted to an early form of a Ponzi scheme, the company issued more stock to pay its dividends, which, by April, inflated stock prices to £360 per share from the original price of £128. By June 1720, the price had risen to £1,000 per share. Many subscribers paid for shares by borrowing at around 5 percent. As confidence in the South Sea Company wavered in August, creditors raised interest rates or suspended loans, thus starving the credit which fed the company. The pyramid began to collapse, and the stock price plummeted into the hundreds of pounds, leaving investors—among them great nobles, government ministers, and the king's mistresses—with massive losses on their hands. The English freethinker John Toland lost a fortune and, in his dying years, could not even pay his doctor. Worse, the crash threatened to undermine the public credit market, industry and business, the stability of the government, and even British national security.

When the Mississippi bubble had burst in France earlier in 1720, the French government possessed neither the tools nor the funds to save the Mississippi Company that had caused the crisis. Believing him to be a financial wizard, the French crown had foolishly contracted out management of the Royal Bank and Mint to a brilliant but untrustworthy Scottish gambler named John Law (in French, his name was pronounced "l'as," meaning "the ace"). After the Mississippi crash, with few financially literate government ministers and no national bank, France had to continue borrowing from the Swiss at unsustainable rates. The French monarchy and public lost faith in the idea of public credit, currency, tools like accounting, and financial markets as a whole. Without effective financial reform, France struggled for much of the eighteenth century without a modern taxation system, near bankruptcy, its industrial innovation and growth stymied.[14]

Yet Britain bounced back from its crash. It did so with something that no other country at the time had: a vibrant and also innovative accounting culture that permeated politics to an extent beyond even what the Dutch had known. This culture allowed Walpole, in particular, to design a government bailout of the South Sea Company and of British credit markets. Walpole's bailout is a vivid story of the promise and failures of financial and government accounting and of how even those politicians well trained in the techniques of accounting can be tempted to break their rules.

Tories had hoped the South Sea Company would balance to the power of the Bank of England, which they saw as giving too much power to England's Hanoverian king and the Whigs who supported him. (A German, George I had inherited the British throne in 1714 through the tangle of dynastic rights brought on by the arrival of the Dutch King William in 1688.) For this reason, Walpole, a Whig, had initially been a foe of the company. In spite of interparty debate over the debt scheme and an admission that he had, at first, found the South Sea scheme "a chimera," Walpole eventually embraced it.

If it seems surprising that Walpole would have gotten entangled in the South Sea bubble, it should be remembered that even Isaac Newton, the great astronomer, lost the immense sum of £20,000 speculating at the height of the scheme. Walpole believed in the scheme in spite of public financial data that put it into question. He was no less shrewd than Newton, but he very well could have been blinded by greed.

In 1720, at the very moment Walpole was both supporting and investing in the South Sea scheme, the lawyer and MP Archibald Hutcheson made a fairly accurate calculation of South Sea stock value. In the pit of corruption and partisan interest that was the House of Commons, Hutcheson was regarded as a man of rare integrity. In works such as *The Present State of Public Debt and Funds* (1718), Hutcheson's skill was to use public financial data to calculate state finance at a level of sophistication that had never, until then, been seen.[15]

In 1720, he published *Some calculations relating to the proposals made by the South Sea Company and the Bank of England*, which, in some ways, was an attack on Walpole's policy, as well as on his fellow Tories who created the scheme. Walpole had come to support the South Sea Company as a way of helping the Bank of England and the sinking fund to alleviate state debt. That way, there were three operations working to lower the debt, something that would prove crucial when the crash came. Hutcheson's calculations went beyond accounting into the new realm of financial analysis.

South Sea stock value was based on profit assumptions. Using present values (the value of past and future money at its calculated present value), discounted cash flow (discounting the value of future money, which loses its value) and annuity tables (how much a payment will be worth over time or at a given time), Hutcheson calculated the shortfall between necessary company profit and the stock's value, on which now depended £43 million of government debt. His calculations illustrated that when the government was paid via new subscriptions, it made money, as did those who invested early and cheaply. However, new investors stood to lose more than 20 percent of their investment. For investors to make a profit, the company would have to make massive and unrealistic profits, otherwise "thousands and thousands of people" would be "undone" in the pyramid scheme. "If the computations I have made, are right," argued Hutcheson, there was no foundation for the company's "Annual Profits." He calculated that the dividends the company paid to new subscribers were simply impossible.[16]

Hutcheson's calculations were complex, based on measuring conversion rates of debt payable to the state, company profit, stock subscription income, and the values of company assets and possible profits with interest rates. But the reasoning was clear. To justify a share price of 300 percent of its original value, the company would need to earn a highly improbable £5.3 million in profit annually, more than ten times the annual military budget.[17]

Walpole knew these numbers, for they had been presented and even debated in Parliament. Indeed, the MP Thomas Brodrick called for the South Sea scheme to be given detailed and public scrutiny, and there were debates about Hutcheson's calculations. The company, investors, and supporters of the scheme published their own analysis of the value of company stock. In April 1720, the *Flying Post* and the *Weekly Journal* both published calculations aiming to prove stock values between £440 and £880 per share. As numbers were bandied about by all concerned, Walpole sided with the company because he believed in it—he needed money to further his career and build his country house.

Perhaps he ignored Hutcheson's analysis because the latter was a political gadfly. In any case, profit and politics all stacked up against
Hutcheson's numbers.[18]

When the bubble burst in August 1720, sending stock value plum-
meting from £1,000 to less than £400 in a matter of weeks, Walpole
was taken by surprise. At his country house in Norfolk, he was in the
process of balancing his own household books, buying properties and
lending money to those who wanted to buy more South Sea stock.
Even more, he had just sent his banker, Robert Jacombe, to London to
purchase £5,000 in shares. When news came that the price of the stock
had dropped over 50 percent in three days, Walpole was faced with
ruin and in shock. He frantically tried to reach Jacombe. When word
finally arrived from London, the news was almost miraculous. Jacombe
had not invested the money. The shrewd banker had gone to the South
Sea offices to meet the directors, whom he found unconvincing, "terrified," and in a "bustle." Jacombe had lost faith in the scheme at the moment it began to collapse and held back the investment, saving Walpole
from even more losses than he had already sustained.[19]

Outrage was palpable as shareholders learned of Hutcheson's calculations. Not a political realist, Hutcheson insisted that the government
forgo £7 million, which the company owed it, to help "the middling
people" who had lost everything in the scheme. In today's terms, he
wanted to bail out Main Street. Influential political critics like John
Trenchard, writing from the republican wing of the Whig Party, made
their own calculations of stock value and public debt and called for a
general audit of the South Sea Company, as well as of all other stock
companies, for the benefit of shareholders and investors. In Trenchard's
words, before paying a dividend, each company would have to present
an annual "state of their stock, as their accomptant shall declare upon
oath, before one of the Barons of the Exchequer, to be the true state of
such company's stock." Only such a public audit, Trenchard implied,
would allow investors to make sound judgment. Trenchard lamented
that financial opacity profited not only the company directors but also
government ministers who enriched themselves in the shadows, while
all others had to "gamble" blindly.[20]

Trenchard was calling for an independent financial auditing office.
But the old-fashioned politician Walpole instinctively resisted public

accountability. His power and, indeed, his personal fortune depended on secret state finance. He would find a way to stabilize the market with neither true political nor financial accountability.

Walpole was politically effective, yet corrupt. And although he coveted power and money, he also believed it was his duty to save Britain's financial and industrial markets. With Britain's economy near collapse and the government's ability to raise and service debt under threat, Walpole had the state intervene to create a rescue package for the South Sea Company. It could not have the same fate as the French Mississippi Company.[21]

Investors in the South Sea Company had hired Charles Snell, a well-respected accountant, to audit the company. Walpole understood the possible ramifications of such a public audit. He felt he needed to stop the audit and stabilize the financial system by restructuring the company. The South Sea Company was, as we say now, too big to fail. With the *Act to Restore Publick Credit*, Walpole's first order of business was to make sure the company retained and continued to service about £33 million in government debt, while also saving investors and the banks that had lent them money to buy shares. To bail out the entire financial system, he first had the government lend money to the company to keep it afloat. He then convinced the Bank of England to take nearly £4 million of South Sea government debt; the South Sea Company was obliged to pay a ransom to the government by transferring its silver holdings to the mint. By keeping the markets and the company afloat, Walpole helped investors recoup £52 on a £100 investment.[22]

But to Walpole, the stability of the markets and the financial class, as well as the monarchy and his own Whig Party, was his first order of business. Figures like Hutcheson and the writer and political critic Daniel Defoe excoriated "stockjobbers," "gamesters," and "tricksters." Parliament moved to "establish Publick Credit by preventing Stockjobbing." Walpole, in turn, attacked his political opponents with the famous saying, "All those men have their price." Nonetheless, he moved in to save his banker friends. Using his close contacts with Nathanial Gould at the Bank of England, Walpole successfully restructured the South Sea Company, the Bank of England, and the East India Company, as well as his own innovative sinking fund.[23]

Rather than a feat of finance, Walpole's restructure was a masterful act of negotiation. Although not everyone agreed on his settlement—Hutcheson protested against it in Parliament—no one else came up with a viable opposing plan. Walpole's skills were political. His plan saved national credit markets and at least propped up the damaged companies and banks. The plan also maintained political stability by averting public audits of either the state or the private companies. Central to managing the fraud was the Secret Committee, a Parliamentary group whose members—including Hutcheson—clearly hoped to uncover the extent of corruption, while Walpole managed damage to the government.[24]

The Secret Committee found a staggering £574,000 in stock bribes made to members of Parliament and the government. Not only had the company directors committed various frauds but also parliamentarians, ministers, member of the royal household, and even the king's mistresses had all accepted bribes of stock in support of the scheme. And all these bribes were found in the company's books. However, they had failed to catch Robert Knight, the cashier of the South Sea Company, who, six months earlier, in December 1720, absconded with the key to the whole affair: the Green Book, the company's secret ledger, which contained full records of its most important bribes. Knight managed to flee from prison to the territories of Liège, in the Austrian Netherlands, where, conveniently, there was a nonextradition clause. He escaped from prison through a hole in the wall with helpful "persuasion" from unnamed British high authorities. Walpole and King George II himself were relieved to hear that the accountant had disappeared. Although many figures were tainted and even prosecuted for corruption, the most important figures in the case—Walpole's allies the Earls of Stanhope and Sunderland—escaped total disgrace. Having shielded select ministers and top financiers from ruin and prosecution, Walpole was now called "the Skreen-Master General."[25]

Walpole's tactics led to public outrage, and he was famously attacked in *Cato's Letters* by Thomas Gordon and John Trenchard, who called for what they believed to be the antique republican virtues of transparent, accountable government through the opening of government books and the auditing of government ministers. Most remarkable, Thomas Gordon equated political liberty and virtue with public accounting. For him, unless government figures literally opened their account books for public audit, there could be no liberty, only political chaos and destruction. Gordon invoked Pericles in making his moralistic demands for transparent government. Pericles, he said, had spent lavishly to perpetuate his power and to avoid a public audit. Even more, Pericles made war to cause political confusion, protect his own reputation, and keep his accounts secret. The collapse of Athens was the fault of the "ruinous folly" of a man who would not render his accounts publicly.[26]

This was a dramatic historical indictment of secretive government finance. The problem was that Walpole was no Pericles. He was proud that his manipulations had kept Britain financially afloat and out of foreign wars. And his restructuring of public credit markets and the sinking fund, although opaque and the very opposite of so-called laissez-faire liberalism, on the whole had worked, at least at first. In the 1720s, the state's debt was about £40 million and the annual interest payment £2 million. By 1727, Walpole had managed to lower interest payments by 1 percent, almost £377,381, nearly the size of the entire military budget. He began putting surpluses of sometimes more than £1 million per annum into the sinking fund, which went to service the debt and lower the debt principal. This brought confidence to the markets and led to a general feeling that the debt was under control. By the time he left office in 1742, Walpole had lowered the debt by £13 million.[27]

In *The Wealth of Nations* (1776)—the defining work of morality and free-market economics—Adam Smith expressed doubt that a sinking fund was a solution to debt. Instead, he considered it a temptation to ignore debt and, indeed, to contract new debts. Smith was thinking of Walpole. Although Walpole was a man of finance who governed during the Enlightenment, he was a politician first, and as political pressure regarding the debt lightened, the sinking fund looked less and less like a debt-servicing instrument and more like a political slush fund.

In 1722, Walpole started raiding the sinking fund. At first, he used it as collateral for £1 million in Exchequer bills that functioned as paper currency. In 1724, £15,144 were taken from the fund to cover treasury losses from the reduction in value of gold coin. By 1727, the fund had become a major policy arm for Walpole: He raided it for £100,000 to raise the capital of the king's Civil List fund (salaries paid directly by the crown) to £800,000. The king could not disagree with this move, but one member of Parliament publicly protested that Walpole was destroying his own sinking fund. Walpole remained silent and continued to raid the fund to pay for East India Company annuities and to reduce the land tax by a shilling. In 1734, he appropriated £1.2 million for government expenses. What Walpole had claimed was a lever to manage debt and balance government books had become a black box through which he circumvented parliamentary oversight of government spending.[28]

These financial maneuverings helped Walpole remain in power. In 1732, King George II made a gift of the residence of 10 Downing Street to his able minister. Ever shrewd, Walpole agreed to inhabit it, but, in an act of public altruism, left it as a legacy to the government as the official residency of subsequent prime ministers. But even Walpole's term as prime minister had to come to an end. After failing in 1739 to prevent the War of Jenkins' Ear over trade disputes with Spain in the West Indies (and over the fact that a British seaman, Jenkins, claimed that a Spaniard had cut off his ear), and after making poor showings in the election of 1741, "the fat old squire of Norfolk" suffered a parliamentary vote of no confidence and fell from power in 1742. Walpole's twenty-one-year tenure in power had been unprecedented—he remains the longest serving prime minister in British history. But the country had tired of this brilliant but unscrupulous minister.

The paintings of William Hogarth (1697–1764) have shaped the modern vision of the British eighteenth century and faithfully represent the contradictions of figures like Walpole. Hogarth showed the gluttonous prosperity of the "Robinocracy," the rich city merchants seen to be pulling the financial strings and, indeed, robbing the public in the age of the Hanoverian monarchs. Hogarth's painting *Shortly After the Marriage*, or *The Tête à Tête* (1743–1745), depicts a hungover viscount slouching on his chair after a night out in a brothel or with his mistress, while his wife begins to wake up after a long card party at home. Their steward, carrying receipts and a ledger, walks away in disgust. Accounting is prominent but ignored. This is a vivid portrayal of the ambivalent relationship of the British elite to a tool they had come to master at a remarkable level. This tool, so respected, so connected to prosperity and salvation, could, like life itself, be wasted and thrown away. The story of Walpole and accounting explains how the English got out of the South Sea disaster, but at the same time, it explains how a culture of self-enrichment and political patronage prevented Britain from creating accountable, transparent government.

Rather than being associated with his financial bailout and other policies, Walpole was called a robber. The greatest writers of his time excoriated him, and Walpole complained that "these scribblers grow so bold of late." In his poem *London* (1738), Samuel Johnson described a city impoverished by financial culture:

> *Explore your Secrets with insidious Art,*
> *Watch the weak Hour, and ransack all the Heart;*
> *Then soon your ill-plac'd Confidence repay,*
> *Commence your Lords, and govern or betray.*
> *By Numbers here from Shame or Censure free,*
> *All Crimes are safe, but hated Poverty.*

Henry Fielding, the satirical novelist and author of *Tom Jones*, also painted a dystopian vision of a Britain not "rewarded by virtue," as the novelist Samuel Richardson had idealistically described in *Pamela* (1740), but riddled by shams. His *Shamela* (1741) was an attack not only on Richardson but also on Walpole's Britain, where even the most apparently virtuous were financial cheats who avoided the auditing of their accounts by any means necessary. In *Shamela*, the maidservant is no paragon of untouchable virtue, but rather a cunning thief who has married her husband to rob his estate: "Sir, says I, I hope I am not obliged to give you an Account of every Shilling; Troth, that will be being your Servant still. I assure you, I married you with no such view, besides did not you tell me I should be Mistress of your Estate?" In bartering sex for forgiveness, she gloats that "I fancy I have effectually prevented any farther Refusals or Inquiry into my Expences."[29]

The public had a right to be deeply skeptical of the corrupt financial culture that Walpole's policies made sure benefited his friends. It also had no reason to believe that its government was accountable. The Parliamentary Commission of Accounts to oversee government spending would not be called again until after the War of American

Independence. Walpole had managed to bail out Britain, but he had not brought the kind of reform and accountability he promised in his first years in politics.

He certainly did not hold himself accountable. In 1722, in the years following the South Sea bubble, Walpole began building Houghton Hall on his lands in Norfolk, one of the great Palladian mansions of the eighteenth century, with a sumptuous interior by William Kent, the great architect and designer who would go on to build the Treasury and Horse Guards buildings at Whitehall. It was a testimony to Walpole's power that when he left office in 1742 and his painting collection was moved to Norfolk from 10 Downing Street, it became one of the great artistic treasures of the world, containing four hundred masterworks. Like Cosimo de' Medici and Jean-Baptiste Colbert, Walpole was a political financial manager and a great patron of art. However, after Walpole's death in 1745, his son was shocked to find that the great man's estate was £40,000 in debt. The inventor of the first bailout died in the red.

CHAPTER 8

"FAME AND PROFIT": COUNTING ON THE WEDGWOOD VASE

> Sum up all the values of all the *pleasures* on the one
> side, and those of all the pains on the other.
>
> —JEREMY BENTHAM, 1781

Eighteenth-century Britain was not only home to the unique financial politics of Walpole's bailout. It also became the great imperial power of the world. As the world's foremost producer, exporter, and importer, the tiny island nation continued to maintain its fearsome navy and overseas empire. And it was the birthplace of the Industrial Revolution or, as some historians have called it, an "industrious revolution," where the Protestant faith in utilitarianism and scientific inquiry, mixed with boundless ambition and relative political freedom, fed unprecedented technological innovation and economic expansion. It was here that religious dissenters and industrialists such as Josiah Wedgwood—the famed inventor of Wedgwood porcelain— would popularize accounting and use it to manage innovative companies and formulate new concepts of human happiness and worth.[1]

Central to British industrial power was that, surpassing even Holland, it had become the center of accounting culture and education. Ever since the Middle Ages, grammar schools had taught accounting to boys who would later be apprenticed. Echoing the old educational model of Italy and Holland, grammar schools prepared boys both for the university and for commercial activity. In a virtuous circle, as industry expanded, so did the demand for accounting expertise. Accounting was seen as something increasingly necessary for a gentlemanly ruling class that valued commerce.

The work of Charles Snell—who was later hired by shareholders to audit the South Sea Company after the crash—showed a ready market for accounting manuals for gentlemen and merchants who wanted to manage their own estates and businesses. He was author of *Accompts for landed-men: or; a plain and easie form which they may observe, in keeping accompts of their estates* (London, 1711). In his 1714 *Gentleman Accomptant*, the Cambridge-educated lawyer, musician, and sixth son of the Baron North, Roger North, explicitly stated that it was a great advantage for gentlemen and "persons of quality" to have a knowledge of accounting so that they could manage their own affairs and follow those of international trade and state. North claimed that accounting had become so perfect that it could be considered one of the sciences. North insisted that those who wanted to rule needed to know accounting. And it made sense. After the Revolution of 1688, excise tax accountants had begun keeping state accounting in double entry. Political power and administration were ever more connected with the knowledge of bookkeeping.[2]

Scotland was a center for this mixture of classical and commercial teaching. In 1727, John Mair was appointed master of arithmetic, bookkeeping, and other sciences at the Ayr grammar school. He would go on to write one of the most influential English-language accounting manuals of all time, *Book-keeping methodiz'd* (1736), which would go through nine editions by 1772 and was the most prominent accounting manual in eighteenth-century North America. Along with grammar schools, accounting schools—or "writing academies," as they were called, for accountants and administrators needed clear writing—taught accounting even to those pupils going on to Cambridge and Oxford because they might later need it for careers in the navy or government.

By the second half of the eighteenth century, accounting and even double-entry accounting had become common in English society because of an unprecedented explosion in accounting schools. By

1740, more than eleven accounting academies were active in Britain. By the end of the eighteenth century, there were more than two hundred. John Rule's Islington Academy advertised that it trained the "gentleman, scholar, and the man of business." Many heads of academies were self-made men, but at least nine were well-known scientists or members of the Royal Academy. A backbone of the Industrial Revolution, these academies mixed scientific, experimental training with practical merchant arts. They taught double-entry accounting, navigating, surveying and gauging, and even military subjects. In a world of expanding opportunity, speed in training was of the essence. A 1766 advertisement for the Islington Academy boasted that gentlemen who intended to go into business could learn double-entry accounting "in a very short time."[3]

With the rise of business and industry in daily life, it became more difficult to bar women's access to accounting education. Indeed, some saw it as a necessary protection for families without men at their head or for single women who could fall prey to the fraud of financial predators. As bookkeeping knowledge spread across classes, aristocratic women, as well as the wives of shopkeepers, industrialists, and simple property owners, increasingly learned double-entry accounting. Indeed, many were said to learn it "at their mother's knee." As one advertisement claimed, private schools for women taught "English, writing, arithmetic as far as it is related to 'keeping accounts,' drawing, needlework, dancing and a little French." Although some enlightened industrialists taught accounting to their daughters, others still felt accounting was a masculine art.[4]

Many accounting academies were led by Dissenters—Low-Church Protestants who, like Puritans, had been excluded from the Anglican Church and the universities for refusing to renounce their religious beliefs. They were imbued with ideals of happiness, self-discipline, scientific progress, and salvation—the heady and unique mix of British Enlightenment Protestantism that Max Weber would idealize as the Protestant work ethic. Their belief in accounting was inspired by religious fervor. Dissenters followed the old English tradition of attempting to marry scientific rationalism and the natural sciences with Christianity. Their beliefs rested on Isaac Newton's ideals of order, harmony, and progress as revealed by mathematics. For these divinely inspired people of discipline and profit, accounting was a tool of personal industriousness, as well as for realizing political freedom and faithfully watching over the God-given gift of prosperity.[5]

Private academies not only afforded Dissenters income but also were a place where they could apply their unique brand of scientific, mercantile learning. Protestant outsiders—Deist Unitarians, Quakers, and Presbyterians—also flocked to academies across Britain. The Warrington Academy in Lancashire was set up to educate the sons of Dissenters, and it focused on "Business and Commerce," as well as the "best methods of Book-keeping." The Standard Hill Academy in Nottingham was founded with the goal of providing a nonconformist discipline that would help young men "distinguish themselves in the professions and in various trades and industries."[6]

There was even an acceptance of this commercial curriculum in the High Anglican Church. British Protestants of all social stripes sought God's work in nature through scientific experiments and observations and tried to fulfill God's will by turning this natural knowledge into worldly wealth. Liberal Anglicans also believed that science and the work of Newton would strengthen Protestant Christianity against other religions and atheism and would be the basis of a new scientific Christianity. They sought to bring Puritans and Dissenters back to the Anglican Church by publicly embracing mathematics and the ideal of profit. As the renowned classical scholar Richard Bentley put it in his Boyle Lecture at Cambridge in 1696, God had commanded "men" to find "profit" and "pleasure" by "pursuing" their "own interest." Accounting was central to these philosophical views.[7]

But Puritans and Dissenters had more important reasons to keep personal accounts. British law forbade them to hold public office or to organize an official church. This imposed lack of hierarchy and oversight meant that this British version of Protestantism, unlike the hierarchical Church of England, truly became a church of all believers, and a new culture of "watchfulness" permeated Dissenter and Calvinist life. The individual would have to "watch" the world to defend against the Devil and aid in the "winning of Christ." To seek the kingdom of God, the faithful would, like spiritual scientists, write down their observations of the world in notebooks and spiritual account books. Dissenters, Quakers, and Calvinists had to account for their own sins and virtue, and they often did this by writing diaries and autobiographies in which good works, sin, and economic success were recorded. In many cases, they wrote not only autobiographical observations but also accounts in order to search for evidence of personal failure or, by predestination, that one was to be saved by God.[8]

Literary figures such as Jonathan Swift kept detailed account books, and the Presbyterian writer Daniel Defoe included descriptions of bookkeeping in *Robinson Crusoe* (1719), a fictional autobiography in which Defoe—who had written expert accounting manuals and was a prolific financial critic—had Crusoe account for himself "like Debtor and Creditor," trying to balance the positive and negative aspects of his life. Like the Jesuit account books of good works and sin, Defoe tried to calculate the good in life.

A successful Leeds clothier and Dissenter, Joseph Ryder, wrote in his diary in 1739 that he used his daily writing and accounting to admire "the Goodness of God In making man a rationall Creature." Wealth was seen as a product of godly conduct and of good accounting. Like the Italian Catholic Datini 350 years earlier, Ryder tallied his moral accounts in his diary and his finances in his ledger. What was new for Ryder was the idea that if one mastered industry or scientific problems through the study of nature—God's work—and gained wealth by it, this success was not sin, but rather a sign of predestination. Good science, good records, and good accounting brought one closer to God and profit. And the better one's accounting was, the more clearly one might see in it possible predestination to salvation. Thus bookkeeping had a special place in the lives of everyone from Anglican, Cambridge-educated, and scientifically minded noble second sons to high merchants and landowners, city businessmen, and financiers, as well as average or middling people—the very literate and often business-minded Dissenters. It was a binding thread in the complex tapestry of British Protestantism.[9]

Of all the Dissenters, the industrialist Josiah Wedgwood (1730–1795) stands out. He not only exemplified the success of industrious Dissenters but also showed the importance of accounting in their project and the heights to which it could be taken in industrial innovation. Inspired by his Dissenting religion, Wedgwood created one of the most successful and innovative companies in history—Wedgwood china is still coveted today, with a six-person dinner set costing well above $1,000. He did this by an intensive study of cost accounting: the calculation of the cost of production time, labor, materials, machinery, and sales. Wedgwood took industriousness and accounting to new levels of innovation and success, but even he struggled to balance morality with his bottom line. He would find that accounting, as he practiced it, could bring him the world's riches but not necessarily the ideals of health, happiness, freedom, and social harmony.

Whereas Walpole was a brash and greedy politician famous for his massive dinner parties and Hogarthian appetites, Wedgwood was a meticulous and moralistic man who ran his famous porcelain factory in Burslem, north of Birmingham, by the time of a famous clock in the courtyard. Like Walpole, Wedgwood used accounting for personal enrichment; his was enrichment not through political tricks, but rather through personal piety and industry, which Wedgwood believed would better his soul and those of his workers.[10]

Josiah Wedgwood regularly boasted to business partner and friend Thomas Bentley that through industry he sought *"Fortune, Fame & the Public Good."* (In his more candid moments, he was less virtuous, simply stating that selling more porcelain would bring *"Fame and Proffit."*) Wedgwood's early letters are full of references to the need for political liberty and the importance of science, but they are also filled with numbers. Sophisticated forms of double-entry accounting were the foundation of the first Industrial Revolution (circa 1760–1840). Walpole used numbers, but Wedgwood lived through them. He loved to count, for example, the numbers in Queen Charlotte's porcelain order for what would become known as Queensware: "The articles are 12 Cups for Tea, & 12 Saucers, a slop bason, sugar dish wth. cover & stand, Teapot & stand, spoon trea, Coffeepot, 12 Coffee cups, 6 pr. Of hand candelsticks & 6 Mellons with leaves." Although he regularly sent Bentley calculations on extraneous things like the cost of building the Stoke-on-Trent Canal, Wedgwood believed that accounting could solve the problem of industrial productivity and profitability.[11]

Whereas medieval and Renaissance painters had regularly underlined the risks of accounting, eighteenth-century British artists reflected the hubris of the young industrial nation's golden age. With profits rolling in, account books appeared to make British merchants, at least the successful ones like Wedgwood, happy. It became common for British businessmen and bankers to pose for portraits smiling and with their account books open on their desks. These portraits were a sign of confidence in modern techniques of accounting. The Baring Brothers—whose bank was founded in 1762 and folded only in 1995 because of the famed rogue trader Nick Leeson, who was also his branch's auditor—were painted by Sir Thomas Lawrence poring over their main ledger like conquering explorers with their fingers on a map. A prominent businessman in India, John Mowbray, was depicted sitting cross-legged at his desk, with an air of satisfied confidence, his account books strewn around him as a local messenger brought him a report. A good accountant could master his books and even the world.[12]

However, this confidence belied the challenges of industry. Although British merchants exuded confidence, the advances they made in accounting were, nonetheless, surprisingly small. Industrialists struggled with the complex accounting needed by factories, and they often gave up. Their goal would be to adapt accounting to industrial production. Wedgwood needed to figure out production costs for his porcelain works to squeeze out higher profits through efficiency. Industrialists began dissecting their factories, breaking down each part of the chain of production through accounting analysis. Although cost accounting had existed in primitive ways since the Middle Ages, there was no publicly recognized method for measuring the costs of labor, machinery, and raw materials. Entrepreneurs also needed to measure returns on capital investments. This was not possible unless one could ascertain whether a new piece of machinery was making a return.[13]

Thus periodic accounts of the cost of various parts of a manufacture were necessary. To effectively run factories and mines, managers had to price the costs of tools and each manufacturing process and decide which mines and mills, for example, to expand or shut down, as the Quaker Lead Company attempted to do in 1774. In 1777, the accountant and mathematician Wardhaugh Thompson wrote one of the most innovative works on the application of double-entry bookkeeping to industry and alluded to the difficulties of accounting for industrial profits. Nonetheless, he noted, without accounting, there was only "guess'd-work." Economic theorists like Max Weber saw the first Industrial Revolution as progress, but accounting and industrial management were still much as they had been hundreds of years before. The techniques of cost accounting, which would seem obvious today, were consistently overlooked. Although companies did do periodic accounts for distinct elements of their factories (materials, labor, production machines, cash, payments, share payments, profit and loss), few ever did general, overall audits.[14]

Yet the leaders of industry knew that their wealth sat on the foundations of accurate accounting. James Watt (1736–1819), scientist, inventor of the steam engine, and Scottish Presbyterian, was deeply aware of the importance of accounting in his various enterprises and factories. As a young apprentice, Watt had borrowed money from his father, and to repay the debt—and to show his father his progress—every day, after working more than twelve hours, he still found time to keep good double-entry books.[15]

Watt's partner, Matthew Boulton (1728–1809), saw the lab, factory, and account books as part of the machinery of industry. He claimed that the same care and exactitude necessary in science was also necessary in keeping books. The chief accountant of the firm Boulton and Watt created a special kind of accounting for the merchant and manufacturer that attempted to show real profit within a production cycle. With increased industrial production and ever more accounts to keep, industrialists such as Watt were challenged by keeping extensive financial paperwork. Indeed, Watt invented a copying machine—which functioned by pressing special thin paper with very strong ink so that the ink would make an imprint on the next sheet—in part to make up for a shortage of accounting scribes to keep his financial records. Aware of just how important accounting was to his competitive edge, he spied on other firms to see how they kept their books. He was one of the first to understand that accounting methods could be an industrial secret.[16]

Like Watt, Josiah Wedgwood was a highly competitive man. He sought not just fame and profit; with his Queensware china, he hoped to "ASTONISH THE WORLD ALL AT ONCE, for I hate piddling you know." He had managed to do just that in 1765, when Queen Charlotte of England placed an order for a full set of china. Wedg-

Jan Provost, *Death and the Miser,* early sixteenth century. Groeningemuseum, Bruges, Belgium (©Lukas—Art in Flanders VZW / Hugo Maertens). Dutch and Flemish Masters painted warning images both celebrating their citizens' prowess in accounting and warning that humans could never fully balance their books. Man would have to be accountable to God, who would always make the final reckoning.

Hendrick ter Brugghen, *The Calling of St. Matthew,* 1621. Central Museum in Utrecht, The Netherlands (©Collection Centraal Museum, Utrecht). The patron saint of accountants, bankers, and perfumers, St. Matthew gave conflicting messages about finance, leaving Christendom with a great moral puzzle: Was it, or was it not, immoral to manage and make money? Matthew insisted that wealth had to be handled competently and honestly but, at the same time, that it was earthly and sinful. This moral ambiguity is still with us today.

Hans Memling, *Last Judgment*, central panel, c. 1467–1471. Pomorskie Museum, Gdansk, Poland (Scala / Art Resource, New York). The director of the Medici Bank's Bruges branch, Tomasso Portinari, commissioned Hans Memling's painting *The Last Judgment* (painted between 1547–1461). In it, the archangel St. Michael holds a scale of final reckoning on which he weighs souls and decides who goes to hell. Life imitated art when, in 1477, Portinari ruined the Medici Bank with risky investments and was cast into poverty and disgrace.

Francesco Sassetti, *Libro Segreto* (Archivio di Stato di Firenze, Italy, Carte Strozziane, Su consessione del Ministro per i Beni e le Attività e Culturali e del Turismo). The pages of the secret account book of the chief accountant for the Medici Bank, Francesco Sassetti, reveal his failings as an accountant. By the time these accounts were made in the early 1470s, Sassetti had become careless about his audits and entries, and the bank was on the brink of financial collapse.

Domenico Ghirlandaio, *Confirmation of the Franciscan Rule by Pope Honorius III*, c. 1485. Detail of the nave of the Sassetti chapel, Santa Trinita, Florence, Italy (Scala / Art Resource, New York). Rather than focusing on disciplined accounting and bank management, Sassetti was consumed by his patronage of Ghirlandaio's Sassetti Chapel in Florence's Santa Trinita Church, a masterpiece of Neo-Platonist civic art. No longer seeing himself as an accountant but rather as a pious and learned patrician, Sassetti had himself painted alongside his employer and the ruler of Florence, Lorenzo "The Magnificent" de' Medici.

Domenico Ghirlandaio, *Francesco Sassetti and His Son Teodoro*, c. 1488. The Metropolitan Museum of Art (©The Metropolitan Museum of Art / Image: Art Resource, New York). Ghirlandaio's portrait *Francesco Sassetti and His Son* (1488) is notable for its lack of resemblance to its subject. It was painted in his absence because Sassetti had left for Lyon to take responsibility for the collapse of the branch and left the painting as a memento of himself to his sons. Once a skilled and respected accountant, the man who helped bring down the Medici Bank would return to Florence a ruined man.

Jacopo de' Barbari, *Portrait of Fra Luca Pacioli*, c. 1500. Museo di Capodimonte, Naples, Italy (Alfredo Dagli Orti / The Art Archive at Art Resource, New York). Jacopo de' Barbari's famous portrait of Fra Luca Pacioli, author of the first printed manual on double-entry accounting. Pacioli's stature as a teacher of mathematics and accounting was such that he was painted in the foreground, with his student and patron, Guido-baldo da Montefeltro, Duke of Urbino, standing behind him. An accountant would never again be painted in a relation of superiority to a nobleman.

Jan Gossaert, *Portrait of a Merchant,* c. 1530. National Gallery of Art, Washington, D.C. (National Gallery of Art, Washington, D.C.). By the early 1500s, Antwerp and its surrounding towns had become the center of world trade and accounting expertise. Jan Gossaert's famous portrait celebrates the wealth and corresponding accounting tools of the successful Dutch merchant Jan Snouck Jacobsz (c.1510–1585).

Quentin Metsys, *The Moneylender and His Wife*, 1514. Musée du Louvre, Paris, France (©RMN-Grand Palais / Art Resource, New York). Quentin Metsys's painting is a study in how merchants can lead pious lives by managing their money well while also being devout Christians. Note that the wife holds an illuminated Book of Hours with a portrait of the Virgin Mary and that accounts and bills of exchange are on the shelf in the background.

Marinus van Reymerswaele, *The Moneychanger and His Wife*, 1539. Museo Nacional del Prado, Madrid, Spain (©Museo Nacional del Prado / Art Resource, New York). In a later version of Metsys's painting, Marinus van Reymerswaele removed the religious aspect, replacing the psalm book with an account book, thus celebrating both Flemish prowess in accounting and the virtue of good stewardship.

Quentin Metsys, *The Money Changers*, c. 1549. Musei Bellas Artes de Bilbao, Spain (Alfredo Dagli Orti / The Art Archive at Art Resource, New York). By the 1540s, however, artists such as Quentin Metsys and Martinus van Reymerswaele began portraying accounting as a possibly fraudulent and immoral financial activity. Both Metsys and van Remerswaele painted a number of versions of this image of untrustworthy and possibly Jewish "money changers" or "tax collectors."

Marinus van Reymerswaele, *Two Tax Gatherers*, c. 1540. National Gallery, London (© National Gallery, London / Art Resource, New York). In this painting of tax gatherers keeping accounts, van Reymerswaele vividly depicts the tools used by accountants: ledgers, bills of exchange, seals, and file boxes. Yet he associates financial management with twisted figures and satirical headdresses, possibly pointing to the human folly of greed and the hubris of hoping to manage fortune. Rather than celebrating accounting and commerce, these paintings warned against the dangers of putting too much faith in human tools of financial calculation and management.

Jan de Baen, *The Corpses of the De Witt Brothers*, c. 1672–1675. Rijksmuseum, Amsterdam, The Netherlands (Rijksmuseum). In spite of the fact that Jan de Witt's financial and accounting sophistication and dedication to the Dutch republican model of politics were a model for modern political expertise, in 1672 he and his brother Cornelis were deposed by the powerful Prince of Orange. At the prince's orders, a mob gutted and lynched them, cutting off their fingers and toes and eating their internal organs.

William Hogarth, *Marriage à la Mode: no. 2, The Tête à Tête*, c. 1743. National Gallery, London (©National Gallery, London / Art Resource, New York). Hogarth's painting *Shortly after the Marriage*, or *The Tête à Tête* (1743–1745) is a vivid portrayal of the ambivalent relationship of the British elite to accounting in the age of Robert Walpole. It shows a hungover viscount propped on his chair after a night out in a brothel or with his mistress, while his wife begins to wake up after a long card party at home. Their steward walks away in disgust, carrying receipts and their clearly unbalanced ledger, which is of no interest to them.

Josiah Wedgwood and Sons, Dark Blue Jasper Dip Medallion of Jacques Necker. c. 1770–1800 (Metropolitan Museum of Art, New York). A fine example of Josiah Wedgwood's valuable jasper pottery, this medallion is a portrait of the French minister and author of the *Compte rendu*, Jacques Necker. While Wedgwood's radical Dissenting friends fought for the political ideals espoused by Necker, Wedgwood satisfied himself by selling profitable cameos of political figures and balancing his books.

Thomas Hickey, *John Mowbray with His Money Agent, Banian,* c.1790. British Library (©British Library Board / Robana / Art Resource, New York). By the mid-eighteenth century, British industrialists and colonialists used accounting with such success that they earned unprecedented wealth. They had such confidence in their skills as financial managers that a series of portraits of leading British merchants were painted showing their subjects smiling over their account books. This happy confidence in accounting would fade by the time of Dickens, a century later.

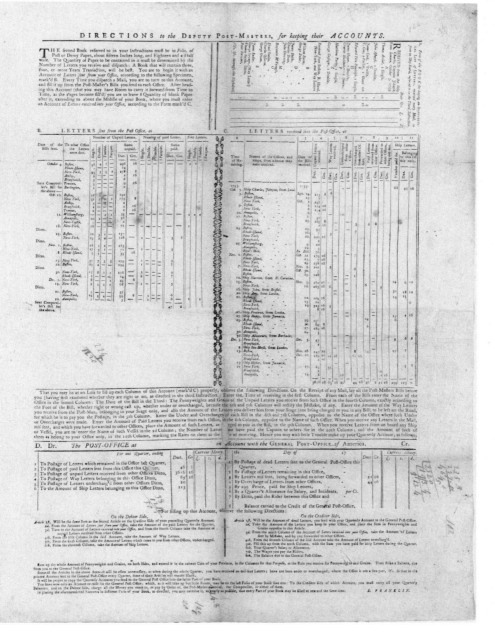

Benjamin Franklin, *Directions to the Deputy Post-Masters, for keeping their Accounts*, Philadelphia, 1753 (Historical Society of Pennsylvania). Benjamin Franklin was fascinated by accounting. He kept double-entry books, wrote about accounting, and even composed his autobiography on the pages of a ledger book. While British postmaster for the American colonies, he created this broadside for every post office. It not only explained to postmasters how to keep postal accounts but also included a minimanual on double-entry accounting so that anyone who came to the post office could learn the basics of accounting, which Franklin considered essential for daily life.

Compte rendu au roi par M. Necker, Paris, 1781 (Rare Books Division, Department of Rare Books and Special Collections, Princeton University Library). The final tally from the French director of finance under Louis XVI, Jacques Necker's revolutionary and best-selling *Compte rendu au roy* (1781). It was the first time that a politician would use the claims of a surplus—in this case 10.2 million livres—as a declaration of political success. Necker began a tradition of using big and often inaccurate numbers as political propaganda, a well-worn tradition that still continues today.

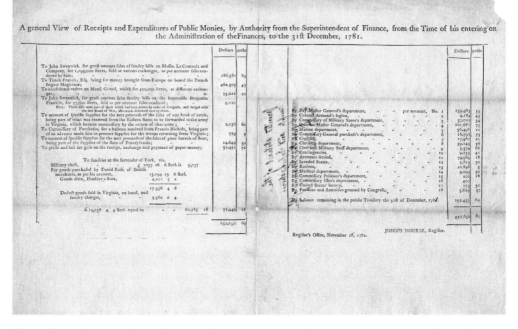

United States Register of the Treasury, *A general view of receipts and expenditures of public monies, by authority from the superintendent of finance, from the time of his entering on the administration of the finances, to the 31st December, 1781* [Philadelphia, 1782]. #Am 1782 United States Treasury Dickinson 60.2 (Library Company of Philadelphia). Inspired by Necker's *Compte rendu*, American Superintendent of Finance Robert Morris published his own copy of the state accounts for the U.S. government. Transparent accounting became central to the American founders and was enshrined in Article 1, section 9 of the Constitution.

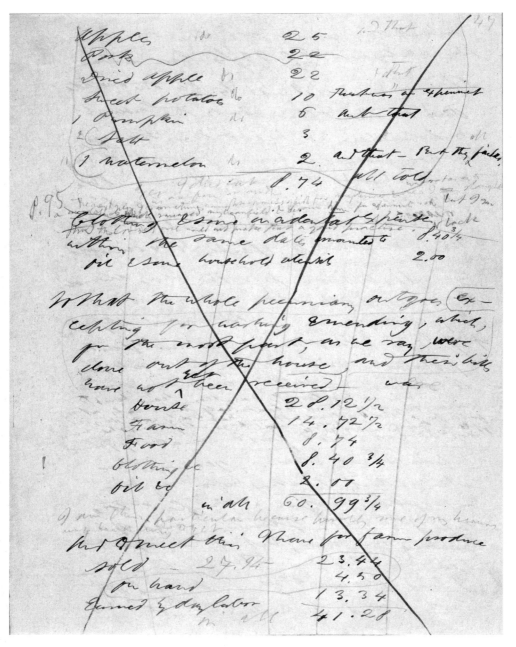

Henry David Thoreau, *Accounts from Walden,* 1846–1847. Huntington MS 924, vol. 1, page 59 (Image: Huntington Library, San Marino, Calif.). As one of the leaders of the American Transcendentalist movement, Henry David Thoreau sought to return to nature and a pure state of spirituality by rejecting material goods. In these rare sheets from the work notes of his classic *Walden,* he turned the principles of accounting on their head by calculating backward, trying to figure out the bare minimum he needed for subsistence.

wood was giddy, as his pious modesty gave way to unadorned pride. He banked that the royal order would create demand and cement the reputation of his china manufacture. Wedgwood had created a marketing strategy. He wrote to his business partner, Bentley, to look to the English peerage for elite clients, for they, he said, were the "legislators in taste." King George III soon followed suit for his own full service of the hand-painted floral Queensware, as did courtiers and diplomats around the world. In 1770, Lord Cathcart, the British ambassador to Russia, ordered a full set for Empress Catherine the Great.[17]

In spite of the success of his Queensware, by 1769 Wedgwood faced a cash flow problem. The company was spending more than it was earning on expensive products for an elite few. Wedgwood worried that the fabrication of replica antique vases might "bring upon us as much *proffit* as *loss*." Paradoxically, more business meant creating a loss for Wedgewood. "Collect. Collect," he wrote his partner Bentley, "set all your hands & heads to work." By the end of the year, they had manufactured pottery worth £12,000 but had debts of £4,000.[18]

Echoing Philip II, this brilliant man of industry also found accounting to be a challenge: "I have been puzzling my brains all the last week to find out proper data, & methods of calculating expense of Manufacturing, Sale, loss &c to be laid upon each article of our manufacture." So Wedgwood went back to the books, but he was perplexed that even when his calculations appeared to allow for the expenses of production, he still managed to calculate only half of the real expense of making and selling his goods. He asked Bentley to verify the books, for he could not figure out his error.[19]

Wedgwood now began to make accounting innovations. He calculated depreciation, administrative costs, the expense of sale, and the interest on capital. He broke down fourteen categories of expenses, from "Wages to Boys, Odd Men, Warehouse and bookkeeping" to "accidents" and "Rent, Wear and Tear, and incidental expenses." He explained to Bentley how he calculated all these things, down to each color of clay, in columns.[20]

His notebooks are filled with accounting notes based on the single goal of lowering labor costs. He would use his books, he said, to produce more for less. Wedgwood concluded that he could mass-produce his extrafine china and recoup his production costs. By examining his accounts, Wedgwood saw the complexities of the production cost over time move "like clockwork." Industry was a machine, which like the universe moved according to fixed intervals. Through accounting, Wedgwood saw clearly that he could price these intervals of labor.[21]

Accounting meant Wedgwood no longer had to guess at his costs. Always grumbling about drunken, "worthless workmen," he now sought to manage them with greater efficiency. He learned that child labor was much cheaper and more efficient than adult labor, as was paying by the piece rather than by the day. He even began to calculate future sales, based on past history, and designed "means to augment" them in the future. He also gained insight into consumer psychology. He was able to see that the rich do not mind paying a little more but that this slight difference in price might scare off the "middleing people." He needed, therefore, to create products for both the rich and the middle class.[22]

Even more, Wedgwood's calculations revealed to him that his chief accounting clerk was robbing him. Wedgwood realized that as the final auditor in the firm, his only way to understand costs and see fraud was constant, real-time auditing. He sent his trusted personal accountant, Peter Swift, "to assist in Examining & settleing the matters with the Clerks so that I may have the accounts weekly, & by every Mondays post, in a way I have mentioned to him, & to put the necessary business of collecting into a way of *perpetual motion*." For accounting to work, the tallying and the auditing could never stop.[23]

Not only did Wedgwood create detailed cost accounting, which allowed him to manage production costs, labor, and pricing, but also he came up with accounting theories. His writings on cost accounting are some of the most fundamental to the history of economics. Wedgwood created a taxonomy or ranking of costs to predict probable costs. Thus probability entered into his equations and his method of management.

And in Wedgwood's case, it paid off. In 1773, a crash in prices spread across Europe, affecting pottery and other consumer goods. Wedgwood had lowered his manufacturing expenses, set prices strategically, and expanded production and his international market presence. As we know from the longevity of the Wedgwood brand, it weathered the long economic storm, and Wedgwood went on to become a very rich man. When he died in 1795, his fortune was estimated at £500,000 ($45 million today, but by its purchasing power, immensely more in the eighteenth century).[24]

Whereas Datini left his fortune to God, Wedgwood left his to his family. His business would "provide for the wants and comforts of the world." Far from the old Dissenting humility, Wedgwood was proud and even vain about his success. But for all of Wedgwood's confidence, even he worried that his success lay on fragile foundations. With increasing social inequity and the challenges of the American War of Independence (1775–1783), the country was in need of reform, indeed, accounting reform. But the now wealthy Wedgwood was loath to call for radical changes. The Dissenter had become a pillar of the establishment.[25]

One reason there had been so few accounting reforms within British government was that the state had, ever since Walpole, been able to manage its public debt. But the American War of Independence sent a financial storm back to Europe, as England and France scrambled to pay for the war that set the colonies free. The shock hit England before France as a heady mix of anti-Catholic sentiment and falling wages brought about the Gordon Riots of 1780, which destroyed a fifth of the buildings in London and rightly terrified propertied elites. Reform was needed. Dissenters would split: on the side of the status quo on the one hand, and for radical reform and even revolution on the other.

As reforming Whig parliamentarians like William Pitt and William Wyndham Grenville looked to fix the crisis caused by the American war, figures like Wedgwood's Dissenting friend Richard Price offered the old solution of a sinking fund. Price's *Two Tracts on Civil Liberty, the War with America, and The Debts and Finances of the Kingdom with A General Introduction and Supplement* (1778) called for a government for "the benefit of the people governed," against the "rapaciousness" of an oligarchy bent on holding onto power and also hoarding wealth. The greatest danger of all, warned Price, was the national debt. Even after Pitt became prime minister in 1783, the debt continued to rise. By 1788, Britain was spending 70 percent of its tax revenue to service a debt that had ballooned from more than £40 million under Walpole to an astronomical £250 million in 1784. Once considered a Dissenting radical, Price was now praised in Parliament as "that able calculator," the term *calculator* having become a compliment.

His treatise contained hundreds of pages of calculations and accounts, showing how his proposed sinking fund would vanquish national debt.[26]

Pitt's administration finally gave real powers to the old, toothless parliamentary Commission of Accounts, which was supposed to oversee state expenditure. Pitt needed more income, and he would now try to harness the old tools of state accounting. Working under Pitt's watchful eye, the commissioners first met on July 15, 1785, at Downing Street but left for Scotland Yard to look over the accounts of the Auditors of Imprest, who audited all crown officers. Their aim was to examine all the accounts and try to bring them together into a single budgetary report. A series of examiners, inspectors, and commissioners would all make audits that would be checked, noted, sent back with objections, and checked again before an official statement was sent to the Lords of the Treasury, who helped make the most important national economic decisions.[27]

In 1806, Pitt's former secretary, George Rose, wrote that there had been no period in British history when the public had been so informed of state accounts. Rose believed that keeping double-entry books for state receipts and expenditures, along with a public rendering of these accounts, would calm worried spirits. The convergence of war, economic crisis, overwhelming debt, and social strife helped bring about many of the accounting reforms cherished by Dissenters, who, ideally, wanted a democratic republic. In spite of Pitt's and Price's reform and Rose's claims, many of the commissioners admitted that they still had difficulty in figuring out state accounts. The Commission of Accounts would finish its reforms only fifty years later, in 1832.[28]

One would have expected Wedgwood to be happy about these reforms, or at least engaged. Here, after all, was one of the greatest accountants of his age, a Dissenter, and a close friend of radical reformers. Wedgwood complained that all who did not have the vote were slaves. He also bitterly complained of slavery itself and about Britain's "obstinate rulers" who had brought "calamity" in the war with America. But he showed a distaste for politics. Wedgwood's letters show the passivity of a man of the establishment. He hoped that his old Dissenting friend Joseph Priestley would find more time for "leisure" rather than the radical preaching that would drive him from England to Pennsylvania in 1791.[29] Wedgwood was ever solicitous to European monarchs and the great aristocrats of his realm, on whose purchases he still relied. As the French Revolution began in 1789, the chief pottery maker to the British monarchy and to the great and the good of the world was less concerned with liberty than with making snuffboxes adorned with the heads of French Finance Minister Jacques Necker and, more prophetically, King Louis XVI's revolutionary brother, the Duke d'Orléans (who would soon lose his on the guillotine). The world was in revolution; Dissenters believed their moment had come, and Wedgwood was focused on making cameos.[30]

In 1791, Wedgwood wrote to support Priestley in the wake of Birmingham's Priestley Riots, which were directed against Dissenters and his friend's revolutionary preaching. An old friend of the family, Priestley—a scientist and Dissenting preacher—was the discoverer of oxygen, a believer in industry, and also an indomitable defender of political and religious liberty. Wedgwood supported Priestley against the rabble that burned down his church. But when Wedgwood read Priestley's appeal in support of the French Revolution and for republican government in Britain, he protested against passages that called for armed revolt and recommended temperance. Wedgwood's discomfort with his revolutionary friend had become palpable, and James Watt, a former radical himself, agreed with him. Watt also warned Priestley that "while Great Britain enjoys an unprecedented degree of prosperity," other countries were in the chaos of revolution and thus he would consider "the overturn of all good government" as folly.[31]

After Priestley was forced to flee to Philadelphia for his safety—where the mayor and Benjamin Franklin welcomed him as a revolutionary hero—Wedgwood's letters contained no more radical talk. In his letters to his close friend Dr. Erasmus Darwin—whose son Robert would marry Wedgwood's daughter Susannah, to beget Charles Darwin, the father of the theory of evolution—Wedgwood remained more focused on calculating the advantages that a good canal system would bring to Britain. In the age of world revolution, Wedgwood continued to take comfort in his very favorable bottom line and his legacy: sound industrial management and tableware for the middling sort.

Yet harsh reality appeared even in the successful factories of Burslem. The effects of industrial pollution on Wedgwood's workers and their families made him wonder why science had not brought more human improvement. As war and violent revolution gripped Europe, tuberculosis ravaged Wedgwood's and other industrial families. Joseph Priestley's and James Watt's daughters both suffered from it, and the lead and coal of the Wedgwood factory damaged the lungs of Josiah's son Tom. In his later years, James Watt wrote, "Nothing now remains, as I can find it [money] can neither bring health nor happiness." With his constant faith in science, Wedgwood spent money on research to cure these diseases, but his heart was more in profit and industry than in medical progress and human well-being.[32] The horrors of industry inspired Romantic poets like William Wordsworth to lament that industry was England's "bane" and had spread darkness "O'er hill and vale." There was poison in this great industry, and even with Wedgwood's true genius, he had not accounted for this heavy cost.[33]

Although Wedgwood the innovator would, in the end, use accounting to try to hold the status quo, economists and philosophers saw that accounting could be a tool for wider social and cultural change and progress. Adam Smith used accounting data to develop free-market theories. It was in ancient accounts, like the Domesday Book—which he called a "very imperfect book of accounts"—that Smith traced the movements of the invisible hand of market prices. He cited the accounts of French, English, and Scottish food markets to understand pricing. A professor of moral thought, Smith mixed the numbers of accounting with theories of moral commerce and liberty in his quest to design a model for human happiness.[34]

Moving beyond profit-oriented accounting, British Protestant thinkers tried to budget productiveness as well as happiness. In 1781, the utilitarian philosopher Jeremy Bentham tried to account for the "greatest happiness principal" with a "hedonic, felicific calculus," which was a double-entry method of valuing pleasure. Bentham called for an account of pleasure and pain: "Sum up all the values of all the *pleasures* on the one side, and those of all the pains on the other." The balance, he said, would show the good and bad tendencies of a person so that he might try to improve his life and find not salvation, but earthly happiness.[35]

Thus the science of bookkeeping became a way of thinking about happiness, well-being, and individual worth, beyond the bottom line.

Bentham pointed out what Wedgwood could not recognize: Holy industriousness could bring both pleasure and pain. The challenge in life, as in business, was to find balance and seek improvement and happiness beyond wealth itself. At the end of the eighteenth century, however, a harmony of human happiness and commerce was still unrealized. As Priestley had tried to tell Wedgwood, there was great inequity in the world, and many felt that only the human reckoning of a revolution could bring freedom and human happiness.

CHAPTER 9

BIG DEBTS, BIG NUMBERS, AND THE FRENCH REVOLUTION

Sire . . . to follow the example of England, which publishes its accounts . . . is an insult to national character. . . .

—COMTE DE VERGENNES, FRENCH FOREIGN MINISTER, TO
LOUIS XVI, 1781

After fifty years, the English budgetary pamphlets of figures like Francis Hutcheson had found no echo in Europe or the Americas. For accounts to become a way of talking about politics and making news, it would take a Parisian argument about numbers and a French revolution. From the beginning of debates about numbers and political accountability, the numbers had been dubious. The French Revolution would begin, in part, as a fight about accountability and accurate numbers in government. This fight would popularize the use of financial accounts in the modern politics.[1]

It is surprising that a lasting language of accounting and accountability emerged not in Holland or England, but in France. As we have seen, Dutch political leaders had a grasp of accounting and maintained relatively open government. With its parliamentary system, constitutional government, and national bank created to manage its debt, England had a system of financial accountability that eighteenth-century despotic France did not. Perhaps it was precisely because of its very lack of open government that a political language of public accounting and accountability emerged more forcefully in France.[2]

John Adams famously noted on his 1778 trip to Paris that the ancient French monarchy and its privileged nobles surrounded themselves in a glittering world of luxury, even as most of France wallowed in increasing poverty. The government had managed to make some spending cuts, but even so, the threat of a government default on debt interest payments spiked interest rates. The only way to lower the debt, inflation, and interest rates was to tax France's proud nobility, the great landowners, who, although less than 3 percent of the population, owned 90 percent of France's considerable wealth. For more than a hundred years, French elites had resisted attempts to make them pay tax above 5 percent and all reforms that might lead to such a thing, especially national accounting audits, which they saw as the first step to measuring their wealth, all the better to tax it.

A culture of accounting and accountability existed, but only among a small group of merchant administrators and political economists. In 1716, one year after the death of Louis XIV, under the bankrupt government of the Regent Philippe d'Orléans, the reforming Pâris brothers— the financial officers who had been given the job of trying to manage the private tax collection system, the "tax farms"—came up with a plan to streamline tax collection and perform audits on the independent tax collectors. Their legal Declaration of June 10, 1716, ordered all tax collectors and state accountants to render their receipts, as well as keep daybooks, to be audited by regional accounting "controllers," who themselves would then integrate all administrative daybooks into a double-entry ledger. As part of this law, the Pâris brothers published abbreviated accounting manuals on small posters that were to be publicly displayed. What had been part of the world of businessmen and accountants, they claimed, would now be a systematic part of their political administration.[3]

Not surprisingly, these reforms met with much resistance. Tax collectors were slow to adopt double entry because of both its difficulty and their unwillingness to give up their privilege to profit from tax collection (or perhaps fearing the competition and the potential domination of the

Pâris brothers, formidable state financiers in their own right). This change coincided with John Law's establishment of a Banque Générale in 1716 and the beginnings of his Mississippi scheme. Clear accounting was not a priority for the brilliant though ultimately disastrous Scottish financier. With enemies among the financier class and the old nobility (who feared taxes and any attacks on their privilege), as well as in Law's influential circle, the Pâris brothers were banished in 1720. As was typical with the vicissitudes of courtly favor, the chief minister, Cardinal Dubois, called them back in 1721, after Law's Mississippi bubble burst, as the French government scrambled unsuccessfully to manage the financial crash.[4]

Although they never came up with a plan like Walpole's bailout, during the next four years, the Pâris brothers continued their accounting reforms. More than simply wanting to use accounting to reform the state, they saw accounting as a new kind of statecraft. In a secret treatise, possibly made for the government, Claude Pâris Le Montagne stated that the only path to an "ordered Government" was financial accountability through double-entry bookkeeping. He maintained that it was to an absolutist king's disadvantage to keep secret the "shadow finance" of private tax farmers. He warned that secrecy caused corruption and that the only antidote was through the "solid and geometric plan" of "faithful tables" of double entry, which would provide a "General Control" of all state finance. Public, double-entry accounting, he concluded, was the basis of "the public good."[5]

In spite of all their reforms, the Pâris brothers had no lasting impact on state policy. Jarred by the collapse of Law's bubble, few in public or in government had the financial literacy to fully understand the basic ideas about accounting and accountability. France was not merchant Britain, and the regent was no Dutchman. The Pâris brothers later complained that the regent "never saw more than the covers of the Books (the Registers of the general Treasurers)." The debate over *comptes rendus*, which the Pâris brothers hoped to spur, never materialized.[6]

Economic debate in France was dominated by the Physiocrats, pioneering economists who believed that wealth came from agricultural production and free markets. Physiocrats had grand ideas and used numbers in their theories, but they did not do the kind of financial analysis of accounts and budgets done by Hutcheson or by the Pâris brothers. The most famous idea that emerged from the works of the French economic philosophers François Quesnay, Vincent de Gournay, and Anne-Robert-Jacques Turgot is what they famously called "laissez faire," a theory of commerce based on the natural law of freedom. Before Adam Smith, it was their hope that by lifting government subsidies, price controls, and guild monopolies, an "invisible hand" would spur agricultural production and national wealth. Large-scale, state financial management was not necessary in a market regulated by the balance of nature itself. Although Quesnay used mathematics to study economic theory and de Gournay and Turgot were skilled accountants, their published work rarely contained analysis of complex numbers, accounts, or budgets. While the English argued about state tax receipts, lending rates, and sinking funds, the French lived in a financial information blackout, imposed by their secretive, absolutist monarchy.[7]

Physiocrats and free market pioneers did, however, believe that public debt undermined economies and society. They echoed the views of the Scottish philosopher David Hume, who, in 1751, had characterized public credit as "dangerous," "rash," and ultimately devastating to nation-states. Hume framed the choice between budget surpluses and deficits in apocalyptic terms: "Either the nation must destroy public credit, or public credit will destroy the nation." At first glance, Hume would appear prophetic: By 1776, the French monarchy, saddled with insurmountable debt and a large deficit in spending, had long been on the edge of bankruptcy. And indeed, when deluge of the revolution came in 1789, it wiped away the old order. Yet the state remained, and so, too, did public credit.[8] The question was how to manage it.

The French public increasingly hungered for the financial details of their own state and its assumed massive debts. During the tumult caused by the American War of Independence (1775–1782), as France's massive debts ballooned, Louis XVI found it harder and harder to borrow. Although earlier reformers had improved tax collection, the basic abuses of a system managed by private tax collectors remained and, given the nation's mounting debts, weighed all the heavier. Without a central accounting system within the state, no one really knew the level of income *or* outstanding debt. The *fermiers* and *regisseurs*, the crown's private tax collectors, kept scant records, turning in primitive and often falsified accounts years after the fiscal year in question. With weak-handed audits conducted every three years, there was ample time to falsify accounts. Some state financiers sent their account books to the Royal Treasury nineteen years late. At the same time, these unac-countable tax collectors, while withholding their tax revenues from the Treasury, lent money to the crown at high interest rates. Corruption, had, in effect, been institutionalized.[9]

Unable to secure loans or raise revenue, in 1777 the crown named Di-rector General of French Finances the famed Protestant Swiss banker Jacques Necker (1732–1804). A commoner, Necker had made his for-tune as a banker and a trader in his native Geneva and in Paris, speculat-ing on grain and administering the French East India Company. His wife hosted a famous salon attended by the leading lights of the Parisian world of arts, letters, and sciences, including Diderot, d'Alembert, Grimm, Mably, and Mme. du Deffand, as well as Madame Necker's former lover, Edward Gibbon, who, at that very moment, was writing his timely and all too apropos *History of the Decline and Fall of the Ro-man Empire* (1776–1778).

Whatever faults Necker had—and acquiring wealth in the French market of grain trading and public companies required a certain moral flexibility—he was a proven manager and a man of high culture and ambition. His brilliance, financial acumen, and access to the world of ideas and public opinion through Madame Necker's salon made him a formidable figure on the Parisian political and social scene. Most im-portant, his connection with Geneva allowed him critical access to credit on behalf of the French crown, whose debts following the Seven Years' War and the War of American Independence had ballooned to more than 3 billion livres of debt. Servicing this debt cost more than 300 million livres annually, at an average of 5.5 to 6 percent interest, which was more than 50 percent of all state expenditure and more than half of state revenue. A country one-third France's size, England, by contrast, successfully serviced a comparable debt, in part with 3 per-cent interest loans from its independent national bank.[10]

Necker worked to stop the tax farmers from lending money to the crown before turning in their revenues and tried to have tax collectors keep accurate, daily books that could be audited at any time. He proposed eliminating three-quarters of the forty-eight tax collectors (*regisseurs*), streamlining them into twelve heavily audited officers. In his accounting regulation of October 18, 1778, Necker attempted to centralize the state financial system into a single *caisse*, or account, based on double-entry books he would closely audit.

Like the reformers before him, he threatened the entire independent financial class of the ancien régime. And, of course, any time any privilege was threatened, the nobles smelled blood. Having resisted reform for more than a century, they were not about to stop now.[11]

It wasn't long before Necker was attacked in the popular press in a burst of publicity and propaganda, which the future Minister of Finance Calonne maliciously called "Neckromania," a "sickness" of public opinion. As a foreign, Protestant finance minister and a magician of Swiss credit, Necker could not have been shocked to see his name dragged through the mud of the popular press. In the Parisian hive of rumor and libel, Necker was an ideal target.[12]

As his even more famous daughter, the writer Madame de Staël, later admitted, her father thrived on publicity and believed, at least in the beginning, that the public was a rational political force. Yet as his reforms continued, the attacks against him became more pointed and potentially threatening. In 1780, one particular libelous pamphlet seized public attention. The Parisian barrister Jacques-Mathieu Augéard's anonymously published *Letter from Monsieur Turgot to Monsieur Necker* was filled with so much financial information that it gave the impression that a government insider had written it. Augéard attacked Necker as a Swiss banker bent on draining money from the state for his own fortune (the grand sum, he claimed, of 1.75 million livres). He critiqued "the Citizen of Geneva's" skill as an accountant, saying, "you know better than I the ABCs of business [accounting and keeping Registers]," and claimed that Necker's vulgar, common manners added up to nothing more than "a little calculation of banks and money." Most seriously, Augéard charged that Necker was another John Law, printing speculative paper money (*billets noirs*) that would lead to a financial crash like the Mississippi bubble. "The example of 1720 is still in sight," he warned.[13]

Although he mocked accounting, Augéard used numbers as his primary weapon in the publicity battle, claiming, for instance, that

Necker's reform of the tax farms had cost the tax farmers 98 million livres. Even more, he accused Necker of falsely claiming that there were 250 million livres to be had by collecting unpaid debts from the companies of state financiers alone: "What an assertion, Sir!, deign to calculate this again with me, for I know the matter well." Numerical proofs and refutations accompanied the narrative of indictment. The influential opinion maker Madame du Deffand claimed that six thousand copies of Augéard's pamphlet quickly circulated through Paris and Versailles. In his own *Mémoires Sécrètes*, Augéard later gloated that his pamphlet was "devilishly successful."[14]

Political publicity was, by 1780, a well-developed, rough-and-tumble art, yet Necker had, until this time, managed to keep his hands clean of it. With these attacks, however—sustained, popular, coming on all fronts, and employing financial calculations authoritative-sounding enough to convince the public—Necker saw no option but to respond. It was unseemly and dangerous for a minister to descend into the mud-slinging world of pamphleteering. Necker could use his position within the state to try to ban the offending pamphlets, but this would have only a minor effect; there was no truly effective censorship machine within the state. Thus he had to turn the tide of pamphlets threatening his position and reputation by taking control of the discourse not just at court, but in the streets.

In 1781, Necker published his *Compte Rendu au Roi* (*Accounts Rendered to the King*), an explanation of the crown's finances for the year. It was the first time in the history of the French monarchy, Necker proudly pointed out, that a finance minister had shown himself accountable for his administration and revealed his calculations to the public, claiming a budget surplus of 10.2 million livres.[15]

As one news pamphlet described it, until then, government had never published an official budget, leaving the real state of royal finances to the "false speculations" of an uninformed public. Secretive state finances had made the French public hungry to understand the workings of the French state that taxed them, prosecuted costly wars, and funded the glory of the court at Versailles. It was into this void of information that Necker stepped. His *Compte rendu* was the key moment when publicly accessible accounts became a central means of assessing the effectiveness of a government.[16]

The response he chose was precisely the sort of mixture of enlightened gesture and reckless bravado that conservative figures in the monarchy feared from their Swiss Director of Finances. A brilliant media coup aimed at the very powers threatened by reforms and at a European audience that included the Swiss creditors of the crown whom he wanted to convince that the state's finances were sound, Necker's *Compte rendu* called the bluff of his enemies. If they sought to use numbers against him, he had at his disposal a weapon they did not possess: the ability to reveal the actual accounts of the government from within. Necker hoped that this "publicity" would neutralize his critics by shining light on "these obscure Writings," the "mystery of the state of Finances." It was, he bragged, "the first moment in which a great State" revealed the truth of its dire finances. Necker was not accountable to the people—there was no real mechanism for this in an absolute monarchy—yet only this publicity, he insisted, could bring order and confidence. And so, with a dose of Calvinist revelation, Necker made the bet that his unveiling the "mystery" of state accounts would gain France good credit with foreign lenders.[17]

Beyond hoping to sway opinion, Necker was offering a new vision of politics. Claiming that England's Parliament printed the state of its finances every year and that he was following suit—he clearly had no knowledge of English political culture or of the debates that were raging even as he wrote—Necker said that balanced books were the basis of "moral," "prosperous," "happy," and "powerful" government. He described in detail his management, state revenues, and expenditures, and at the end of his description, he provided his accounts for public opinion to see the justice of his claims. The numbers of his accounts were to represent the virtue of his administration. In short, open good books were open good government. Public prosperity and public accountability were central to the defense of the state and the power of its sovereign. This was literally revolutionary, for Necker was implying that it was not the king's personal will that constituted political power, but rather the management of state accounts, for which he himself took credit.[18]

The *Compte rendu* revealed the finances of each major institution and office in the state and its expenditures and revenues. Total revenues were 264,154,000 livres. Out of the total "ordinary" expenditures of 253,954,000, the king spent 65.2 million livres on the military, 25.7

million on the court and his household, and 8 million for the comte d'Artois's household. This was in comparison to 5 million livres for roads and bridges; 1.5 million for Paris police, lighting, and city cleaning; 900,000 for the homeless poor; and 89,000 for the famed Royal Library. The royal priorities here were painfully clear.

These revelations shocked the public, not just for the gross disparities of expenditures they made plain, but for the very way they demystified the sacred realm of the king's household and the careful theater of power played out at Versailles. The *Maison du Roi* was not represented as a royal, legal, personal, or even mystical entity, but rather as a set of shocking numbers. In a particularly daring affront to the crown in an age of famine, Necker took the opportunity to critique the king's dining expenses, claiming that with better management they could be cut by half.[19]

The pièce de résistance of the *Compte rendu* was its annex of accounts. Necker provided what appear to be full state accounts, followed by a final tally on a large table on the last page. Necker claimed that all these calculations could be backed up by "verifiable documents," state accounts signed by those who made them, which he kept in a box and would go on to produce as evidence. At the end of his calculations, Necker declared: "Revenues exceed Expenditures by . . . 10,200,000." All the numbers were there, and they showed a surplus. As would later be revealed and even acknowledged by Necker himself, he omitted about 50 million more in deficit military and debt-related spending, which he deemed extraordinary, thus beginning a venerable tradition of underreporting, or keeping military spending off the books, out of national interest.[20]

Ever on the sideline of events (save that of his own downfall), the hapless Louis XVI had clearly not realized what his minister was doing in publicizing the accounts. For his part, Necker, sure that he would improve his political standing, did not imagine his numbers would be challenged. He had the *Compte rendu* published by Panckoucke, publisher of the *Encyclopédie*, who sensed this was to be a major success, as indeed it proved to be. If Augéard's print run of 6,000 was considered a success, it is hard to characterize the phenomenon of the *Compte rendu*. Within a month, the 60,000 copies Panckoucke had printed sold out. More than 100,000 copies were sold in 1781 alone, changing the very notion of what constituted a best seller. Thousands more copies were printed in foreign editions and translations. The *Compte rendu* became one of the most successful works of all time and a media phenomenon. Seditious material had long circulated clandestinely. What Necker did was to redefine the very substance of debate. It was no accident that Necker paired the *Compte rendu* with a royal declaration of accountability on March 3, 1781, requiring all tax collectors to present their account books and a future budget. Necker's proposed "Law of Accounting" offered to the king the possibility of putting order in both ordinary and extraordinary finances. In the past, debates about good government had been fought with words and even images and songs. With the *Compte rendu*, debates would now be waged not only with increasing fury but also with cold numbers of accounting.[21]

Necker's *Compte rendu* had the appeal of a secret truth. Yet as Necker himself had made clear in his earlier criticisms of the state's financial institutions, although a truly accurate account of state finances was nearly impossible, his accounts were more accurate than those of his detractors. Many of Necker's critics accepted his numbers but attacked his act of revelation, especially that of royal expenditure. His method of exposing royal accounts was seen as undermining the very religion of absolute monarchy: secrecy. Foreign Minister Vergennes attacked the idea of revealing government secrets, seeing the *Compte rendu* as a direct threat to the personal authority of the king; he, like much of the public, assumed that Necker had been not only truthful, but accurate. In a letter to Louis XVI, Vergennes called the *Compte rendu* "an insult to national character, which is sentimental, confident and devoted to its Kings. All is lost in France, Sire, if Your Majesty allows his Ministers to cite English Administration for which your predecessors have shown a just aversion."[22]

One particularly reactionary aristocrat, the Marquise de Créquy, made a bilious rant against the *Compte rendu* that reveals just how threatening the idea of accountability was to the court nobility. Créquy understood that part of the *Compte rendu* was an act of public theatrics, but the idea that a Protestant banker would reveal royal secrets touched on ideas of privilege based on rank, blood, religion, and nationality. Accountability, or the revelation of secrets of state, was a subversive act in itself and showed the qualities of an enlightened "encyclopedist" and "Jew-like" Protestant banker who lowered himself to the burlesque and base activity of merchant accounting. It was the royal minister Maurepas's fault in the end, Créquy lamented, for leaving state secrets in the hands of a foreign Protestant like Necker.[23]

One critic warned that the "illusion" and media sensation created by the *Compte rendu* had to be "snuffed out," precisely because Necker's numbers were a chimera. At first objecting simply to numbers, Necker's critics soon got in on his act. The only way to fight these bad numbers, they saw, was with "the evidence of numbers." Here was the model of modern political debate: an arms war of impossibly hard to substantiate numbers. The fact that few could actually verify calculations made numbers a perfect cover for fraud.[24]

For the next decade, the unscrupulous courtier Charles Alexandre, Vicomte de Calonne—called "Monsieur Déficit" by his enemies— would be Necker's archrival in debates over state accounting and accountability. A protégé of Vergennes himself, Calonne was a royal tax lawyer, or intendant, and as such sufficiently acquainted with state finance to attack Necker with counternumbers. The decade-long battle between these two men would take on epic proportions, forming the first public polemic about state accounting numbers.

Calculated critiques like Calonne's pierced Necker's political armor, and it is hard to imagine that these attacks against a crown minister, no matter how independently he might have acted, did not pique Louis XVI's royal sense of dignity. In the end, however, the remote king finally ceded to the parties of privileges—the queen, the court, his brother Artois, royal financiers, and the Parlement of Paris—and dismissed Necker on May 19, 1781. Exiled to the country to fulminate, Necker took this time to write his masterful and best-selling *Treatise on the Administration of Finances* (1784), thereby cementing his place as the world's leading financial writer. His daughter Germaine, by marrying the Swedish ambassador, became Madame de Staël, the famed French Romantic writer. Necker's quitting of the scene did not change the fact that he had let loose the genie of accountability into the world of politics.

Over the next six years, attempts at reform were mostly in the ways Necker had suggested. Then in February 1787, Calonne became Controller General of Finances and came face-to-face with precisely the same financial problems that Necker had. Meeting with the Assembly of Notables at Versailles in yet another attempt to combat the gangrene of French state finances, Calonne sought to explain the reasons for the financial deficit, and deflect blame for it, and he proposed a despised general land tax that included the nobles. Although not responsible for the debt, he, politically, owned it. Like all those before him who had failed to reform state accounting and impose the tax on nobles that was so sorely needed, Calonne fell in 1787, later fleeing to London.

The now reviled Calonne had to rescue his reputation and career. He saw his solution in blaming Necker for the deficit by showing that the calculations of the *Compte rendu* had been incorrect: Rather than a surplus of 10.2 million livres, there was instead a deficit of 46,329,000, a difference of 56,529,000 from Necker's rendering. Calonne made the same argument about accountability that Necker had: Calculations were the only way to prove the success of an administration. He claimed that Necker had forced him into doing this "painful revelation," which would break the "armor of illusion" with "incontestable truth." "Quelle masse d'erreurs!"[25]

It is not at all clear that the public was able to judge sums like 10.2 million livres. By 1785, the Affair of the Diamond Necklace, in which Marie Antoinette had been falsely implicated and discredited in the complicated theft and resale of jewels, had familiarized the public with sums like 2 million livres. Wages were counted in sous, not livres, and the average laborer earned between fifteen and twenty-five sous a day (around the value of one livre). Skilled artisans earned about double that. Daily bread averaged about seven to fifteen sous, anywhere between 50 and 100 percent of a journeyman's wages. Few could understand the immense sums being discussed, let alone the calculations accompanying them. Nonetheless, the numbers entered into the everyday parlance of the literate, and soon enough Necker's 10.2 million livres became a commonly bandied number. What was clear to the general populace, literate and illiterate alike, was that the sums discussed were incredible and scandalous and that they discredited the crown.[26]

From 1781 onward, newspapers such as the *Gazette de Leyde*, the *Mercure de France*, and the *Courrier d'Avignon* closely covered the debate over Necker's *Compte rendu* and the subsequent *comptes rendus* of his enemies. They often discussed numbers and in some cases critiqued accountings. In 1788, the *Courrier d'Avignon* reviewed various *comptes rendus* and reproduced extracts of royal accounts and calculations. Although not truly analyzing accounts in any professional or technical way, journalists nonetheless compared accounts and highlighted the differences between the total tallies of Turgot, Necker, and Calonne. Throughout 1788, *comptes rendus* and numbers appeared in newspapers, which more and more equated credible calculations with political legitimacy. Clearly, the public was enthralled not just by sedition and slander, but by the power of numbers, of accounting.[27]

In 1788, Necker triumphantly returned to his position as director-general of finance. Allegories now likened him to liberty itself. For obvious reasons, Louis XVI had not wanted his old minister back, but Necker rode back to power quite literally on a wave of public acclaim, and Louis XVI became more and more powerless. Crowds thronged the streets to celebrate Necker's triumph. Yet the old problems remained, and Necker once again was tied to these problems and numbers.

On June 23, 1789, rumors that the queen had forced the king to fire Necker brought protesting crowds into the streets of Versailles, pressing against the gilded gates of the chateau. Necker went to the front gates to bask in the approbation of the crowd. Some presciently worried that such mass demonstrations posed a danger to authority, yet the crowds were not dispersed, and the king began to amass troops in Paris and Versailles. On July 11, 1789, Necker protested the presence of soldiers in the capital. This was one disagreement too many, and the king fired him yet again. Necker, claiming the full support of the Third Estate—the increasingly influential non-noble political representatives who had declared a National Assembly at Versailles—was stunned. He alone held back "famine and bankruptcy," he pronounced.

On the July 14, an angry mob gathered in front of the Bastille, a medieval fortress on the edge of Paris, now a royal prison and weapons magazine. It had been used as a royal prison since the fourteenth century, and although it held only seven privileged prisoners (one was an Irishman who thought he was God), it was a symbol of royal power and repression. "Citizens, there is no time to lose," yelled Camille Desmoulins, a radical leader of the revolution who would help open the doors to the Terror, only to lose his head on the guillotine by the hand of his friend Robespierre. "The dismissal of Necker is the knell of a

Saint Bartholomew [a famous French massacre of 1572] for patriots! This very night all the Swiss and German battalions will leave the Champ de Mars to massacre us all; one resource is left; to take arms!" By the end of the day, the royal governor's head was on a stake, weapons and gunpowder had been commandeered by the mob, hundreds of years of police archives had been thrown into the streets, and the royal flag was lowered. When the Duke de Liancourt announced the news to Louis XVI, the king asked, "But is it a revolt?" The duke famously replied, "No Sire, it is a Revolution."[28]

As the old regime crumbled, Necker was recalled yet again, returning to Versailles once more through the adoring throngs of the public. But events were now beyond this moderate, who, if anything, now appeared hapless as the juggernaut of revolution started rolling. Necker was a reformer, not a revolutionary, and there would be no reforming the old order. Through the National Assembly, the revolutionaries wanted to wipe away aristocratic privilege and royal fiat. The accounting Necker wished to use to reform could just as easily be used to build a new government. Over the next two heady years, Necker slowly faded from the scene, but accounting reforms and the public discussion of big numbers remained.

Numbers not only remained part of political debate; accounting became central to the language of the revolutionary constitutions. The English word *accountability* might derive from a translation of the French term *comptabilité* into *accomptability* or finally *accountability*. Whatever the first usage, it was the way the English rendered the term in their translations of the French revolutionary constitutions. The French revolutionary Constitution of 1791 legislated that all financial and political actions had to be published in the form of *comptes rendus* ("public accounts").[29]

In 1792, the Convention Nationale (now the legislature) organized of a Bureau of Accountability. The bureau had eight accounting commissioners and gave an accounting of its own annual expenditures—they spent 499,001 livres, a considerable sum. However, creating the bureau was not easy; few officials were expert enough in accounting to take the posts. That same year, Deputy Antoine Burté published a pamphlet (of what was probably a speech to the Convention) titled "Rapid Observations on the Conditions of Eligibility of the Commissars of

Accountability." In it, he discussed how to do accounts, the scarcity of skilled accountants, and the difficulty in training accounting commissioners.[30]

With the abolition of the tax farms in 1790 and the rise of a central state taxation office, there were improvements. Not only did all bureaus of government publish their own accounts (*comptes rendus*, or *états*) but also the ministries of finance and the navy published regular accounts. Every office and agent of the government had to produce financial accounts and receipts for their actions. Through these little account pamphlets filled with numbers, the state revealed its workings and publicized its virtue.[31]

Far from the scene of momentous events, Necker returned to his roots, passing his last years in his Chateau of Coppet, near Geneva. Madame de Staël, meanwhile, took the family's moderate mantle and fought ardently against Napoleon. Necker died at age seventy-one in 1804.

The revolution failed to secure representative, accountable government; still, it introduced a culture of financial literacy and accountability into politics that in turn planted the seeds for future accounting reforms. In creating a language for judging politics through state balance sheets, Necker's *Compte rendu* was a precursor to the modern budget and, indeed, to financial newspapers. It was emulated across Europe and even in America. The Grand Duke of Tuscany and future emperor of Austria, Pietro Leopoldo, published his own *Rendiconto* of state accounts in 1790. Even constitutional England and the nascent United States paid close attention to the *Compte rendu* and to French accounting reforms. France, which had for so long failed in any sort of state financial accountability, provided an exportable method for building a modern accountable state.

CHAPTER 10

"The Price of Liberty"

A regular Statement and Account of the Receipts and
Expenditures of all public Money shall be published
from time to time.
—UNITED STATES CONSTITUTION, ARTICLE 1, SECTION 9

Jacques Necker's *Compte rendu* not only played a role in the French
Revolution. His writings and accounting reforms provided inspiration to the Founding Fathers of the United States. State build-
ers and administrators across Europe and the New World were finding
new uses for the old methods of accounting. Those methods would find
fertile ground in a young nation whose constitution was based on the
ideal of political accountability. Here, in the newly formed United States,
there would be a chance to build a government around the principles of
accounting.

Before it was the nation of the Constitution, America was the land of
the account book. The noble enterprise, as many saw it to be, began as
a commercial venture. The Mayflower Compact of 1620—the undertaking of the Puritans to make a sea voyage to the New World—was
made in the form of a commercial contract, signed by investing partners, to share expenses and profits. And contracts went into account
books. It should never be forgotten that although they were religiously

inspired, the early American colonial ventures were organized to make a profit. Like the Dutch, French, and English East India Companies, the early colonial ventures in America were chartered companies, with trade monopolies granted by the British Crown, founded to colonize British North America.

The Massachusetts Bay Company was a private shareholder company, founded by "undertakers," with a charter from King Charles I and officers: a governor, a deputy governor, and a treasurer. Leader of the Boston Puritan pilgrims John White's project for a "plantation" on the Massachusetts Bay was a colonial business venture as well as an attempt to find safe haven and religious freedom for Puritan Calvinists, who were persecuted in Charles I's Anglican England. In 1629, in Cambridge, England, the shareholders met to sign the Cambridge Agreement. Some shareholders stayed behind, and others, led by John Winthrop and Thomas Dudley, made the arduous, two-month Atlantic crossing in a ninety-foot wood and tar boat to the unknown (although already populated) land to found the cities of Boston and New Towne, which would become the new Cambridge, placed on the easiest crossing from Boston, across the "great oyster bank" of the respectfully named Charles River.

As might be expected, and in the great tradition of the Italians, any multipartner seafaring company depended on the quality of its books: those of the home office, those of the boat, and those of the trading post or, in this case, colony. Colonies relied on account books even more than factories did, for how was one to assess a far-flung investment without conducting a personal inspection? Early in the Mayflower settlement, the Pilgrim Fathers encountered accounting problems when their treasurer failed to keep accounts: "Mr. Martin saith he neither can nor will give any accounts; he crieth out unthankfulness for his pains and care, that we are susspitious of him and flings away, and will end in nothing." In 1629, to calculate what the Massachusetts Bay Company owed to each partner, an audit was made: "But for that there is a great debt owing by the joint stock, it was moved tha some course might be taken for the cleering thereof, before the gouvmt bee transferred; and to this purpose it was first though fit that the accompts should bee audited, to see what the debt is." Indeed, the accounts showed that the North American colonies could produce great wealth but that they were often in debt. The early history of America is, in part—along with religion, colonialism, trade, slavery, education, and philosophy—the history of accounting for the management of that debt. From 1636 onward, the Massachusetts Bay Company would proceed in the "audite," or "taking" of treasurer's accounts. The same was happening in the Dutch colonies. In 1651, the Dutch directors of the North American trading companies, in what is today New York, hired Johannes Dyckman as "Bookkeeper in New Netherland."[1] The founders of the United States were not just religious idealists, merchants, smugglers, philosophers, and slavers; they were also accountants interested in accounting for profit, for God, and ultimately for the people of the United States. Until then, no country had ever been founded under the watchful eye of a bookkeeper.

Unlike Britain, however, America was not yet a land of shopkeepers. It was a rural place, of farms and plantations. Among the general population, especially in the early colonial years, double-entry accounting was not common and actual money was scarce (and often a motley mix of guineas, bits, and Spanish dollars, from which the word *dollar* is derived). Most towns were small, and few residents paid any taxes. Some made their money smuggling, and the majority of transactions took place by barter.[2]

However, the American elite and urban classes did come from the world of the British financial revolution, and whether landowners or merchants, English, Scottish, French, German, Dutch, Swedish, Swiss, and even some Jewish colonists brought with them traditions of merchant accounting. Early Puritan merchants were well versed in bookkeeping. In 1653, Robert Keayne, a tailor, speaker of the House of the Massachusetts general court and a military man, wrote about his account books: "the third is bound in white vellum, which I keep constantly with the sum of most of my accounts contracted wherein there is [*sic*] accounts between myself and others with the accounts balanced on either side and also an account of my adventures by shipping with their returns and also an account of what debts I owe and far they are discharged." In cities, accounting culture flourished much as it did in England. In the early 1700s, British-style "writing schools" had emerged in most large towns, advertising instruction in "merchant's accounts." By the third quarter of the eighteenth century, the colonial population had swelled to 2 million, and Philadelphia, with 20,000 inhabitants, was the second biggest city in the British realm. From Bostonian booksellers and Philadelphia traders to the plantation owners of the south, British eighteenth-century bookkeeping was almost universally known.[3]

A number of British accounting manuals circulated in the early United States. Among them, John Mair's *Bookkeeping Methodiz'd* was found in many colonial libraries. Accounting was often taught in families with manuals like that of Mair. A copy owned by the Library Company of Philadelphia is an eighth edition with the owner's signature, "Sam Mickle's, 1776," and those of his heirs, "George Mickle, 1830" and "Joseph Mickle Fox, 1906." By the 1790s, American accounting manuals were appearing in the trade capital, Philadelphia. Thomas Serjeant's *An Introduction to the Counting House* was published there in 1789. But Mair's book dominated the market, for it advertised double-entry accounting as a tool for "merchant-accounts" and plantation owners. Without it, Mair warned, it would be difficult to use accounting for the management of estates, farms, and, indeed, government. For the top and the bottom of society, Mair advertised double entry as a tool for "real business," colonial nation building, trade, agriculture, and domestic life and gave examples as specific as "The Produce and Commerce of the Tobacco Colonies."[4]

Obadiah Brown, a former ship's captain—of the Providence, Rhode Island, Brown family—taught himself accounting by using a British accounting manual. Much of his early accounting was haphazard and single entry, although effective enough. Brown mixed his accounts with a personal diary. Joining his family firm, Brown made a fortune in cocoa, rum, molasses, and slaves. Members of the Brown family would become academics in the mid-eighteenth century and, using their wealth from trade, in 1833 helped turn the Baptist College of the English Colony of Rhode Island into Brown University.[5]

Accounting played a major role in the lives of the founders of the early American republic. Merchants such as John Hancock were sent to London to learn accounting as apprentices. Hancock made errors in his books, but the accounts were extensive and reflected his background in British overseas trade. And he used these skills to make a fortune profiteering during the war. But accounting was not simply a way to get rich. In the case of Benjamin Franklin, it formed his vision of the world and was a central tool of nation and state building.[6]

In *The Protestant Ethic and the Spirit of Capitalism* (1905), the sociologist Max Weber held up Benjamin Franklin as what we now recognize as a caricature of the Protestant capitalist strain. Double-entry bookkeeping was at the center of Weber's work ethic theory, for he considered it "rational." Weber quoted Franklin's famous sayings that "*time* is money" and "*credit* is money," and he cited Franklin's financial maxims on accounting and thrift as his prime examples. Weber concluded that earning money and denying self-gratification were not simply good capitalist tools; they were a holy Calvinist ethic. And he quoted the Bible: "Seest thou a man diligent in his business? He shall stand before kings" (Proverbs 22:29).[7]

At one level, this was Franklin, the most diligent and enterprising of men. And he was certainly endowed with staggering talents. His account books show how he organized all levels of his life through accounting. As a polymath, inventor, printer, businessman, scientist, musician, politician, author, bibliophile, scholar, journalist, philosopher, diplomat, and householder, Franklin clearly saw accounting much like Colbert in seventeenth-century France: as an organizing principle for his disparate interests. He learned accounting as a printer's apprentice, and it took a major role in his life. He wrote accounts for his family business, for his household, for his position of Postmaster General of the British colonies, and for his diplomatic missions representing the fledgling American republic.

In Franklin's early years, he kept ledgers for his business as a printer in Philadelphia. Franklin admired those who knew how to do double-entry accounting, noting it as a great virtue in his *Autobiography* (1771–1790). He described how his friend, the future poet and writer James Ralph, was expert in double entry, "which he thought himself well qualify'd to undertake, as he wrote an excellent Hand, & was a Master of Arithmetic & Accounts."[8]

Franklin's shop book accounts between 1735 and 1739 recorded all sales and transactions in meticulous detail. Entries include "an almanac," "an ounce of inks for Cristefer the Fisherman," and the debit of sixpence "lent to the Stranger from Boston." Franklin was impressed that the Dutch wife of one of his journeymen—who himself could do no accounting—"born and bred in Holland," was fluent in accounting and could run a printing shop. Franklin recommended that all women be trained in accounting, not only to help run businesses, but to teach it to their children, which would bring "lasting Advantage and enriching of the Family."[9]

Here, then, was an ideal of the Protestant work ethic, learned from the discipline of accounting and taught as a family work ethic for women and children. Indeed, for Franklin, accounting was central to the order of life. As with the Jesuits before him, accounting helped Franklin order not just his finances but also his thoughts, writings, and moral well-being. He kept moral account books, in which he tallied his own virtues and failings in columns he "cross'd . . . with thirteen red Lines, marking the Beginning of each Line with the first Letter of one of the Virtues." Franklin, too, believed in being watchful through accounting in anticipation of God's judgment.

Even more, Franklin believed that accounting should be a general tool for institutional management, tailored to the needs of a specific business. When Franklin became Postmaster General of the Royal Post in the Colonies in 1753—a lucrative post—he set out to design a system with which local postmasters could do the complex accounting for the mail. In *Instructions Given By Benjamin Franklin, and William Hunter, Esquires, His Majesty's Deputy Post-Masters General of all his Dominions on the Continent of North America* (1753), Franklin outlined how to manage a post office. For postmasters, the care of their letters was paramount—they had to keep them in "good Order," keep them closed and out of the view of all other private persons. More than that, each letter had to be stamped and taxed, for much correspondence was official, and some contained taxable goods. Even more, packets often contained things like jewelry, and their value had to be accounted for. The only way postmasters could organize and manage their offices was by keeping good accounts of all letters and packages. Franklin pointed out that he made the process easier by sending each postmaster forms he printed to facilitate their accounting.[10]

In a founding text of management and organizational theory, Franklin explained how to keep these complex accounts, in which letters had different values in stamps, taxes, and type of letter, and they had to be accounted for as they came, left, stayed, and were paid for or not. Thus Franklin not only created a manual for keeping these accounts, with printed illustrations of how to keep them, but also explained postal double-entry bookkeeping, which was part managerial, part mathematical. In any case, it was one of the most innovative accounting manuals of all time because of its specific design for a complex office system, with a detailed list of specific expenditures and unpaid letters "On the Debtor Side" and other miscellaneous and dead letters plus income "On the Creditor Side." He signed the instructions "B. Franklin."[11]

Aware that these complex instructions might be hard to follow, he also made a large broadside—a foldout poster measuring two feet in diameter and 18.8 inches in height to be put on the walls of post offices—that explained all this in abridged form, with illustrations and a minimanual of double-entry bookkeeping. Thus all post offices in early America had double-entry manuals posted on their walls, with instructions on how to use them. Franklin was not only making the post office work in the colonies but also spreading his vision of how to order and manage the world.[12]

For all Franklin's espoused work ethic (early to bed, early to rise, etc.), he may have had ulterior motives in some of his accounting projects. His enthusiasm for teaching women accounting had an outcome not necessarily in line with the ethic of delayed gratification. In the early years, his wife, Deborah Read Franklin, kept books at the counter of their Philadelphia shop, recording sales transactions. Franklin took Deborah's shop book and his own transaction journal and transferred the entries into his main ledger in classic form. He kept debit and credit columns, numbered pages, and, as he noted later, before leaving on a political mission to England in 1757, "I have drawn a red Line over all such Accounts in this book, as are either Settled or not likely to be recovered." With America a fledgling nation, Franklin left America as ambassador to France after his wife's death in 1774, where he stayed for ten years between 1776 and 1785, in great luxury and in the company of some of the most beautiful and sophisticated women of Paris.[13]

Throughout his many diplomatic missions to Europe, Franklin kept concise books. Once installed in Paris, Franklin set up a foundry and printing press in Passy, a little village to the west of Paris on the Seine, in what is today the sixteenth arrondissement. Here, in 1779, Franklin printed pamphlets for the American cause, comic writings, and the first American passports. He also created the first American typeface, called "le Franklin," which he had to ship to America twice to get through the British blockade. Franklin was so happy when he finally made his typeface that he recorded in his "Cash Book" that he threw a lavish party for Independence Day in Passy to celebrate, with "more than a hundred bottles of wine" and a cornucopia of summer delicacies from the French countryside. Fittingly, the feast was held under a portrait of the gourmand war hero George Washington. Franklin even printed the invitations himself. Franklin certainly felt no need to delay any gratification. It was not Paris that corrupted the great man. It was that good ledgers did not always reflect a moral Protestant life.[14]

Although it was a pillar of his life, Franklin could grow tired of accounting, and even in politically sensitive situations, he sometimes failed to keep accounts. As ambassador to France, Franklin made numerous accounting errors (he accidentally reported a French loan of 4 million as 3 million) and often gave up when major audits proved too taxing. He corresponded with Jacques Necker around the very time the *Compte rendu* was published, but he had to negotiate American loans with the eccentric Pierre-Augustin de Beaumarchais (1732–1799), famed author of *The Barber of Seville* and *The Marriage of Figaro*, satirist, watchmaker, inventor, arms dealer, spy, and Louis XV of France's agent in charge of funding the American Revolution. Franklin complained that his fellow genius was not a good accountant. In a letter dated August 12, 1782, to Robert Morris, America's powerful Superintendent of Finances, Franklin described his difficulties in dealing with Beaumarchais and hoped that a commissioner to settle public accounts in Europe would have "better success with M. Beaumarchais than I have had. He has often promised solemnly to render an account in two or three days. Years have since elapsed and he has not done it. Indeed, I doubt whether his books have been kept so well as to make it possible." Franklin recognized that in the realm of politics, accounting did not always work as desired. Yet in his own case, he was confident of accounts. He promised Morris that he had "no doubt" that with an audit, Congress would approve his books. America was lucky that

Franklin was so skilled and principled an accountant, given that he managed America's international finances and loans.[15]

Not all founders, or indeed Protestants, were professional merchants, financiers, or industrialists. Although plantation owners such as Thomas Jefferson used extensive accounts to run their plantations and manage their own trade, they were not exactly the sort of thrifty, hardworking Protestants that Weber would later idealize. Jefferson was an aristocratic landowner with pretensions to live in the high style of eighteenth-century French nobles, whom he so admired. Yet accounting was still central to American planters and slave owners' lives and ethics. Slavery and accounting fit well together, for as Josiah Wedgwood showed, accounts made it easier to turn the labor of a child or a slave into a number in a column. Just as slaves were brought to America chained in rows in boats, so they were accounted for as merchandise and sold the same way, in neat columns. The slave-trading Royal African Company kept double-entry ledgers. The very nature of international, seaborne trade made double entry necessary for financially successful slave trading, as human assets were ordered and moved through the Atlantic trading routes.[16]

Rich, learned, and a lover of luxury, science, architecture, books, and fine food, Jefferson kept meticulous account books for sixty years, leaving records of the minute details of his life and his value system. One account book was labeled "Indispensables," reserved for books and wine. Along with numbers, his account books acted as diaries in which he wrote such details as the price of a tomb for his dead sister and the project of building it, and one for a slave, too: "one half of the burying grounds at Monticello might be appropriate/d . . . to the use of my own family . . . other of strangers, servants, &c, . . . on the grave of a favorite and faithful servant might be a pyramid . . . of the rough rockstone, the pedestal made plain to receive an inscription," to which he appended his poem, the oddly lyrical 1771 poem, *Inscription for an African Slave*. A fine violin player, Jefferson noted the cost of "fiddle strings," as well as his and his wife's losses at cards and backgammon. Accounting revealed how America's greatest and most influential modern thinker on human liberty and democracy, and a not necessarily repentant practitioner of slavery, could coldly calculate human life, as he did in 1817: "bought a horse . . . a light bay, with *a* star in the forehead and small snip on the nose, right hindfoot white . . . 120 D.; bought a negro woman Lucretia, her 2 sons John & Randall, and the child of which she is pregnant, when born, for 180." Among the last entries in Jefferson's account books were payments for "shew of horsemanship," "Dr. Emmet for a book," "Lee for veal," and "Isaacs for cheese."[17]

A gentleman planter and a slave owner like Jefferson, George Washington gave extra thought to his account books. He was trained in daily accounting and rough double entry—John Mair's accounting manual, found in his library, shows heavy wear—and his accounts had particular significance as he was responsible for managing the expenses of the War of Independence, a heavy and difficult task of both military and financial management, and later, with the aid of Alexander Hamilton, the first presidency of the United States. Rare for an early American, Washington was responsible for the management of great sums, for the army and government as well as for his wife Martha's extensive estates and, of course, his many slaves. The Library of Congress's collection contains Washington's account books, both professional and personal, from 1750 to 1794. Like those of Jefferson, they are a vivid window into his life of public and military service, landownership and slavery, and luxury.[18]

As good an accountant as he was, Washington often struggled with his accounts. From August 1775 to September 1783, he received a total income of £80,167 but was dismayed that he was unable to calculate what part of this sum equaled profit on his enterprises. But Washington was skilled enough to calculate "cash lost, stolen, or paid away" and balanced his books when he could. His militia and Revolutionary War accounts reveal these same practices. Indeed, Washington's own staff and soldiers admired the managerial skills that helped him defeat the British.[19]

But Washington's accounts also reveal something else: Washington recorded his exorbitant personal expenses and almost compulsive spending on luxury goods in the midst of the war. His lawyer, Edmund Pendleton, wrote Washington's 1775 declaration, refusing a $500 a month salary as commander in chief of the Continental Army:

> As to pay, Sir, I beg leave to Assure the Congress that as pecuniary consideration could have tempted me to have accepted this Arduous employment (at the expense of my domestic ease

and happiness). I do not wish to make any Proffit from it. I will keep an exact Account of my expenses. Those I doubt not they will discharge, and that is all I desire.[20]

In 1783, when his enemies accused him of profiting from the war, Washington took the extraordinary measure of handing his *Revolutionary War Expense Account 1775–1783* to state auditors (and through their hands, he assumed, to the public). Washington calculated the accounts of his personal expenses during the war, for which he requested a reimbursement of $160,704, the equivalent of millions today. The accounts are, for the most part, meticulous. At the very end, Washington wrote a personal note explaining that he had not felt it necessary to publish the accounts of his personal expenditures during the war, but with the "embarrassed situation of our Public Affairs," he now found himself "obliged" to do so. He noted that his "disbursements" fell "a good deal short of my Receipts" and that he had covered much of the expenditures himself. The government audit agreed, finding that the U.S. government still owed General Washington a little less than one dollar to cover his expenses.[21]

Washington's act of rendering his account books public was a daring, although perhaps politically necessary, move. Many of the tens of thousands of dollars Washington spent during the Revolutionary War were on luxuries. The pay of army generals was $166 a month, and Washington, out of a sense of honor, had forgone $40,000 in salary over the course of the war, a risky venture. Washington could not have known he would win the war. Had he lost, the British might have hanged him. He therefore spent accordingly: thousands on Madeira wine, fine tablecloths, the best English horse-drawn chariots, luxurious clothes and thread, and grand dinners. Between July 24 and August 6, 1776, in New York City, before the Battle of Long Island, his accounts show he went on a feasting spree, hiring a French chef and dining on pigeons, veal, squash, eggs, dozens of very expensive limes, ducks, hurtleberries, and his endless casks of Madeira, on which he regularly spent five times the monthly salary of one of his generals. He spent $27,665.30—a massive portion of his war budget—on Martha Washington's visits to his winter quarters. Not surprisingly, Washington gained twenty pounds during the war.[22]

As self-indulgent as Washington was, he managed to do something neither Necker nor Walpole dared. He revealed his true accounts and, with them, his princely expenditures, all without compromising his power. He also did something few others have ever done: He won a war to found a nation. This surely made his accounts seem less outrageous. On April 30, 1789, little more than a month before the outbreak of the French Revolution, he was elected unanimously by the Electoral College as the first president of the United States, a post he might have kept for life, but which, luxury-lover though he was, he did not and stayed in, devoted to the republic, for only two terms.

It was a good thing that America's founders were literate in accounting, for the young nation was born into war and debt. By 1776, little gold or silver specie remained in circulation. The $241.5 million in paper currency issued by Congress in 1781 was worth two cents on the dollar. Congress then began to borrow money through domestic loans and IOUs for food and military supplies. The individual states were more than $200 million in debt. Congress had to turn to loans, ironically from a bankrupt France, where Franklin used his considerable influence to borrow nearly $8 million. These loans were more serious than the domestic ones because they had to be paid back at face value and not in worthless paper Continental dollars.[23]

By 1780, the public debt threatened to literally gobble up the young nation. Many rightfully worried that if the United States could not pay back its debt to France, then France could claim large tracts of U.S. territory. For the first time, public debt threatened the very existence of a nation. Congress turned to America's leading international trader, Philadelphia businessman Robert Morris.

Born in Liverpool in 1734, Morris was the epitome of the eighteenth-century international merchant. When he was thirteen, his father moved to Maryland to work as a tobacco factor. Morris was sent to Philadelphia to apprentice in a commercial firm, which meant he was learning the basics of accounting and finance on the shop room floor. He made his fortune in shipping, land, mills, privateering, securities, slaves, and sugar, and he invested in Mississippi slave plantations. Even as the U.S. economy faltered during the war and its currency plunged, Morris's fortunes rose, and his worth was said to be in the hundreds of thousands of pounds, rivaling Josiah Wedgwood's. Morris excelled in complex international financial transactions. The nearly bankrupt U.S. government was sorely in need of such skills.

When the Continental Army ran out of munitions and even uniforms, Morris helped fund the Revolutionary War. But mostly, Morris provided the service of his deep financial knowledge based on a firm idea: If the United States were to pay back its debt and obtain much needed loans for the military, it would have to show good management in its books. This may sound familiar. As Philadelphia's leading merchant, Morris was a merchant in the British tradition, but he was also an innovative financier and, as such, a reader and admirer of Jacques Necker.

In 1776, Congress had established the Treasury with an auditor general and a team of "competent" assistants and clerks. All accounts of public expenditure were audited twice, by two different offices. A copy of the receipt went to the comptroller, who managed day-to-day operations for the Treasury. In 1779, a Treasury Board was founded: two members of Congress and two outside members. The auditor general kept accounts and records for the board.[24]

Immediately, there were complaints that this process did not work. As the auditor general himself noted, "The machine is so clogged, as to defeat in a great measure the intention of having the public accounts speedily settled." In 1780, a Congressional committee reported that the "Demon of Discord pervaded the whole Department." It concluded that the Treasury Board be disbanded and run by one individual. In 1780, the Virginian delegate Joseph Jones declared, "Our finances want a Necker to arrange and reform them, Morris is I believe the best qualified of any our country affords for the arduous undertaking." On February 7, 1781, Congress appointed Morris as the first American superintendent of finances. Washington had no illusions that his wealthy friend could "by any magic art . . . do more than recover us by degrees from the labyrinth into which our finances are plunged."[25]

Although America's situation was grave, Morris knew of a place with finances even more labyrinthine and dire than those of the United States. Morris studied Jacques Necker's accounting reforms in France and how Necker proposed to raise revenues by centralizing tax collection and teaching double entry to tax collectors and treasurers. By

1781, Necker had published the *Compte rendu*, and Morris was now titled after Necker (and indeed Colbert) as the American superintendent of finance. Morris then wrote to Necker, asking for advice and expressing his "ardent wish . . . to tread in the footsteps of so disinterested and successful a Financier as Mr. Necker." Like Necker, Morris had been attacked by figures such as Thomas Paine as a corrupt "financier." But the government needed Morris and gave the superintendent "Absolute Power" to manage his team of accountants.[26]

Morris followed Necker's example. In 1782, he published *A general View of Receipts and Expenditures of Public Monies, by Authority from the Superintendent of Finance, from the Time of his entering on the Administration of the Finances, to the 31st December, 1781* (Philadelphia: Register's Office, 1782). America began its days indebted to France to pay for its war with England. The entries concerned receipts, much of which came from French loans, and expenditures, which were almost entirely military provisioning. Morris concluded that the "Balance remaining in the public Treasury the 31st of December" was $852,650.59.

Morris's *compte rendu* differed from Necker's in that America's budget was tiny in comparison with that of France. Even more, Morris did not know in 1781 that Necker's numbers were off by more than 25 million livres of unaccounted-for debt. And Necker would never have the chance to implement the financial reforms laid out in his *Treatise on the Administration of French Finances* (1784), which would further inspire Morris and politicians such as Silas Deane and Alexander Hamilton.

Morris's job was to produce plausible financial statements not only to manage state monies but also to restore public credit to obtain loans for war. Under Morris, the organization of the American financial administration happened precisely so that it could obtain debt. For this, Morris would have to rebuild the auditing system of the Treasury. Morris's reforms echoed Necker's hopes and the later achievements of the French Revolutionary government. He trained his clerks so that "every account ought to be first stated in one certain form, so that a person once acquainted with that form, could go through the public Accounts with equal Facility." All clerks and auditors would have to be "checked," but to do this, there had to be a clear, central ledger. Thus the logic of double entry worked its way into the organization of the American administration.[27]

Following Necker's reforms and even French administrative terminology, Morris appointed Continental receivers to collect taxes. As Necker had recommended, Morris required each receiver to publish every month "in one of the News papers of the state" the names and receipts from each taxpayer. This way, all could verify the accounts. The publication of tax receipts, he wrote in 1782, would stimulate curiosity about which counties had paid their taxes and which had not. Along with a system of accounts, Morris was trying to create a culture of political and financial accountability and transparency. This was no small thing. Morris felt it was "proper and necessary that, in a free Country the People should be as fully informed of the Administration of their Affairs as the Nature of things will admit."[28]

Morris himself published further *compte rendus*, or operating statements, for the following year, this time with a breakdown of state tax receipts of $422,161.63. Statements would be sent to the Treasury, Congress, Washington, and Franklin in France. Morris had made good on his promise. He was bringing in revenue and could thus obtain more debt. But like Necker, he also needed to silence his critics, and so his published accounts became political tools. He republished state financial sheets, directed at state legislators, to remind them of their own dire debt and the need to service it.[29]

When Congress audited Morris in 1783, it found that he had kept good, "regular" accounts. However, Morris had just built up the administration of the Treasury and the taxation arm of the government. The next step was to build a political system around these reforms, as neither taxation nor state finance had yet been fully centralized in 1782. That would take the Federalist movement, which, in part, was based on the simple but incredibly elusive concept that to govern a nation, its executive or representatives needed a well-kept, central account ledger.

Robert Morris was a good accountant and financial manager, but he was no philosopher. The challenge at hand for the U.S. government on the eve of writing the Constitution was to establish a philosophical and political framework to enshrine Morris's reforms so that public credit could be maintained on a large, national scale. This would allow the United States to protect its interests in the hostile world of international trade and empires. It was, therefore, lucky for Morris and those who thought like him that he received a letter requesting work from Alexander Hamilton (1755–1804), a brilliant young officer and war hero on Washington's staff.

Born on the Caribbean island of Nevis, Alexander Hamilton had a turbulent family upbringing. He was born out of wedlock, and his mother died in 1768, when he was thirteen. No other founder, not even Franklin, was forced to work so early. Recognized for his prodigious talent and energy, Hamilton was frustrated with his job as apprentice accountant in St. Croix, and at the age of twelve he wrote to a friend, "My Ambition is prevalent that contemn the grov'ling and condition of a Clerk, or the like and would willingly risk my life tho' not my Character to exalt my station." He wished "there was a war."[30]

At the age of fifteen, Hamilton set sail to New York with only a bundle of letters of introduction, but one introduced him into the house of William Livingston in Elizabethtown, New Jersey, where he attended the College of New Jersey, now Princeton, and later, in 1773, King's College, now Columbia University in New York City. Hamilton was a keen reader of the classics and such Enlightenment philosophers as Hobbes, Locke, Montesquieu, Blackstone, and Hume. His mix of accounting and international trade expertise and philosophical interest would, after the Revolutionary War, drive Hamilton to run the Treasury and formulate the federal plan of finance that transformed America from a series of colonies into a nation with a national bank, mint, and a healthily funded public debt.[31]

Hamilton was short and strikingly handsome, and his heroism at the Battle of Princeton—he fired a cannon directly at Princeton University's now revered Nassau Hall, supposedly decapitating a statue of George II—piqued the interest of Washington, who made the "little lion" a member of his staff. It was from this relatively high position that Hamilton wrote to Robert Morris of his ambitions to help build the American financial system. Hamilton shared with Morris an admiration of the centralized financial administration of the French. France had found prosperity, he wrote, due to the "abilities and indefatigable endeavors of the great COLBERT." Hamilton had no patience for laissez-faire, as the very existence of the United States hung in the balance of books. America must take foreign loans, he insisted. And for that, there was no way it could follow a "hands off" economic policy, as the country suffered from a negative trade balance and a costly war. The American government needed to centralize its financial system or risk disappearing.[32]

In his now famous 1780 letter to the New York lawyer and politician James Duane, Hamilton laid out his vision for federalist government, based on a centralized financial and auditing system, like the one Morris was struggling to build. Congress needed power over the states to raise money to wage war. Congress, he insisted, "should have complete sovereignty" not only in all that related to war, national defense, and diplomacy. And for this, it needed the means to pay for it.

Thinking perhaps of Colbert and Necker, Hamilton insisted that the state be run by a series of powerful ministers, "as those in France," who would be experts—as he would later insist in the *Federalist Papers*, 35—in their respective fields, like finance. Their power extended to the nation's "general account of revenues and expences." Hamilton understood that the power of the state was reduced to a central ledger. Power, he claimed, "holds the purse strings absolutely." Central financial control would, he maintained, "give reality to its authority."[33]

In 1782, Congress chartered the Bank of North America. In 1789, when Washington sought to appoint Morris the first secretary of the Treasury, he declined, suggesting Hamilton in his place. It was in this office in 1790 that Hamilton wrote his extensive *Report Relative to a Provision for the Support of Public Credit*, in which he insisted that public debt was "the price of liberty." Some considered him the greatest genius in American politics, but Madison and Jefferson vehemently opposed Hamilton's embrace of debt for war and state building. Yet seventeen years after his arrival in America as a penniless accountant clerk, Hamilton had helped design and implement the American financial system, not only on the idea of private property but also on effective taxation and the concept of a central state account ledger. Article 1, Section 9 of the Constitution stipulated that "No money shall be drawn from the Treasury, but in Consequence of Appropriations made by Law; and a regular Statement and Account of the Receipts and Expenditures of all public Money shall be published from time to time."[34]

In hindsight, one might conclude that good state accounting, political accountability, and effective collection of taxes were elusive goals, even with the grand designs of great planners and worriers like Hamilton. But even if Article 1, Section 9 looks much like basic fourteenth-century northern Italian or Dutch administrative practice, in late-eighteenth-century America, truly innovative things began to happen. The federal government and various politicians published numerous versions of state accounts, in particular in Pennsylvania. In 1791, the House of Representatives of the Commonwealth of Pennsylvania published a detailed account of state finances. Tucked in the tables, calculations, and claims of surplus is a truly revolutionary statement. The authors note: "We also think it would be an advantage to the public and individuals, if a set of Books were kept in the Register-General's Office, where accounts should be kept" for access to all citizens. All accounts would be kept in the same office, in dollars, with strict time-tables, audits, and open books whose calculations all citizens could verify with their own eyes. In the 1795 *Accounts of Pennsylvania*, State Comptroller John Nicholson claimed that citizens were more likely to pay taxes, and even enjoy paying taxes, when they are "faithfully accounted for." This would build credit and protect property, business, and American democracy. It was a noble dream.[35]

CHAPTER 11

RAILROADED

The professional accountant is an investigator, a looker
for leaks, a dissector and a detective in the highest acceptation of the term. . . . He is the foe of deceit and
the champion of honesty.

—*THE BOOKKEEPER*, 1896

By the early nineteenth century, England, France, the United
States, Prussia, Italian states like the Grand Duchy of Tuscany,
Austria, and other countries had created clear, accountable state
financial systems. Ever leaders in reform, the British would continue to
centralize by giving the Bank of England responsibility for its own
administration in 1848, and further centralizing reforms were made
until 1862. States produced budgets and planned for the future, which
often meant large amounts of military spending. After five hundred
years of fits and starts, with the rise of professional accounting and of
increasing government involvement with accounting standards and
reforms, it appeared that the age of the modern, accountable state had
dawned.

The nineteenth and early twentieth centuries were a time of iron,
steel, empire, and capital. But it was also the age of gilded robber barons,
Dickensian poverty, financial distress, colonial mass murder, and wars of
startling deadliness. The Industrial Revolution would eventually bring

unparalleled living standards and popular democracy, but also the guns, trains, and meticulous administrations that coldly planned mass death and mutilation in the Congo and from the Marne to Auschwitz. Ever-present and Zelig-like, accounting was there at the scene of triumph and of crime. In hindsight, it is obvious that as accounting became more complex, so did the possibility for fraud. Thus two faces of accounting emerged in modern consciousness. Some thinkers began to mistrust accounting, seeing it as a tool for exploitation and fraud; others held it up as a model of modern rationality. This was truest in Britain and America, one a world empire, the other a transcontinental powerhouse.

In spite of all the reforms of the eighteenth century, in Britain in the 1820s and 1830s, there were public outcries against the corruption of Parliament. In 1819, more than 60,000 people protested in Manchester about food prices and gerrymandered, rigged elections. They were met with a military cavalry charge that killed fifteen and injured hundreds. Whig reformers complained that Parliament was "in the pocket" of great landowners. In 1821, the reforming Anglican clergyman Sydney Smith proclaimed, "The country belongs to the Duke of Rutland, Lord Lonsdale, the Duke of Newcastle, and about twenty other holders of boroughs. They are our masters!" Working men and now women were demanding the vote. Britain was faced with the specter of revolution. The government had to act.[1]

Whig Prime Minister Earl Grey—remembered now for the tea that bears his name—sought to reform not only the British voting system but also state accounting. Political corruption could be cleaned up only if state accounts were clear. After all the reforms of the eighteenth century, a parliamentary commission in 1822 noted that it was not only "impossible to strike a Balance between Income and Expenditure" but also impossible to manage debt and major government projects or to understand "errors." A reformed state would need a "simple, intelligible" central account.[2]

This report should make readers pause. After hundreds of years of reform and advances in accounting, the home to the Industrial Revolution, Britain, still could not balance its books. And so the wheels of reform again began to turn. Earl Grey hired one of the most extraordinary minds in Britain to figure out how to do it. Dr. John Bowring (1792–1872) was a disciple and friend of the utilitarian philosopher, Jeremy Bentham, who, on his death, made Bowring his literary executor. It was a fitting role, for Bowring, a Unitarian, was not only considered the most skilled linguist in Britain—it was claimed he could speak at least a hundred languages—he was also a political economist with deep expertise in accounting. In 1831, the Commission on Public Accounts gave Bowring the mission to go to France and Holland to examine how they kept their government books.

Bowring found Holland's financial administration opaque and damaged by the Napoleonic wars. France, which had come out of decades of Napoleonic empire and restoration monarchy, interested him most. Bowring was given remarkable access to the accounts of Britain's old foe. What sparked Bowring's attention was France's centralized system, which allowed French bureaucrats to have a "unified" account of all the state's finances. Bowring reported back to the House of Commons that Jacques Laffitte, formerly head of the Banque de France and now prime minister to the new King Louis Philippe, had assured him that the French accounts were so good that he believed the present system neared perfection and that the "machinery" worked so well that not only did the French government always know the exact state of its finances but also it provided security against all fraud. The prime minister personally, and "by hand," drew up the public balances of the treasury, and the government was able to show how under the preceding minister of finance, the Count Chabrol, France had saved £800,000 a year in personnel costs and £14.8 million in payments on the national debt by bringing "harmony and order" to the day-to-day operations of the government. Through double entry, Chabrol was able to produce a monthly balance sheet and an annual return to the Commission des Comptes, the legislature, and the public. Bowring attested to personally witnessing the system and how "an uninterrupted chain of operation and inspection thus descended from the highest to the lowest of authorities, while uniform returns ascended from the lowest to the highest." The whole of the "books of Treasury" of all the administrations were admirably centralized. He would note in a later report that this system even made it possible to "perfectly audit" the military. Bowring would go on to be governor of Hong Kong. Empires and industry were expanding, and those, like Bowring, who mastered the administrative account books had every reason to believe they could master the world.[3]

Of all the advances of the Industrial Revolution, the railroad was the most revolutionary, for it not only transformed the world—peasants who had never gone out of sight of their village's church steeples could now travel to capital cities in a matter of hours—but also transformed financial accounting and government regulation. If Bowring thought governments had solved the problems of managing their own affairs, he was wrong. The advent of railroads not only brought great industrial innovation but also brought new and quicker avenues of financial complexity and corruption.

By 1803, the British inventor and industrialist Richard Trevithick built the first high-pressure, steam-powered carriage. He and his competitors would develop his "Puffing Devil" into the steam-powered rail engine. From Merthyr Tydfil, Wales, to Paris, Cologne, and Philadelphia, inventors rushed to create railway steam-engine patents. Oliver Evans, the Philadelphia designer of the high-pressure steam engine, saw how the railroad would transform experiences of space and time: "The time will come when people will travel in stages moved by steam engines from one city to another, almost as fast as birds can fly, 15 or 20 miles an hour. . . . A carriage will start from Washington in the morning, the passengers will breakfast at Baltimore, dine at Philadelphia, and sup in New York the same day."[4]

Railroads transformed culture and the human perception of time and space, as coasts, factories, ports, warehouses, and military barracks were linked, and remote towns had access to an enormous national rail system connected by managerial systems of timetables (a term invented for railroads), wireless communication, and interlocking account books. The concept of miles-per-hour came with the railroads. By 1840, the United Kingdom had six thousand miles of track, and the European continent and the United States each had seven thousand. By the 1870s, the United States had 51,000 miles, as much as Britain, Europe, and the rest of the world combined. America would become the center of world industry.[5]

The problem was that this unprecedented growth needed to be funded by investors, and there was simply not enough American capital to fund investment in American railroads. In the 1850s, British investors stepped in to buy railroad securities on the New York Stock Exchange. By 1869, $350 million of capital stock was listed on the NYSE for thirty-eight railroad companies. This massive capital influx, spent on the most complex industrial undertaking in human history, required accounting methods that allowed companies to coordinate high volumes of swift traffic and trade. From tracks, transcontinental landholdings, coal supplies, stations, ticket sales, and personnel of all sorts to onboard restaurants and voluminous freight, all had to be accounted for and managed. Teams of accountants from each division of the railroads would send their audits to the central accounting office. Rather than fixed ledgers, the loose-leaf notebook was adopted, and special account books, journals, and vouchers were mass-produced to cut down on duplicate work and manuscript copying.[6]

Railroad engineers and accountants had to calculate the price of a ticket in relation to the proportional use of the entire rail system. In 1844, the French railroad engineer Adolph Jullien used averages and ratios to establish the real cost of running a single train. He took into account the price of operating each carriage of the train as well as the cost of each passenger per kilometer. To these operational costs, he added administrative and debt interest costs to establish the fair price of a ticket.[7]

By 1860, it was common to find audit reports from various divisions of railroad companies in shareholder reports. An 1857 annual report from the Boston & Worcester Railroad included a four-page auditor's report that explained both accounts and how they were made: "Each of the departments is in charge of an efficient head, and in their respective offices it is ascertained which of the several agents on the road account for all the tickets or the freight bills with which they stand charged." Also included was an explanatory letter recommending that, based on analyses of the accounts, improvements be made in areas such as verifying ticket sales and in managing the risks of shorter railroad lines, which had the same costs but less possibility for profit.[8]

With the new demands of railroad management came innovation. Benjamin Franklin had famously said, "Time is Money." This was more than an abstract idea for railroads that had to make trains run on time while working out cost accounting for assets that were always in movement and in need of constant repair, from steam engines to tracks. Managing the railroad meant auditing, recording, and calculating hundreds of daily financial transactions and standardizing time itself into zones to measure the movement of trains. Whereas the largest textile mills typically had four sets of accounts, by 1857 the Pennsylvania Railroad had 144 sets of accounting records, which were compiled and often printed monthly and then tabulated for the annual report.[9]

Like nations unto themselves, railroad companies had internal comptroller's offices whose duty it was to calculate profit and loss and the new concept of the "operating ratio." Even with statistics, the problem was figuring out how much revenue was needed to pay for operating costs and still make a profit. Herein lay the problem of depreciation. How was a railroad to account for the depreciation of a steam engine and the obsolescence of tracks? An 1839 report from the Reading Railroad calculated that repairs and depreciation of an engine along with its fuel were 25 percent of a total cost of $8,000. Money would have to be available for constant repairs and the replacement of machines and matériel. Managers started charging these costs to the operating budget, but this procedure did not recognize that these costs were not one-time necessities of operation, but built-in, recurring expenses. An auditor or a stockholder could not see the real cost of depreciation if it was hidden as single costs charged to the operating budget. This meant that without a depreciation account statement, investors had no idea of the real costs over time of maintaining a railroad.[10]

As capital poured into railroads, vast profits were made by the robber barons Morgan, Vanderbilt, Gould, Rockefeller, Drew, and Fisk, among others. This vast power had malign effects on public reporting and on government financial management—the state could not tax entities whose financial reports were inaccessible and indecipherable. Not only did the great industrialists of the age manipulate their stock through opaque public reporting but also investors could not fully understand the true financial workings of the railroads. Even the steamship and railroad entrepreneur Daniel Drew stated, "To speculate in

Wall Street when you are not an insider is like buying cows by candle-light." Not only was there no oversight requiring the railroads to make accurate reporting to both shareholders and the public but also Gould, Drew, and Fisk corrupted the New York and California legislatures by permitting them to profit on public land, make insider trades, and create monopolies. In 1867, Mark Twain wrote to a San Francisco newspaper: "A railroad is like a lie—you have to keep building it to make it stand." Oversight could not keep up with either industry or its increasingly complex accounting methods. Increasingly, railroads were associated not with rational statistics, but rather with the fraud of gilded excess.[11]

Many of the financial scandals of the age arose from faulty balance sheets, and not just those from the overly complex railroads. The authority of a balance sheet could be used as both objective proof and false evidence. In 1855, the Irish financier and MP John Sadleir sold 19,000 falsified shares in the Royal Swedish Railroad Company; then he and his brother James produced a falsified balance sheet for Tipperary Bank, the balance that promised a dividend of 6 percent invested. As directors of the bank, the Sadleirs used bogus accounting to hide £247,320 of their own debt to the bank, which they could not pay back. By 1856, Tipperary Bank was insolvent, and James Sadleir was presented with his false balance sheets and forced to sign them, admitting his and his brother's fraud and bankruptcy. Soon after, John Sadleir committed suicide behind Jack Straw's Castle Hotel on Hempstead Heath and was found with a jug of poison and a jar of "Oil of Bitter Almonds" by his side. Sadleir would come to symbolize the craven, sallow-faced financial swindler of the Victorian era. Charles Dickens would base his character Mr. Merdle, the failed fraudster of his novel *Little Dorrit*, on the man he called that "precious rascality, John Sadleir."[12]

As capitalism expanded across continents and empires, government followed in slow but methodical pursuit. The massive scale of railroad management produced streams of financial information and potentially crippling financial scandals and crises, and government would have to expand to regulate the gargantuan companies. The railroads had laid bare the risks and even impossibilities of a laissez-faire economy. If railroads collapsed or swallowed investors, capitalism—and indeed governments and nations—could not function. Oversight was needed, and accountants now stepped up as the official regulators of modern capitalism. Government regulators and private accounting companies developed around the accounting information produced by railroads, and the railroad companies, in turn, had to tailor their accounts to either respond to or hide from government regulators.

Governments did not necessarily have the means to audit giant industrial corporations. Private accountants developed to work as middle agents between private companies and the state. In 1854, Scotland took steps to organize an official framework for recognizing Chartered Accountants who would have the proper training and ethical reputation to audit and stamp books, and England followed suit. New York began financial auditing requirements in 1849, and the American Association of Public Accountants was established in 1887. That same year, the government created the Interstate Commerce Commission to regulate the railroads.[13]

America had become the biggest and most complex economy in the world, which, with the British Empire, might explain why so much accounting innovation happened in the Anglo-Saxon world. However, then as now, where there was industry and complex trade, there was, by necessity, modern accounting. Chartered accountants began stamping and validating balance sheets. By 1899, France, Germany, Italy, Holland, Sweden, and Belgium all had professional accounting associations. Not surprisingly, in Italy, the Florentines led the drive with a National Congress of Accountants in 1876. In Holland, the Nederlands Institut van Accountants was founded in 1895. These chartered, government-regulated groups led to national accounting schools, textbooks, professional journals, and regulations about private and state accounting standards.[14]

But this was not the positivistic science for which some had hoped. Accountants and government regulators still did not have the authority to make companies report, and there was no effective legislation to force audits. Even more, many classically trained elites resisted rules based on quantification. The relationships between corporations, the state, and professional accounting associations remained loosely defined. Sparked by financial fraud and failure, the British Parliament passed the Bankruptcy Act of 1831, which gave accountants a leading role as "Official

Assignees" in managing bankruptcies, auctions, liquidations, and debt trials. In 1844, it passed the Joint Stock Companies Act, which aimed to regulate the finances of hundreds of companies. Trained accountants began trying to audit companies, but the job was arguably too big without an enormous bureaucracy of actuaries. The English baron, politician, and stockbroker Sir William Quilter testified to a parliamentary committee in 1849 that audits were based on personal judgment, not "dry arithmetical duty." Attempting to predict earnings using probability was still in its infancy and, as today, was a speculative science. Without compliance, regulation could not effectively function.[15]

Accountants needed authority, as well as large auditing teams. By the 1840s, major accounting firms appeared across Britain. Deloitte, Price Waterhouse, Ernst & Young, Touche, and many others sprang up in Edinburgh, the Midlands, and London. Price Waterhouse—today the biggest auditing firm in the world in the form of PricewaterhouseCoopers—was founded when Samuel Lowell Price (1821–1887), the son of a Bristol potter, teamed with William Hopkins Holyland and Edwin Waterhouse, the University College–educated son of "somewhat austere" but wealthy Quaker mill owners, to create the partnership of Price Waterhouse & Co. Holyland and Waterhouse held a 25 percent share, and Price held 50 percent. As became the custom in accounting firms, partners had to invest personal capital in the firm.

Founded on principles of accounting, America still did not have an adequately developed accounting profession to handle its industrial expansion. In the 1870s, America was filled with English and Scottish accountants pouring over company records from Charleston to Rochester. Price Waterhouse & Co. would distinguish itself by its early success in the American market. September 11, 1890, the firm sent Lewis Davies Jones to open a New York office at 45 Broadway to handle work in North, Central, and South America. In the 1890s, J. P. Morgan began a series of huge corporate consolidations, buying some thirty companies to merge into American Steel and Wire, as well as five farm machinery companies that would become International Harvester. Morgan wanted audits of the companies he purchased, and Price Waterhouse got the job, making more profit in 1897 than it had in the previous five years combined. With this base, Price Waterhouse & Co. would become the leader of the American accounting industry.[16]

But early professional accountants still struggled in the wild and unregulated American market. The incapacity of governments to regulate railroads inspired the pioneering financial analyst John Moody. The founder of what are today Moody's Analytics and Moody's Investor Services, he began as a crusader for public financial information and came to symbolize the move for financial accountability. In addition, he saw a market in extracting and analyzing inaccurate accounts. Highlighting the persistent problem of holding the railroads accountable, he published *How to Analyze Railroad Reports* (1912), which became the basis for his recurring *Moody's Investment Analysis*. In his *Railroad Reports*, Moody stated that the stockholder is like a partner, and to invest successfully, the stockholder had to understand true earnings potential. Therefore, a uniform method analyzing "property in motion . . . annihilating time and space" would be based on statistics. "It is not so easy to realize the financial significance of the aggregate motion and wear and tear which are ceaselessly going on, daily, throughout the year and decade, without beginning and without end." His major conclusion was that depreciation was a necessary concept to measure expenses and fair value over time.[17]

Arguably the most important reform was the insistence that depreciation be calculated separately from operating costs, as a constant set of necessary expenses rather than a one-time payment. The question that accountants strove to ask was: "What is profit?" With depreciation (the costs of maintenance over time), it was a very tricky question. An asset that brought in revenue could hide long-term costs, and eventually, it could eat up profit. In 1880, Charles E. Sprague created an "algebra of accounts," based on the notion that accounting is a "history of values." His equation, $\text{Assets} = \text{Liabilities} + \text{Proprietorship}$ $(A = L + P)$, took into account the depreciations and risks in valuing capital. In other words, capital, equity, or proprietorship—what one actually owns—is one's assets minus various liabilities, such as debt, necessary expenditures, and depreciation. Through Sprague's equations, it was possible to calculate transactions and determine net wealth, or one's holdings minus all liabilities. This allowed accountants to calculate profit and fair values in complex data sets like railroad accounts, in which an untrained eye could not separate equity and liability from all the moving parts. At the end of the 1800s, depreciation became central to account-ing theory, as accountants like Frederick W. Child insisted that special accounts be created not only to measure depreciation but also to pay for it. In his view, cash reserves were necessary to balance out (or pay for) depreciation costs and therefore had to be listed.[18]

Yet with all these advances and reforms, government regulators still could not obtain accurate financial reports. Once again, account-ing appeared like Ariadne's thread in a maze of financial and political accountability, only to disappear the moment reformers tried to seize it. A general refusal of large companies to open their accounts per-sisted. The *Commercial and Financial Chronicle* of 1867 noted that "in-formation upon the finances of the roads is suppressed and accounts are falsified." Like the Medici, modern corporations kept "private led-gers" with lock and key that only a few trusted partners would ever see. The respected banker Henry Clews suggested officially trained and certified accountants would help businesses by producing conclusive, public accounts. But with railroads and companies like Westinghouse Electric and Manufacturing neither publishing annual financial state-ments nor even holding shareholder meetings, a 1900 government re-port pointed out that "the chief evil of large corporations is a lack of responsibility of the directors to the stockholders" in publishing balance sheets. J. P. Morgan—whose holding company owned the *Titanic*—complained that President Theodore Roosevelt's trust-busting reforms would make it so that "we'd all do business with glass pockets." And although Morgan helped found the Federal Reserve to ward off finan-cial crises, the only thing he revealed through glass was his legendary book collection, fit for a Medici.[19]

There was a great mistrust of accounting in the hands of financiers, industrialists, and politicians. Indeed, trained originally as an accoun-tant and auditor, John D. Rockefeller, the richest man in the world, would be revered but also referred to in pejorative terms as "that blood-less, Baptist bookkeeper." Gone were the great paintings of accountants as glorious patrons, dramatically fallen sinners, or smiling captains of finance and industry. Instead, dour portraits of professionals in black suits would come to define accountants until this day as serious, even dull arbiters of financial numbers. Their role was ambiguous: They could aid capitalism and government or, through cooked books, impede them both.[20]

Yet accountants themselves were making a stand for the integrity of their profession and its role in fighting the corruption of the Gilded Age. In 1896, an editorial in *The Book-Keeper* enthused about the great reforming powers of accounting: "The professional accountant is an investigator, a looker for leaks, a dissector and a detective in the highest acceptation of the term. . . . He is a reader of hieroglyphics, however written, for every erasure, altercation [*sic*], interlining, dot, dash or character may have meaning. . . . He is the foe of deceit and the champion of honesty."[21]

The bookkeeper as a financial Sherlock Holmes, bringing light and reason to the mysteries of finance, became a powerful idea among education reformers and the influential pioneers of the new profession of accounting. From a prestigious family, Charles Waldo Haskins—the nephew of Ralph Waldo Emerson—was among the first Chartered Public Accountants. An erudite and learned philosopher of accounting, he wrote works on how to do both financial and domestic accounting. Haskins's *Business Education and Accountancy* (1904) bemoaned "men of business" who derided "men of education." He believed that through accounting, businessmen had to unite with "men of science" to create a method of business administration. Haskins thought that from the ancient world to his own time, accounting provided a rationalist, professional tradition of business for the educated "entrepreneur."[22]

Perhaps influenced by his family's cultural tradition, which valued women's education, Haskins placed women firmly in his vision of a society managed through accounting. Women would not run businesses, in his eyes, but rather households, and to do this, they, too, would draw on the science of accounting. In his learned *How to Keep Household Accounts: A Manual of Family Accounts* (1903), he used a long history of accounting to prove that accounting applied as much to "domestic" life as it did to "finance and administration." He cited the French Renaissance philosopher Montaigne to defend the idea that men as well as women should learn the "science" of managing households. Thus the scientific management of household accounts created a great chain of rational administration, from federal and municipal government to businesses to households. Economic utilitarianism could be systematized through business schools (in particular at New York University, Haskins's own institution) and home economics courses. It now seemed that Americans trained in accounting could stand against the menaces of fraud and ignorance.[23]

CHAPTER 12

The Dickens Dilemma

Whatever was required to be done, the Circumlocution Office was beforehand with all the public departments in the art of perceiving—HOW NOT TO
DO IT.

—CHARLES DICKENS, *LITTLE DORRIT* (1855–1857)

Not everyone, however, was convinced of the rationality of accounting. Given the extent of economic fraud and distress that accompanied industrialization, it is not surprising that nineteenth-century observers of the world of finance were skeptical about accounting's power to do good and about the very possibility of both personal and political accountability. The accountant could be respectable, but fraud was rife and potent. The old dilemma remained: Accounting offered neither a sure path to reason and order nor a convincing model of morality or happiness hoped for by industrialists such as Josiah Wedgwood and philosophers such as Jeremy Bentham. Great writers of the nineteenth century would struggle with the dilemma of whether accounting was an instrument of good or of corruption.

In his 1828 novel *L'Interdiction* (*The Ban*), the French author Honoré de Balzac showed that accounting was best suited to measure the "misery of the human heart." Balzac described how the Parisian magistrate

Popinot not only looked into financial fraud but also developed an accounting system to deal with life in the twelfth arrondissement of Paris, just above the Place de la Bastille: "All the miseries of the neighborhood were numbered, and filed in a book where each misfortune had its own account, in the style of a merchant who recorded his various debtors." His system measured neither finances, moral rights, wrongs, nor even happiness. In the tradition of Colbert, it was a tool of policing.[1]

A precursor to Sherlock Holmes, exposing frauds and extraordinary crimes, Popinot had to manage the details of the lives of his jurisdiction's miserable constituents so that they did not bubble up into the world of high society. The affairs of the heart—the nuanced shades of "the Human Comedy," as Balzac called it—could be of great use to a judge who had to regulate and manipulate the often dark affairs of the streets of Paris. Popinot did not try to balance out sin. Accounting did not bring happiness. Popinot considered social evils part of the operation of everyday life. Like costs, he simply tried to manage them.

Of all the authors of the nineteenth century, Charles Dickens had the most vivid view of accountants and accountability. In Dickens's world, the accountant had been reduced to a good-hearted but hapless clerk, a malicious swindler, or a nightmarish bureaucrat. Accountants could be good men like Bob Cratchit, the father of Tiny Tim in *A Christmas Carol* (1843), who loyally kept the books of the counting house or bank of the miser Ebenezer Scrooge. Both Scrooge and his ghostly partner in banking, Jacob Marley, had trained as accountants. Where Cratchit filled out his books without question, took his meager pay, and accepted his suffering with decency and Christian generosity, Jacob Marley was damned for his financial dealings. He came to warn Scrooge of the dangers of becoming a prisoner of account books and greed. Marley's ghost appeared to Scrooge, bound by a chain: "It was long, and wound about him like a tail; and it was made (for Scrooge observed it closely) of cash-boxes, keys, padlocks, ledgers, deeds, and heavy purses wrought in steel." Not just money, but the ledgers and deeds of accounting had ensnared the wily banker and imprisoned his soul. Scrooge risked the same were he not to make amends, in the logic of Pacioli, paying to the poor on Christmas to balance his accounts with a moral, Christian God.[2]

Dickens saw two roads for accounting. There were the Scrooges of the world, and then there was the good, honest clerk like Bob Cratchit, or like Mr. Micawber, in *David Copperfield*, who exposed his employer, Uriah Heep, as a swindler. Micawber made the now famous financial truism that discarded the philosophical elegance of Bentham but retained his simple message: "Annual income twenty pounds, annual expenditure nineteen pounds nineteen and six, result happiness. Annual income twenty pounds, annual expenditure twenty pounds ought and six, result misery." Micawber was speaking with Dickens's personal experience, as the author's own father, John Dickens, was himself an accountant, a clerk in the naval paymaster's office. And the Dickens family knew misery. In 1821, John Dickens lost his post and, overwhelmed by debts, was arrested and sent to the Marshalsea Debtor's Prison in Southwark. Charles Dickens was only twelve and, until his grandfather died and left his father a big enough inheritance to get out of jail, Dickens grew up there, scavenging for jobs among the dregs of London.

Dickens made Marshalsea Prison the setting for *Little Dorrit* (1855–1857), a novel about the absurdity of finance, debts, and his father's own predicament. Thrown in prison for debts, William Dorrit, like Dickens's father, could not work to pay them back. In the book, a family friend, Arthur Clenham—who suspects his mother has something to do with the misfortune of the Dorrits—goes to the Circumlocution Office to inquire about the debts. Based on the British Treasury, the office shows no resemblance to the proud, rational machine of administration about which John Bowring bragged. Rather than a bulwark of utility, Dickens's fictional proto-Orwellian ministry was an archival maze into which all went, but "nothing came out." Directed by the ever-absent Tite Barnacle, this was where statesmen made their reputations by taking in the "bamboozling air of how not to do it." Those charged with the accounts of the nation made sure all accounts were turned into incomprehensible bundles.[3]

For Dickens, the willfully opaque accounting and management of the Victorian treasury pointlessly ruined honest men like Dorrit and opened the door for swindlers like Sadleir, whom Dickens immortalized as Mr. Merdle, who ruins Arthur Clenham and then, true to life, commits suicide. Only luck could save Dickens's accountant father and the Dorrit family. And with no mode of government or financial accountability, only ruin could bring men like Sadleir some form of justice.

The logic and metaphors of accounting permeated not just literature but also philosophy. Accounting was central to the project of Henry David Thoreau (1817–1862), the American critic of industry and finance. Thoreau and his fellow Transcendentalists were Harvard-educated Unitarian idealists who fought industrial development, resisted taxes, believed in civil disobedience, and opposed slavery. Fascinated by the study of nature, Thoreau was a pioneering environmentalist. He was famous for his work *Walden, or Life in the Woods* (1854), in which he called for a return to nature. "Men labor under a mistake," he warned, "and dig their graves as soon as they are born." Mixed with a Puritan critique of modern Rationalism and inspired by Romanticism, Thoreau called for spiritual purity through meditation and self-sufficiency through communing with nature. "Digging in the dirt" was better, he said, than building a railroad around the world.[4]

As an experiment in "home economics," he lived two years on Walden Pond in Concord, Massachusetts. Part of Thoreau's process of finding a path to purity was to account for that which was absolutely "necessary of life" and that which wasn't. Thoreau outlined his accounts in single entry, detailing "outgoes" on his farm and all his living expenses, and earnings from selling his farm produce. He calculated he had earned $13.34, the "expense of food . . . though I had lived there more than two years—not counting potatoes, a little green corn, and some peas, which I had raised." Although the accounts in *Walden* are simple, Thoreau's personal papers contain a packet of account calculations, revealing that he worked on his accounts in earnest before putting them in print. In the end, Thoreau was accounting backward, away from the profit logic of industrialists like Wedgwood, and instead calculating the bare minimum needed for an ascetic, spiritual life in nature.[5]

Brought up by Transcendentalist parents with close contacts to Emerson and Thoreau, who gave her lessons as a child, Louisa May Alcott (1832–1888) also saw the dilemmas of accounting. In *Little*

Women (1868), Alcott illustrated how keeping accounts was a necessary tool of home management but could bring stress into the marriage of a poor couple: "Till now she had done well, been prudent and exact, kept her little account books neatly, and showed them to him monthly, without fear. But that autumn the serpent got into Meg's paradise, and tempted her, not with apples but with dress." When Meg's husband, John, brought out the books that revealed her spending, she felt real fear. Their joint accounting was a precursor to the arrival of an unwelcome and revealing bill.[6]

Numbers and mathematics increasingly played a role in all aspects of industrialized life. Probability had set the basis for insurance companies, and statistics had become part of modern society and a basis of how to judge science and society. The French philosopher Auguste Comte's work on social statistics was part of attempts to subject not just nature to the will of humanity but also social life and industry to numerical regulation. From maps, biology, human behavior, and railroads to the probabilities of life and death and the management of time itself, all now came under the purview of the men of numbers. The spread of science into all aspects of life brought great advantages in industry, technology, and medicine, but it was also used for more morally ambiguous purposes.[7]

Whereas Jeremy Bentham had used a double-entry model to try to calculate happiness, Thomas Malthus used the analogy of a numerical balance in his *Essay on the Principle of Population* (1798). In a pessimistic parallel to Bentham, Malthus also believed in two sides balancing each other out. In a biological reckoning, human subsistence requirements and the fatalities of vice would balance human population in a natural system of checks and balances, by which "the superior power of population is repressed, and the actual population kept equal to the means of subsistence, by misery and vice." An accountant of mortality, Malthus used the stark medieval terms of balance and reckoning in the new language of the laws of nature and population statistics. Before Balzac and Dickens, Malthus grappled with the concept of balancing human survival with "misery and vice" but with a soulless modern echo of Dante.[8]

Malthus was not alone in seeing the very essence of life and death through the analogy of balanced books. In 1859, Charles Darwin—a reader of Malthus—wrote *The Origin of the Species*. The word *species* comes from Aristotle's Greek term for the classification of animals, but *specie* was also a medieval term for money. For Darwin, there was a link between his categories and lists of species that showed the course of evolution and nature's fine but violent system of balance, on one hand, and the world of accounting on the other. Darwin's notebooks of observations from the Galápagos Islands are some of the most famous in history. Darwin, it should be noted, was Josiah Wedgwood's grandson.[9]

In 1873, Darwin's cousin, the explorer, polymath, and scientist Francis Galton (1822–1911), sent a number of members of the Royal Society a questionnaire about their daily habits. Among Galton's interests were geography, statistics, and, like his cousin, the idea of inherited traits. Galton was the grandson not of Wedgwood, but of his best friend, Erasmus Darwin, whose Quaker offspring made their fortune as gun manufacturers. In this case, Galton wanted to see if there were daily activities or inherited habits that explained the intellectual prowess of members of the society as compared with their fathers. And so Darwin filled out his cousin's questionnaire. In the left column, he listed his own traits, and on the right, those of his father. It contained questions like "temperament," to which Darwin responded with admirable candor, "Somewhat nervous." For his father, he respectfully listed "sanguine." He listed his height, hair and eye colors, politics, and religion. For the question "studious," he claimed that he was "very studious," but in the column for his father he was again frank: "Not very studious or mentally receptive, except for facts in conversation—great collector of anecdotes." It was a notable moment in the history of evolution: Darwin the son had balanced his faculties with those of his father.[10]

It should come as no surprise that Galton was a pioneer of eugenics and the even more sinister anthropometric studies that sought to improve the perceived quality of superior, literally "well-born" groups of human population through genetic and social selection. It was the basis of the nightmarish modern oxymoron of scientific racism, which would have catastrophic effects in the twentieth century. One of

Galton's most pointed questions revealed the origins of Darwin's own method. In the line "Special Talents?" Darwin answered, "None, except for business as evinced by keeping accounts, replies to correspondence, and investing money very well. Very methodical in my habits." In hindsight, this seems like an understatement. For his father, Darwin responded, "Practical business—made a large fortune and incurred no losses."

Accounting was central to the life of Josiah Wedgwood, and he taught it to his sons and daughters. Accounting remained important in the Wedgwood-Darwin family. Its methods of comparative lists and balanced formularies remained the model of how to think and balance life for both Darwin and his cousin Francis Galton. Darwin himself admitted that he was "methodical in his habits." He kept detailed account books for all his activities, both in business and managing his household affairs, breaking each one down under its own topic headings: "Science, Gardens, Personal, Household (which included servants' salaries)." As was common to Victorian roles of men and women, Darwin's wife, Emma, managed the details of the domestic accounts, keeping books for food, clothes, servants, entertaining and furniture, taxis, piano tuning and sheet music, concert tickets, and children's education. The biggest expenditure of the household of the discoverer of biological evolution was meat: In 1867, the Darwins spent £250 on it, as opposed to £213 on clothing.[11]

Charles's son Francis Darwin wrote, "In money and business matters he [Charles Darwin] was remarkably careful and exact. He kept accounts with great care, classifying them, and balancing at the end of the year like a merchant. I remember the quick way in which he would reach out for this account-book to enter each cheque paid, as though he were in a hurry to get it entered before he had forgotten it." The habits of old Josiah Wedgwood had been passed down to a new generation that took its notebooks and accounts with equal seriousness. And like Wedgwood, Darwin had great success in business, mostly from investment in ventures like his grandfather's beloved canals and in railroad stock. Although he suffered from a number of crashes, the wily investor was good enough at analyzing his investments that in the mid-1860s, he sold his railway stock and invested in government bonds.

The books show that Darwin began married life with a marriage bond of £10,000, £573 in the bank, and £36 in petty cash. A year before his death in 1881, when his brother drew up a will showing capital holdings of £282,000, Charles's son William ribbed his father, "Did you ever expect to be worth over ¼ of a million?"[12]

Like merchants and British diary writers before him, Darwin also kept a journal in which he tallied his personal life, balancing sick days with healthy ones and hours spent on work. He tried to measure the utility of social institutions, as early in his life when he wrote, "Marry, Not Marry. This is the question." Darwin was even more calculating than his grandfather, who was clearly a more passionate man. Darwin even tallied the hours he and his wife spent playing games. Natural scientist that he was, he could not help drawing conclusions from his personal observations. In the *Descent of Man* (1871), he echoed Malthus and even the tone of Wedgwood when he stated that "all ought to refrain from marriage who cannot avoid abject poverty for their children." Like his cousin Galton, Darwin believed that wealth brought scientific, industrial, and artistic progress. "Well-instructed men," he thought, could carry out the necessary "intellectual work." Galton went one step further: He believed his family members' long tradition of achievement showed them to be of a superior, industrious race. Biological science, accounting, and utilitarian values were leading to a new and not necessarily Christian or even Dickensian approach to valuing life.[13]

A generation later, the Polish writer Joseph Conrad saw the role of accounting as hiding human crime and suffering. In his novel *Heart of Darkness* (1899), a grim critique of colonial atrocities, "the company" is decadent and steeped in murder and death in its African plantations, and its accountant is always nattily dressed, well informed, and with an aversion to error. Only the trained accountant could keep up the veneer of civilization in the killing grounds of the jungle. "Thus this man had verily accomplished something. And he was devoted to his books, which were in apple-pie order." The protagonist Marlow respected this paragon of order at the very heart of darkness. The accountant was able to turn decrepitude and death into neat and tidy numbers to be sent back to the main office. Seen through the accountant's numbers, Conrad's classic imperialist character Kurtz, and his nightmarish operation of slave labor, looked clean and efficient.[14]

The problem of financial success represented by numbers outweighing human rights plagued the Industrial Revolution into its later stages. From an established Philadelphia family of Mayflower stock, Frederick Winslow Taylor (1856–1915) chose to be an apprentice patternmaker and machine mechanic at the Philadelphia Hydraulic Works and then, in 1871, for the Midvale Steel Company. Taylor is now known for Taylorism, his "scientific management" approach to industrial and labor efficiency. In many ways, Taylor can be seen as the Josiah Wedgwood of the age of steel. He focused on tight management of mechanical and labor costs in relation to time. Central to Taylor's model was detailed cost accounting based on a monthly closing of books and detailed balance sheets and income statements. Taylor claimed that these were the "features in which my system of accounting differs from ordinary commercial and manufacturing accounting, and, so far as I know, no other system has as yet attempted to accomplish the above."[15]

Taylor not only organized a new system of how costs were reported and information circulated in a corporation but also moved the accounting office into the planning room so that industrial and management strategy could be made directly from account analysis. Each part of the manufacturing process produced cards listing costs. These cost cards were then gathered and analyzed in the cost department, with each cost classified and totaled so that every part of the production chain could be analyzed. To guarantee accurate cost assessment, he created a specific costs office that then reported to the accounting office. Profit, he concluded, was based on accurate determination of costs, which was based on accurate assessments of the costs of labor, matériel, and the time needed for labor to make production. Efficiency played out into profits as it made up for the laziness and ignorance of workers. Following Taylor's logic, John Dewey believed that Jeremy Bentham's calculus showed that workers equated work with pain and therefore were intrinsically lazy. Taylorism made up for this loss in the calculus.

Taylor's methods were successful on many levels. Not only was he able to make enormous profits at Bethlehem Steel by increasing production but also he became the first management consultant, and his acolytes came up with theories to manage railroads and workers' psychology. Harvard Business School was founded in part by Taylor's inspiration, as was the storied consulting firm McKinsey & Co., started by University of Chicago accountant James O. McKinsey.

America developed a fetish for efficiency and speed, and President Herbert Hoover advocated the idea that work should be done "as quickly as possible." Henry Ford took inspiration from Taylor and his methods (and his desire to do away with unions—Taylor believed his methods linking pay to production made them unnecessary), as did industrialists around the world. They were able to mass-produce, and this brought staggering wealth but also social discord and eventual chaos. Taylorized workers often went on strike, complaining of inhumane conditions, as happened at the Watertown, Massachusetts, Arsenal in 1912. They also maintained that in the quest for higher production, Taylor suppressed data and evidence that revealed the suffering of workers and undermined his theories.[16]

Lenin was interested in Taylor's work, as was Stalin. Hitler gave Ford a medal and admired Taylor. Albert Speer proclaimed, "When Hitler appointed me his Minister of Armaments, I threw out the military chiefs and turned to the professionals, industrialists, and engineers. Then I borrowed the ideas of Walter Rathenau, the great Jewish chief of the German economy during the last war: Standardization of parts, the division of labor, and the maximum use of the assembly line." It was a dark irony: Rathenau was the German Jewish pioneer of Taylorism.[17]

Hitler may have liked the idea of rationalized mass production and the reduction of workers into obedient cogs in the machine, but he did not like the idea of financial accountability. In the end, the Deutsche Reichsban (railway) executives did away with detailed cost accounting as ideology trumped profit. In spite of the entreaties of managers, Walter Speiß, the head of the Reichsban, rejected cost accounting based on the idea that the railways were a public utility that could not be based on profit, but rather had to be measured against the political objectives of the Reich. On January 1, 1936, the officers in charge of cost accounting were reassigned to other duties, and accounting data collection was scaled back. As in the time of Philip II, Necker, and the British Imperial Navy, war—now on an ever-greater scale—was an extraordinary expenditure that could not follow the rationales of returns on investments or clear accounting. The military juggernaut would move forward until war itself provided a terrible reckoning.[18]

At the beginning of the twentieth century, accountants had regained much of the respectability that Dickens had taken away from them. Like Charles Waldo Haskins, the pioneer of accounting education and standards, they were servants of rationality and public, secular inquisitors who sought to understand and manage the mysterious accounts of business and finance. Interestingly, although anti-Semites painted Jews as unscrupulous international financiers and businessmen, accountants remained symbols of national public service and the common good. Their role as the silent arbiters of the modern economy was solidified in the new accounting companies. By the 1920s, in America, now the largest industrialized democratic nation on earth, publicminded accountants and democratically minded politicians were working to make both industry and government more transparent and rational. Industry, accounting, and government had evolved and seemed confident that they no longer had a dilemma. Haskins and those who followed him developed equations, methods, manuals, schools, professional institutions, and even laws and government auditing agencies, all for what appeared to be a modern art of how to do it.

CHAPTER 13

JUDGMENT DAY

God would have us pay the debt we owe.
Don't dwell upon the form of punishment:
consider what comes after that; at worst
it cannot last beyond the final Judgment.

—DANTE, *PURGATORIO*, X

In late October 1900, Arthur Lowes Dickinson arrived in New York from London to head the American office of Price Waterhouse & Co. From a distinguished family of painters and philosophers, with a Cambridge degree in mathematics, Dickinson was a methodical man devoted to British accounting traditions of ethical independence and public service. Under Dickinson's watch, PW, as it became known, prepared the 1902 financial statement for U.S. Steel, which *Scientific American* lauded as "the most complete . . . report ever issued by any great American corporation." Through his work setting up offices in Chicago and St. Louis, Dickinson became a leader in the Illinois Association of Accountants. He worked tirelessly to standardize audits for the Federal Trade Commission and wrote influential accounting pamphlets such as *Accounting Practice and Procedure* (1913).[1]

The model of a gentleman accountant, Dickinson was knighted by King George V in 1919, after returning to Britain to work in the London office of Price Waterhouse & Co. and then for the British government during World War I. Dickinson saw the accountant as impartial referee between business and government, dedicated to numbers and order. It was a stance not always easy to maintain, particularly in the rough-and-tumble of the New World. Dickinson found American business unpredictable, fast-paced, and unregulated. "Annual audits which in England are always the backbone of a business are few in number," he complained, "and the largest of them being dependent on the caprice of a few individuals cannot be considered certain."[2]

Dickinson soon discovered that American clients did not know "good from bad" audits. This meant that Price Waterhouse's U.S. business would have to engage in "speculative" audits based on incomplete books, a practice considered unethical in Britain. Dickinson was forced to adopt unorthodox methods, like modern advertising, and to compete for accounts. Worse, Americans did not want "the bare statement of facts," but rather advice on how to run their businesses, something he felt that accountants—empirical calculators—were not meant to be dispensing. Nonetheless, Dickinson focused on his quest to provide the finest audits possible. By the late 1920s, PW was the biggest auditing company in the United States and, indeed, as *Fortune* magazine would note, "the foremost in the world," representing 146 of the 700 companies on the New York Stock Exchange. With venerable firms like Charles Waldo Haskins's homegrown Haskins and Sells, as well as other British firms like Deloitte now working on American soil and the flourishing of business schools, it appeared, from Dickinson's perspective, that reason and order had arrived in the Wild West of American business.[3]

Yet Dickinson's dream of an orderly world of business, well governed by rational, private auditors, did not come to pass. Throughout the twentieth and twenty-first centuries, modern accounting firms have served, at best, as impartial referees and skilled financial analysts. In many cases, though, they have been hapless in exposing rogue firms and irresponsible politicians. At worst, they have acted as skilled enablers of financial fraud. As modern finance became more complex, lurching from one crisis to the next with reform and financial accountability ever harder to achieve, so the role of accountants became more fragile and even ambiguous.

If, in the early 1920s, Arthur Lowes Dickinson could feel proud that he had established professional British accounting in the United States, he did not foresee the great crisis of accountability that would soon lead to the Great Depression and a brutal day of reckoning for the accounting profession itself. In 1926, the Harvard economics professor William Z. Ripley published in the *Atlantic Monthly* a widely read article, "Stop, Look, Listen! The Shareholder's Right to Adequate Information." According to Ripley, the world of well-kept account books touted by figures like Haskins and Dickinson was an illusion. Business, he warned, was "still too largely carried out in twilight." He was incredulous that advertising had trumped clear financial statements. "On my table is a great pile of recent official corporate pamphlets. The premier concern on the list is the Royal Baking Powder Company, which fails to register in this collection at all, in as much as it has never issued a balance sheet or financial statement of any kind whatsoever for more than a quarter of a century." For corporations like the Singer Manufacturing Company, the National Biscuit Company, and the Gillette Safety Razor Company, "such newfangled gewgaws as income accounts or depreciation simply do not exist," and accrual (or liabilities) was completely ignored.[4]

Ripley predicted that a lack of corporate transparency would undermine the American economy. To make sound investments, the public needed more information, as "corporate obscuration has long outlived its day." The stock market could function only if corporations disclosed their true value. There were, he charged, no rules to govern corporate reporting and balance sheets. In spite of companies such as Price Waterhouse, many family firms kept especially poor accounts, and big companies simply did not report their earnings. American business, insisted Ripley, was still a jungle.

George O. May, now senior partner of Price Waterhouse & Co. USA, responded to Ripley, insisting that audits were an imperfect art. Any company can prepare false books, which, he insisted, were very hard to verify. "No amount of regulation will make a dishonestly managed company a satisfactory investment," he claimed. Yet try as he did to defend the work done by accounting firms, May conceded that he, too, was concerned about the lack of financial regulation and the accuracy of audits based on poor reporting. He recommended vigilance at the firm and insisted that each auditor provide a certificate stating that the report was "fairly presented, in accordance with the accepted principles of accounting."[5]

During the 1920s, the New York Stock Exchange emerged as the major world financial entity. Trading grew exponentially, with the Dow Jones Industrials Index climbing from 95.51 in 1922 to 340 after January 1929. Yet the growth of the Roaring Twenties would be revealed just as Ripley had warned—as but so much glossy advertising on the false balance sheets of American corporations. Months later, between October 24 and 29, the stock exchange lost more than 30 percent of its value. At its low point, American gross domestic product dropped 30 percent, wholesale prices dropped 32 percent, nine thousand banks failed, and unemployment spiked to 25 percent. By 1933, the New York Stock Exchange had lost 89 percent of all stock value. This was not simply a convergence of poor economic performance. Never had an economy so rich and so sophisticated, based largely on publicly traded stock, been allowed to remain so opaque. Ripley was right; the account books were rotten. Bad accounting did not cause the Great Depression, but it exacerbated it. Months after the crash began, Wall Street traders knew perfectly well that the stock they were selling was worthless. "If there must be madness," the economist John Kenneth Galbraith lamented, "something may be said for having it on a heroic scale." Those in the soup lines, however, would not have agreed.[6]

In response to the crash, in 1933 Congress enacted the Glass-Steagall Act to separate the activities of investment and commercial banking and prevent investment banks from putting depositors at risk by making risky and often difficult to regulate trades. It would also facilitate the auditing of their assets and liabilities. Spurred by the reforming zeal of the former New York District Attorney Ferdinand Pecora (1882–1971), who had unearthed J. P. Morgan's list of preferred stocks that he shared with privileged investors, including former U.S. President Calvin Coolidge, the Roosevelt administration enshrined these reforms with the establishment of the Securities and Exchange Commission in 1934, chaired by Joseph P. Kennedy, founder of the political dynasty and, more to the point, a known master of insider trading. The SEC was to standardize accounting and reporting for publicly traded companies. Roosevelt did not believe he could stop fraud and misreporting, but he believed that the SEC could prevent "malicious misinformation" being given to stockholders, limit insider trading, and ban the preferred stock lists that had helped destabilize the market.[7]

The Securities Act of 1933 gave a new oversight commission the authority to require more complete balance sheets and earnings statements, "appraisals" or "valuations of assets and liabilities," calculations of "depreciation" and "depletion," and detailed, consolidated audits of all branches of firms. Armed with a "Chief Accountant" in 1935, the SEC set the rules and regulations governing financial reporting by companies listed on the stock exchange. But even then, leaders of the audit firms worried that the reforms put too much onus on them, as opposed to on the corporations, which could still doctor the books they gave to accountants. The auditing firms wanted a certificate attached to each audit that stipulated: "We have made an examination of your accounts for the purpose of expressing an opinion in connection with such statements, which have been prepared by you."[8]

Leading partners in U.S. auditing firms worried that the government would take too large a role in regulating financial markets and stifle financial independence and innovation. There was a concern on the part of the auditing companies—which had since the mid-nineteenth century provided the U.S. government with its audits and standards—that compulsory audits would replace the role of the public accountant with a government auditor potentially hostile to financial firms. These arguments, however, lost relevance in the chaotic aftermath of 1929, with confidence in the crippled financial sector at an all-time low. Realizing regulation was inevitable, a leading partner at Price Waterhouse, George O. May, hoped that helping to reform and regulate the market would continue to ensure the trusted, independent role of auditors. Still respected, private accountants could lead the regulatory charge of the government. And so, volunteer accountants designed the SEC filing forms for financial statements and wrote the official guide for auditing. May himself helped write the fundamental rules of the generally accepted accounting principles, still known today as GAAP.[9]

In the years following the Depression, the ripples of standards reform spread worldwide. In 1949, the Conferencia Interamericana de Contabilidad met to create standards in South and Central America. In 1951, Austria, Belgium, France, Germany, Italy, Luxemburg, the Netherlands, Portugal, Spain, and Switzerland created the Union Européenne des Experts Comptables; Denmark, Ireland, Norway, Sweden, and the United Kingdom joined in 1963. The 1957 Treaty of Rome created the European Economic Community (EEC) and, with it, the International Accounting Standards Committee (IASC). That same year, the Far East Conference of Accountants was formed. Postwar nations were creating a global accounting framework to manage the new global economy. By the 1960s, Price Waterhouse & Co. would call for common standards that could be used for assessing "true and fair value" of the foreign subsidiaries of American and British companies. Global trade brought a need for what accountants called "harmony." Sir Henry (later Lord) Benson (1909–1995), a leader of the IASC (which, in 2001, became the IASB, the International Accounting Standards Board), a British war munitions expert and president of the Institute of Chartered Accountants of England, continued the push for GAAP, which gradually became accepted by international accounting bodies.[10]

The period between 1946 and 1961 has been called a golden age for accountants, with trust in the industry widespread and robust. Clear auditing standards and regulations accompanied economic expansion in the Western economies and Japan. Yet something in the culture of accounting had changed since the nineteenth century. The rise of massive government institutions, bureaus, laws, and tax codes had perhaps inevitably made accounting more complex. The list of acronyms in the preceding paragraphs attests to the depersonalized character of twentieth-century accounting. It now was a subject only for the expertly informed, inscrutable even to the best educated citizen. Accountants now became synonymous not only with professional success but also with the dehumanizing large-scale number crunching of the mainframe computer age.

Like postwar economic growth, the golden age of accounting did not last, and the role of the accountant as a leading, even gentlemanly, social figure and neutral arbiter of business and regulation soon enough began to erode. Competition between the auditing firms became fierce in the mid-1950s. Peat Marwick outpaced Price Waterhouse & Co. in revenues, and Andersen & Co., founded in 1913 by Arthur Andersen, the son of Norwegian immigrants and trained by Price Waterhouse & Co., brought a new, distinctly American culture to accounting. Shocked by the mayhem of Chicago business in the prohibition age, Arthur

Andersen had looked to bring order to a corrupt city dominated by figures like Jake "Greasy Thumb" Guzik, Al Capone's notorious book-keeper, whose account books provided the tax evasion evidence that was Capone's ultimate downfall. Andersen was meticulous about ethics, insisting that auditors answer first and foremost to investors. "To preserve the integrity of his reports," Andersen insisted, "the accountant must insist upon absolute independence of judgment and action." He said that there was "not enough money in the city of Chicago" to make him sign off on books he thought were inaccurate or false, even if that entailed losing a major account.[11]

Discipline and high standards, Andersen believed, came through thorough training. He looked to build a utopia of accounting based on what he claimed were the simple principles of his Norwegian mother: "Think straight, talk straight." Andersen's ideals of moral rectitude, discipline, and fierce competitiveness would be the basis for a new business model. Instead of tapping the ranks of the Ivy League and other competitive universities, Andersen looked for Midwestern strivers he could train himself. He created his own accounting university on the 55,000-acre former campus of St. Dominic College in St. Charles, outside Chicago. At its peak, it had a 500-member permanent staff, 1,800 full-time residential students, and 68,000 part-time students who would pass through the campus annually. In this perfect world of accounting, "green bean" recruits lived and trained on campus, in close quarters with partners who instilled a cultlike conformity, with a strict regimen of shirts, ties, and hats—felt from Labor Day to Memorial Day and straw after—that hung on specified hooks. Sometimes referred to as "Androids," all Andersen employees, whether from Chicago, London, or Kuala Lumpur, were to be trained to fit the same model of clean-cut standards, competitiveness, and hierarchical loyalty. This model remained unchanged even beyond the 1970s. In the 1990s, one new recruit described beginning the Andersen training process: "It is year Zero with the Khmer Rouge. You have just been born."[12]

From the beginning, Arthur Andersen broke from the very British traditions of Price Waterhouse & Co. So long as it was done with strict integrity, Andersen believed, accountants should also act as consultants on the "advisability of investment in a new enterprise or the extension of an old business." Cost-accounting models could be used to redesign entire businesses; such was the direction the industry was moving in. And with competition now fierce among the Big Eight auditing firms—Price Waterhouse & Co.; Deloitte, Haskins and Sells; Peat Marwick Mitchell; Arthur Andersen; Touche Ross; Coopers & Lybrand; Ernst and Whinney; and Arthur Young & Co.—all now had to stretch their reach into consulting, thus blurring the lines of independence, as they received massive consulting contracts from the very companies they were supposed to independently audit.[13]

It was only a matter of time before these conflicts caught up with members of the Big Eight. In the 1970s, a slew of accounting scandals rocked the industry, as imaginative bookkeeping allowed companies like the railroad Penn Central to post a $4 million profit right before going bankrupt. Against the social turmoil of the Vietnam War, accountants and Androids were the definition of *square* and so hardly popular cultural figures. By 1971, under the Nixon administration, inflation rose to 5 percent. Prices jumped 38.2 percent between 1971 and 1976. Many critics blamed accountants for failing to agree on "inflation accounting techniques." Fairly or not, accountants were blamed when companies cooked their books by overstating profits, understating depreciation, or inaccurately gauging the monetary values, which were fluctuating violently. In the tumult of inflation, accountants were seen as unable or unwilling to give objective and independent audits.[14]

Inflation undermined the very idea of how to measure value and, hence, the old certainties of accounting. When inflation undermined the value of currency, then depreciation, or historical value—based on a calculation starting from an original purchase price and evolving over time—did not always reflect the true value of assets or, in accounting-speak, the difference between replacement costs and original purchase value. Companies were able to hide income and manipulate values by misstating the values of depreciation and appreciation.

Looking for a way to manage corporate accounting tricks, accountants devised the concept of "impairment recognition," by which they sought to take into account false reporting in order to establish true corporate asset values. They used a "market-to-market" method to assess the "fair value" of corporate assets. This means a company is valued by its price on the current market, not on calculations of depreciation based on a historical or original purchase price. "Fair value" accounting was also based on the idea that the value of a dollar is not always the same. Today's dollars would have to be calculated in terms of what a dollar used to be worth, using a general price index. This means the past dollar amount is changed to its current "real" purchasing power. But not all accountants agreed that fair value was the best tool, as it, too, could be manipulated. With the idea of value now uncertain, accounting had become more speculative, and account books, harder to accurately audit.

Most damaging, the public would not only be lost in these arguments, it would simply ignore them, as trust in auditing and balance sheets continued to ebb in the constant flow of accounting scandals and arcane economic debates. Herman Bevis, then head of Price Waterhouse & Co., complained that there was an "expectation gap" between what the public wanted of auditing companies and what they could actually do. The problem was not just the confidence of the public. By 1966, auditing firms had become liable for the frauds committed by the companies they audited through the Federal Rules Procedure and application of the standard of the 1931 Ultramares case, which deemed an auditor responsible to single stockholders. If a company submitted false books or misstatements, and the accounting firm failed to recognize it or did not report fraud, both the company and the auditor faced legal action.[15]

By 1974, the Big Eight firms had come under a hail of two hundred lawsuits. In 1976, Congress stepped in with a committee led by Montana's powerful senior senator, Democrat Lee Metcalf. The Metcalf Report was damning. Auditing firms, it stated, had "over-delegated" authority to the very firms they were supposed to audit, demonstrating "an alarming lack of independence." The Metcalf Committee condemned the SEC as well for having "seriously failed to protect the public interest and to fulfill its public mandate"; it insisted that the SEC regulate the accounting firms to guarantee compliance with standards of independence when both auditing and consulting for firms. No longer would auditing companies be entrusted to make their own rules. Bad accounting had become an affair of state, and the U.S. government, which for two hundred years had left accounting standards and rules to companies, now took over, with Congress exercising oversight of accounting practices and standards.[16]

But the knife of accountability cut both ways. If the government was now the chief auditor, who would audit the government? In the 1960s and 1970s, the U.S. government slowly began to open its own books to scrutiny. Congress had argued with President Lyndon Johnson over the budget of the Vietnam War, and with the economic havoc caused by inflation in the 1970s, a consensus emerged that a nonpartisan state accounting office was needed to settle political arguments over public finance. When President Richard Nixon demanded that Congress raise the debt ceiling by $250 billion in 1972, Congress responded to conflicts over spending priorities by creating a Joint Study Committee on Budget Control—to give Congress a greater role in budget and debt decisions—to counterbalance the President's Office of Management and Budget. President Nixon signed into law the creation of the nonpartisan Congressional Budget Office (CBO), which would be responsible for providing data to Congress for fiscal analysis—from taxation to spending—and for forecasting state finance and budgeting. In turn, the old credit rating firms—Moody's, Standard and Poor's, and Fitch—initially designed to analyze railroad stocks, were authorized by the SEC to become Nationally Recognized Statistical Ratings Organizations (NRSROs) and officially rate bond investment securities for private companies and the state.[17]

In the late 1980s, ratings agencies aggressively analyzed countries' creditworthiness in order to rate the value of their currency, as well as government debt bonds (the capacity of a country to successfully pay its debts), moving from three rated countries to fifty. Before 1985, most countries received a AAA bond rating, but that changed in the early 1990s, when government debt and currency value became ever more complex and difficult to assess. The ratings agencies and their critics recognized that assessing sovereign debt (government bonds issued by a government to sell to foreign investors) to determine a country's credit rating was highly speculative. Nonetheless, ratings companies maintained a sacrosanct status.[18]

The reputations of auditing companies were damaged, however, by the perceived conflict of interest in their active role in corporate consulting. The Metcalf Report had criticized the consulting services of the auditing companies, calling them "particularly incompatible with the responsibility of independent auditors and should be prohibited by federal standards of conduct." Auditing companies continued to provide this service, insisting it was compatible with their roles as independent auditors of the same companies for which they consulted, often for fees ranging in the tens of millions of dollars. In 1981, the journalist Mark Stevens wrote a savage critique of what was happening "behind the pinstripe curtain," as he called it, of the Big Eight, accusing them of having "a lock" on the massive auditing accounts, and in spite of the Metcalf Report, he called the industry "derelict in its duties." Accounting was a damaged brand, yet the big accounting firms remained the only ones with the expertise for audits on such a massive scale. As mistrusted by the public as they were valued by corporations, the Big Eight dominated the auditing industry.[19]

In 1989, Ernst & Whinney merged with Arthur Young to form Ernst and Young, and Deloitte, Haskins & Sells merged with Touche Ross to become Deloitte & Touche (there were different mergers in the United Kingdom); the Big Eight became the Big Six. In 1991, Stevens wrote yet another attack on the profession, *The Big Six: The Selling Out of America's Top Accounting Firms*. Unchecked, he argued, the Big Six "behemoths" were lining their pockets by working as consultants for the companies they also audited. A good audit meant higher corporate value, which, in turn, could mean a payoff for the consulting arms of the accounting firms. According to Stevens, the accountants were even robbing the bankers by providing misleading audits. Wall Street, he went on to charge, sustained a naïve faith in auditing firms to look after anyone's interest except their own.[20]

Less strident critics, too, began to question the integrity of the large auditing firms. For instance, a financial analyst and bureau chief for *BusinessWeek*, Richard Melcher, asked in a 1998 piece for the magazine, "Where Are the Accountants?" Rather than fulfilling their roles as impartial referees, Melcher charged auditors allowed their clients too much leeway in risky although legal accounting tactics.[21]

Melcher critiqued the fact that more than 50 percent of all income of auditing firms now came from consulting, which was beginning to outweigh the value of their accounting business. With many top-level corporate managers coming from the ranks of firms like Andersen, and with massive, cozy double contracts for consulting and auditing, "suddenly, environmental or other legal liabilities are minimized, or inventory depreciation gets stretched out, or a big push is made to drum up end-of-quarter sales." The SEC, he hoped, would take notice. Senior partners at Andersen actually discussed Melcher's article in a meeting and even expressed some concern about their own reliance on consulting. But no steps were taken to ensure independence, let alone examine company ethics and risk taking.[22]

Most accountants stuck to the rules, terrified of the constant flow of litigation stemming from poor audits. Yet the public by now had come to distrust accountants. It was not hard to see why. Corporate clients were clearly less interested in audits than they were in consultants promising ever-greater profits. The consulting business boomed. And the worst was yet to come.[23]

In the 1999, with little public or investor protest, the U.S. government, in the name of economic freedom, replaced the Glass-Steagall Act with the Gramm-Leach-Bliley Act, which allowed the consolidation of commercial banks, investment banks, securities firms, and insurance companies. It enabled banks to take deposits and make loans, as well as underwrite and sell securities (such as pools of mortgages). Signing the act into law on November 12, President Clinton recognized that it made "the most important legislative changes to the structure of the U.S. financial system since the 1930s." He claimed that repealing Glass-Steagall and allowing the "affiliation" between banks and securities firms would spark competition, "enhance the stability of our financial services system," and help it to "compete in global financial markets." Clinton insisted that the bill contained "important safety and soundness protections." But the safeguards for accounting and corporate accountability of the Great Depression were falling away with an "irrationally exuberant" confidence that the boom of the age would last forever with lighter regulation and ever more complex financial products.[24]

Meanwhile, by the 1990s, the Big Six employed literally hundreds of thousands of accountants around the world. The problem was that the audit market was saturated, with little possibility for growth, and profits dropped. Companies now wanted what Arthur Andersen had first proposed—that auditors use their unique quantitative insights for consulting purposes. So strong were their reputations as business fixers that at Andersen, for instance, Andersen Consulting soon eclipsed

Andersen Auditing and, in doing so, became a lead player in the disastrous corporate frauds of the 1990s. Visitors to the Andersen headquarters in Chicago were struck by the fact that Andersen Auditing had drab offices, yet Andersen Consulting operated out of plush, well-furnished digs. Although other auditing companies also made huge fees in consulting, Andersen let the consulting tail wag the whole company. Doing so made sense purely as a matter of profits. Between 1992 and 2001, profits—70 percent of which were from consulting—more than tripled. Andersen would consult for high-profile "new economy" firms like Waste Management, WorldCom, and, most notoriously, the Texas energy firm Enron, while also acting as their auditor. All of these companies inflated their stock value by using false accounting statements. Eventually, all, even the once-venerable Andersen, went bankrupt. Andersen & Co. was indicted in Texas in 2002 for producing false financial statements for Enron, and the SEC found fraudulent Andersen audits for companies such as Waste Management and WorldCom.[25]

Andersen was sunk by the sheer massiveness of the Enron fraud along with its clear complicity in inflating the company's stock price—when it fell, shareholders lost $11 billion. So infamous were Andersen's false audits that President George W. Bush joked about them at the 2002 annual Alfalfa Club dinner in Washington, DC. The president claimed he had good news and bad news from Saddam Hussein: "The good news is he is willing to let us inspect his biological and chemical warfare installations. The bad news is that he insists Arthur Andersen do the inspections."[26]

What is tragically ironic in the Enron case is that certain basic Andersen audits actually worked. In 2001, well-trained, midlevel auditors made smoking-gun reports about questionable Enron transactions and false accounts. Yet, faced with the loss of $100 million in annual consulting fees, top management ignored the audits. The account was just too big to lose. With evidence building that Andersen had covered up its knowledge of Enron's malfeasance, the partner in charge of the Enron account, David Duncan, was terrified of being charged with violating securities laws and ordered his office staff into an orgy of document shredding. It was wishful thinking. The fraud was so large, the collusion of Andersen with Enron so criminal, that Enron's collapse quickly brought down Andersen, too. Duncan would turn state's witness against his company, and to this day, neither he nor any other Andersen employee has served jail time for cooking the books in one of America's worst and most costly financial frauds. Today, Andersen employs a skeleton staff of two hundred to manage its continuing litigation, down from 85,000 worldwide.[27]

In response to Enron and a cascade of other corporate accounting scandals and bankruptcies (among them giants like Tyco International, Adelphia, and Peregrine Systems), President George W. Bush signed the 2002 Sarbanes-Oxley Act, which set up the Public Company Accounting Oversight Board, an attempt to guarantee auditor independence and corporate governance and to clarify the rules of corporate auditing and financial disclosure. This was a pure corporate accountability law. "The era of low standards and false profits is over," President Bush said. "No boardroom in America is above or beyond the law." The day of reckoning had come, he intoned, at least for the accountants: "Free markets are not a jungle in which only the unscrupulous survive, or a financial free-for-all guided only by greed. . . . For the sake of our free economy, those who break the law—break the rules of fairness, those who are dishonest, however wealthy or successful they may be—must pay a price."[28]

Supported by leaders from both political parties, the legislation was seen as so essential and effective that similar laws were subsequently passed in Australia, France, Germany, Italy, Israel, India, Japan, South Africa, and Turkey. In New York, it was hoped that the law would bring confidence to the American stock market after the debacles of Enron and WorldCom. However, a consequence of strict accounting regulation was that weaker accounting firms faced ever more Goliath-like banks and companies that, with their own high-paid teams of internal creative bookkeepers and lobbyists, could remain one step ahead of the auditors.

This would be an issue in the financial crisis of 2008, when unsound and overvalued mortgage securities bundles (CDOs) caused a world financial meltdown. The New York Federal Reserve, the New York offices of the SEC, and the Big Four firms—PricewaterhouseCoopers (PwC), Deloitte Touche Tohmatsu Ltd., Ernst & Young, and KPMG, with nearly 700,000 employees—were only blocks away from Bear

Stearns and Lehmann Brothers, whose collapse led to the federal emergency bailout of most remaining investment banks through the comically titled Troubled Asset Relief Program (TARP). The auditing firms had warned the banks and regulators that CDOs were Class 3 assets (Class 1 being cash) and that their values were speculative and highly risky. Yet they had no power, and possibly no will, to make the case that the CDOs could lead to a financial crisis. In spite of the proximity of regulators, auditors, and bankers, few seemed aware of the impending crash.

Highlighting the weak position of the auditing companies, in the immediate aftermath of the collapse, the investment banks blamed the Big Four for causing the crash, insisting that their new, risk-averse low assessments of the CDOs' values fed the flames of crisis by undermining confidence in their value. Caught between a public that suspected the accounting firms of failing to provide correct audits and the corporate and finance leaders who accused them of undervaluing assets, the Big Four continued to tread lightly out of fear that any accounting or legal misstep could lead to Andersen-style litigation and the implosion of the accounting industry. Indeed, regulators in Britain had begun to worry that the monopoly of the Big Four was itself a risk to the industry. Much like the investment banks, all firms' large accounts have become interconnected through the complex tentacles of finance. The collapse of one of the Big Four firms could bring down the other three. It would seem, then, that the Big Four are too big to fail but too weak to effectively audit their corporate clients.[29]

Dickens would have appreciated the conundrum. To stop fraud at auditing companies, the U.S. and British governments worked to clip their wings, only to find that without effective auditors, it is impossible to oversee finance and industry, let alone government. In spite of the hundreds of thousands of auditors working for accounting firms, the SEC, and the Department of Justice (not to mention European regulatory bodies), no one, as yet, has gone to jail for the 2008 financial crisis. Identifying those who have committed financial crimes, or criminally negligent oversight, and actually sending them to jail—part of the jobs of auditors and government regulators, but something the United States and Europe inexplicably have not elected to do in the years following the 2008 crash—is the sort of aggressive response that might spur reforms and, in their wake, better financial practices. Eric Holder, U.S. Attorney General, has gone on record saying that the size and importance of major investment banks "has an inhibiting influence" on prosecuting financial malfeasance. He has expressed fears that sustained legal action against financial institutions—beyond fines—could destabilize the financial system.[30]

In spite of laws, regulations, and an active financial press, powerful forces are aligned against financial transparency. By the sheer complexity and scale of their operations, banks, corporations, and government bodies have rendered themselves unauditable. How many accountants, really, would it take to truly audit Goldman Sachs, were this indeed a realistic task? Ten thousand? Forty thousand? It might not even be possible. The fact is that government and the auditing companies cannot, for the moment, keep up with the ever-mutating, bacteria-like financial tools and tricks of banking. At the same time, it is unclear that governments can effectively audit themselves. The world financial system is threatened by disaster from bad municipal and government accounting, as countries like Greece and major cities like Detroit go bankrupt because of poor planning but also poor bookkeeping. Government accountants too often calculate that states and cities can pay for pensions. There has been little outcry about bad government accounting by a public unfamiliar with the risks of long-term municipal and government obligations. And despite recent threats by the Department of Justice to pursue financial crimes and the fines meted out to major banks, there have no reckonings on Wall Street or in government. And without one, there can be little incentive for true reform.[31]

Conclusion

From the Renaissance to the nineteenth century, great artists and philosophers painted and discussed accountants and their complex role in society. But great artists don't paint accountants anymore. It is not surprising. In the wake of fiascoes like Enron, accountants have come to be perceived not only as boring but also as venal and inexpert. Few political and financial commentators discuss accountants or accounting. Due to their dour image and the indecipherable aspects of their profession, accountants have become separated from everyday culture. Our financial world has no artist at the level of Charles Dickens to bring alive the complicated world of financial accounting with a brilliantly multilayered social and moral analysis. Yet over the course of the last century, even as they have disappeared from cultural awareness and imagination, accountants have become ever more numerous and ever more skilled in the large-scale number crunching necessary to make and untangle financial operations, and ever more essential to the process of accountability.

As we have seen, this follows a pattern: From Renaissance Italy and the great monarchies of Spain and France to the commercial societies of Holland, Britain, and America, accounting arrives on the scene with great effect, only to retreat into dangerous obscurity. Even in the most financially literate cultures, finance, as Dickens so eloquently wrote, is "splendid, massive, overpowering, and impracticable." Indeed, Dickens felt that accounting was so beyond human control that only luck could extricate his characters from the labyrinth created by numbers and paperwork.[1]

Considering that there have been centuries of struggles over financial accountability, our own recent inability to effectively audit and hold companies and governments accountable seems incomprehensible. And yet, our predicament follows a historical pattern: No sooner is an accounting reform made than we find a way to resist it. Indeed, the rise of technology has made the task of accountability even more daunting, as regulators and even auditors come up against labyrinthine big numbers and financial logarithms, high-speed trading, and complex financial products such as bundled mortgages.

As governments struggle with the paradox of the power and frailty of the Big Four accounting firms, their own account books are in increasing disarray. Risky mortgage bundles are still difficult to value and pose a threat to banking and the stock market. American municipalities have gone bankrupt, and parts of Europe teeter on the brink of insolvency. The International Accounting Standards Board has characterized municipal and government accounting as being in a stage of "primitive anarchy." All countries, rich and poor, hide the true costs of their pension benefits and health care, as well as of infrastructure, off their balance sheets. Credit rating agencies (Moody's, Fitch, and Standard and Poor's) have downgraded leading industrial nations—the United States, France, and, more dramatically, Italy, Spain, and Greece—not without scandal or error. In a vicious cycle of mistrust, many critics, in turn, cast doubt on the integrity and skill of rating agencies as well as on the Big Four.[2]

Why, one may ask, don't democratic governments do more to stabilize the world of finance, from the most sophisticated leveraging of Wall Street to the dime-a-dozen mortgages of Main Street? One reason is that the public is as disengaged from these hard questions as it is unknowledgeable in even the most basic principles of accounting or political economy. The other is that government and the auditing companies cannot keep up with the ever-mutating, bacteria-like financial tools and tricks of banking.

Citizens and investors, in turn, cannot have confidence in multinational businesses or, indeed, their governments, when their own auditing firms and public agencies seem so powerless to obtain accurate numbers. To foster serious and constructive policy debate, the International Monetary Fund's Timothy Irwin has suggested that governments publish balance sheets with their net worth, revealing their assets, liabilities, and budgets up to fifty years into the future. Others have simply called for corporations to publish clearer balance sheets. These seem to be simple prescriptions, but are they possible? None of these proposals addresses the historical difficulties of transparent accounting. And none of these proposals addresses the challenges posed by the rise of China. Its economy blankets a huge percentage of world manufacturing and finance in what is essentially a closed society. The *Economist* magazine refuses even to list Chinese state-generated economic statistics, which it has called an untrustworthy, "aberrant abacus" for an inherently unaccountable superpower. Other nations and markets, while arguably more open, suffer still from a troubling lack of transparency. Beyond economic cycles, then, failure seems to be built into a world financial system that is opaque not at all by accident, but rather by multiple designs.[3]

If there is any historical lesson to be learned here, it is that those societies that managed to harness accounting as part of their general cultures flourished. Republican Italian city-states like Genoa and Florence, Golden Age Holland, and eighteenth- and nineteenth-century Britain and America (to name just those places discussed in this book) all integrated accounting into their educational curriculum, religious and moral thought, art, philosophy, and political theory.

In Holland, for example, accountability was not simply an idea one learned or the work ethic of one religious or ethnic group. It was embedded into all facets of culture. One would learn accounting at school and practice it in business, civil, and domestic life and, at the same time, read religious texts about accountability and view masterworks of art that placed warnings about accounting and financial hubris on the backdrop of scenes or messages from the Bible. Politicians discussed the importance of accounting and accountability, and political pamphlets called for audits using religious language. Among educated citizens, there was an expectation that those in power, from municipal administrators to educators to princes, knew accounting and had a sense of just how essential financial accountability was to their republican system.

Today, economics has too often been reduced to complex number crunching and theories about human behavioral patterns or economic cycles. And yet, economics was born as not just a mathematical field of inquiry but as a historical study of culture. The French economist Jean-Baptiste Say called economics the "simple exposition of the every day life of wealth," and Max Weber insisted on studying both "economy and society." Indeed, those societies that avoided disastrous financial reckonings did so by putting finances in a meaningful cultural context.

Perhaps the salvation of our stumbling, hyperfinancial societies lies not only in the personal, disciplined accounting of Josiah Wedgwood or in the historical and moral approaches of economic thinkers like Adam Smith or, indeed, in the analysis of modern-day number crunchers, but also in the old lessons of paintings such as Jan Provost's *Death and the Miser*, which illustrates so powerfully the importance of bookkeeping and financial management by grounding it in piety, ethics, civic politics, and art. By separating finance into its own sphere, we have lowered our financial and political aspirations. Once, we asked those who thought about and practiced finance to consider the numbers of accounting as an integral part of society and culture, even elevating the mundane numbers of account books to the analysis of religion and great literature. It is this cultural ambition that we will need to recapture if we are to face down our future reckonings.[4]

Acknowledgments

A profound thanks to David A. Bell, who worked on this book with me at every stage and without whose help, I could not have done it.

For helping me to conceptualize this book, thanks go to Rob Mc-Quilkin, Sophus Reinert, John Pollack, Ted Rabb, Peter Burke, Anthony Grafton, Will Deringer, Dan Edelstein, Keith Baker, Peter B. Miller, Jim Green, Matt Kadane, Sean Macaulay, Peter Stallybrass, and Alex Stirling.

A special thanks goes to Istvan Hont who is much missed.

Many thanks also to Alessandro Arienzo, Enzo Baldini, Alastair Bellany, Ann Blair, Robert Bloomfield, Gianfranco Borelli, John Brewer, Janet Browne, Joyce Chaplin, Paul Cheney, Bill Connell, Bill Deverell, Jan de Vries, Kate Epstein, Lynn Farrington, Moti Feingold, Steve Ferguson, Boris Fishman, Rob Fredona, Wantje Fritschy, Beth Garrett, Oscar Gelderblom, Peter Gordon, Orsola Gori, Amy Graves Monroe, Karen Halttunen, Colin Hamilton, Deb Harkness, Randolph Head, Carla Hesse, Steve Hindle, Blair Hoxby, Lynn Hunt, Matt Jones, Richard Kagan, Bruce Kahan, Béla Kapossy, Julius Kirshner, Christopher Krebs, Tom Lacqueur, Inger Leemans, Marie-Laure Legay, Alex Lippincott, James Livesey, Mark Lotto, Peter Mancall, Alex Marr, John McCormick, Siobhan McElduff, Michael McKeon, Darrin McMahon, Ken Merchant, Wijnand Mijnhardt, Peter N. Miller, Ken Mills, Tony Molho, Craig Muldrew, John Najemy, Christopher Napier, Diego Navarro Bonilla, Vanessa Ogle, Derek Parsons, Renato

Pasta, Nathan Perl-Rosenthal, Steve Pincus, John Pocock, Maarten Prak, Paolo Quattrone, Daniel Raff, Jack Rakove, Diogo Ramada-Curto, Orest Ranum, Neil Safier, Maurie Samuels, Margaret Schotte, Vanessa Schwartz, Catherine Secretan, Richard Serjeantson, Andy Shankman, Christina Shideler, Michael Sonenscher, Nomi Stolzenberg, Naomi Taback, University of Michigan Press, Charles van den Heuvel, Ellen Wayland-Smith, Caroline Weber, Carl Wennerlind, and Isser Wolloch.

Especial thanks and credit are due to my clairvoyant editor Lara Heimert, for her unwavering faith in this book, and to her crack team at Basic Books, Katy O'Donnell, Michele Jacob, Cassie Nelson, and, in particular, Roger Labrie, as well as copyeditor Joy Matkowski and production editor Melody Negron.

I am deeply indebted to my indefatigable agent, Rob McQuilkin, and his sterling literary agency, Lippincott, Massie, McQuilkin.

I'm grateful for funding from the John Simon Guggenheim Memorial Foundation and the John D. and Katherine P. MacArthur Foundation and for the funding and unparalleled support of the Dornsife College of Arts and Letters and the Department of History of the University of Southern California.

Thanks also for sustained support and sustenance from Bibou Restaurant in Philadelphia, the Choay-Lescar family in Paris, and the Bartoli family in Florence.

This project would not have been possible without great libraries and librarians. Thanks go to the University of Pennsylvania Rare Books Collection, the Rutgers University Libraries, the Library Company of Philadelphia, the Bibliothèque Nationale de France, the Firestone Library Collection of Rare Books at Princeton University, the Archivio di Stato di Firenze, the Huntington Library, and the University of Southern California Libraries.

The ideas in this book were fleshed out in conferences at the Columbia University Eighteenth Century Seminar, University of Buffalo Early Modern Seminar, Yale University French Studies Seminar, TEDx New Wall Street, the Maison Française de Columbia University, the Harvard Business School Seminar on New Perspectives on Political Economy, the Wharton School Economic History Seminar, the Stanford Humanities Center, the USC-Cambridge University CRASSH seminar on material culture, the Cambridge University Economic

History Seminar, the Borchard Foundation, the Huygens Institute in the Hague, the Descartes Centre in Utrecht, the Felix Meritis Foundation in Amsterdam, the Other Canon Foundation in Oslo, the University of California Berkeley Seminar on the Enlightenment 2.0, the Rutgers University Seminar on Political Polemics in Early Modern Britain and Europe, the *Journal of Interdisciplinary History*, the Fondazione Luigi Firpo, the University Federico II di Napoli, the Early Modern Studies Institute and the Center for Law, History and Culture at the University of Southern California, and the Caltech/Huntington Library conference on Debates over Early Modern Taxonomies. Also thanks and gratitude go to the students of my undergraduate seminar on accounting, politics, and ethics at the University of Southern California, who helped me think through this book.

Notes

Introduction

1. Louise Story and Eric Dash, "Lehman Channeled Risks Through 'Alter Ego' Firm," *New York Times*, April 12, 2010.

2. Alain Desrosières, *The Politics of Large Numbers: A History of Statistical Reasoning*, trans. Camille Nash (Cambridge, MA: Harvard University Press, 1998), 177; Keith Thomas, "Numeracy in Early Modern England," *Transactions of the Royal Historical Society* 37 (1987): 103–132. On eighteenth-century North America, see Patricia Cline Cohen, *A Calculating People: The Spread of Numeracy in Early America* (Chicago: University of Chicago Press, 1982); Daniel Defoe, chapter 20 in *The Complete English Tradesman* (Edinburgh, 1839); Ceri Sullivan, *The Rhetoric of Credit: Merchants in Early Modern Writing* (Madison, NJ: Associated University Presses, 2002), 12–17.

3. Domenico Manzoni, *Quaderno doppio col suo giornale* (Venice: 1540), sig. ii verso. Paul F. Grendler, *Schooling in Renaissance Italy: Literacy and Learning 1300–1600* (Baltimore: Johns Hopkins University Press, 1989), 322.

4. A. C. Littleton, *Accounting Evolution to 1900* (New York: American Institute Publishing, 1933), 25.

5. Max Weber, *General Economic History*, trans. Frank Hyneman Knight (New York: Free Press, 1950), 275.

6. Werner Sombart, *Der Moderne Kapitalismus*, 6th ed. (Leipzig, 1924), 118. The translation is from J. A. Aho, *Confession and Bookkeeping: The Religious, Moral, and Rhetorical Roots of Modern Accounting* (Albany: State University of New York Press, 2005), 8. Also see Joseph A. Schumpeter, *History of Economic Analysis*, ed. Elizabeth Boody Schumpeter (New York: Oxford University Press, 1954), 156. Schumpeter cited in Yuri Bondi, "Schumpeter's Economic Theory and the Dynamic Accounting View of the Firm: Neglected Pages from the *Theory of Economic Development*," *Economy and Society* 37, no. 4 (2008): 528.

Chapter 1

1. Suetonius, *The Twelve Caesars*, trans. Robert Graves (Harmondsworth, UK: Penguin Books, 1982), 69; *Res gestae divi Augusti*, trans. P. A. Brunt and J. M. Moore (Oxford: Oxford University Press, 1973), stanza 17.

2. Salvador Carmona and Mahmous Ezzamel, "Ancient Accounting," in *The Routledge Companion to Accounting History*, ed. John Richard Edwards and Stephen P. Walker (Oxford: Routledge, 2009), 79.

3. Ibid., 14; Max Weber, *The Theory of Social and Economic Organizations*, trans. and ed. A. M. Henderson and Talcott Parsons (New York: Free Press, 1947), 191–192; also see Aho, *Confession and Bookkeeping*, 8.

4. Littleton, *Accounting Evolution*, 83; Richard Brown, *A History of Accounting and Accountants* (Edinburgh: T. C. & E. C. Jack, 1905), 17.

5. Augustus Boeckh, *The Public Economy of Athens* (London: John W. Parker, 1842), 185–189, 194; Aristotle, *The Athenian Constitution*, trans. P. J. Rhodes (London: Penguin Books, 1984), 93–94.

6. Boecke, *The Public Economy of Athens*, 194.

7. Brown, *A History of Accounting and Accountants*, 30.

8. David Oldroyd, "The Role of Accounting in Public Expenditure and Monetary Policy in the First Century AD Roman Empire," *Accounting Historians Journal* 22, no. 2 (1995): 121–122.

9. Ibid., 31.

10. Cicero, *The Orations of Marcus Tullius Cicero (Philippics)*, trans. C. D. Yonge (London: Henry J. Bohn, 1852), 2:34.

11. Oldroyd, "The Role of Accounting," 123.

12. *Res gestae divi Augusti*, stanzas 15–16; Oldroyd, "The Role of Accounting," 125.

13. Oldroyd, "The Role of Accounting," 124.

14. Moses I. Finley, *The Ancient Economy* (Berkeley: University of California Press, 1973), 19.

15. Edward Gibbon, *History of the Decline and Fall of the Roman Empire*, 4th ed. (London: W. and T. Cadell, 1781), 1: chap. XVII, 55.

16. M. T. Clanchy, *From Memory to Written Record: England 1066–1307* (London: Blackwell, 1979); F. E. L. Carter and D. E. Greenway, *Dialogus de Scaccario (The Course of the Exchequer), and Constitutio Domus Regis (The Establishment of the Royal Household)* (London: Charles Johnson, 1950), 64.

17. Clanchy, *From Memory to Written Record*, 2–92.

18. Robert-Henri Bautier, "Chancellerie et culture au moyen age," in *Chartes, sceaux et chancelleries: Études de diplomatique et de sigillographie médiévales*, ed. Robert-Henri Bautier (Paris: École des Chartes, 1990), 1:47–75; Brown, *A History of Accounting and Accountants*, 53–121.

19. Brown, *A History of Accounting and Accountants*, 54.

20. Thomas Madox, *The Anqituities and the History of the Exchequer of the Kings of England* (London: Matthews and Knaplock, 1711); Clanchy, *From Memory to Written Record*, 78.

21. John W. Durham, "The Introduction of 'Arabic' Numerals in European Accounting," *Accounting Historians Journal* 19, no. 2 (1992): 26.

22. Quentin Skinner, *The Foundations of Modern Political Thought* (Cambridge: Cambridge University Press, 1978), 1:3.

23. Quotations from Grendler, *Schooling in Renaissance Italy*, 307; Ingrid D. Rowland, *The Culture of the High Renaissance: Ancients and Moderns in Sixteenth-Century Rome* (Cambridge: Cambridge University Press, 1998), 110–113.

24. Grendler, *Schooling in Renaissance Italy*, 307.

25. Ibid., 308.

26. Carte Strozziane, 2a serie, n. 84 bis, Archivio di Stato, Florence. Also see Geoffrey A. Lee, "The Coming of Age of Double Entry: The Giovanni Farolfi Ledger of 1299–1300," *Accounting Historians Journal* 4, no. 2 (1977): 80. On Italian origins of double-entry bookkeeping, see Federigo Melis, *Storia della ragioneria* (Bologna: Cesare Zuffi, 1950); Federigo Melis, *Documenti per la storia economica dei secoli XIII–XVI* (Firenze: Olschki, 1972); Raymond de Roover, "The Development of Accounting Prior to Luca Pacioli According to the Account-Books of Medieval Merchants," in *Studies in the History of Accounting*, ed. A. C. Littleton and B. S. Yamey (London: Sweet & Maxwell, 1956), 114–174; Raymond de Roover, "The Development of Accounting Prior to Luca Pacioli," in *Business, Banking and Economic Thought in Late Medieval and Early Modern Europe: Selected Studies of Raymond de Roover*, ed. Julius Kirschner (Chicago: University of Chicago Press, 1974), 119–180; Pietro Santini, "Frammenti di un libro di banchieri fiorentini scritto in volgare nel 1211," *Giornale storico della litteratura italiana* 10 (1887): 161–177; Geoffrey Alan Lee, "The Oldest European Account Book: A Florentine Bank Ledger of 1211," *Nottingham Medieval Studies* 16, no. 1 (1972): 28–60; Geoffrey Alan Lee, "The Development of Italian Bookkeeping 1211–1300," *Abacus* 9, no. 2 (1973): 137–155.

27. De Roover, "The Development of Accounting Prior to Luca Pacioli," 124, 122.

28. Edward Peragallo, *Origin and Evolution of Double Entry Bookkeeping: A Study of Italian Practice from the Fourteenth Century* (New York: American Institute Publishing Company, 1938), 4–5; Brown, *Accounting and Accountants*, 99; Alvaro Martinelli, "The Ledger of Cristianus Lomellinus and Dominicus De Garibaldo, Stewards of the City of Genoa (1340–41)," *Abacus* 19, no. 2 (1983): 90–91.

29. For an analysis and reproduction of the Genoese pepper account see Alvaro Martinelli, "The Ledger of Cristianus Lomellinus and Dominicus De Garibaldo, Stewards of the City of Genoa (1340–41)," *Abacus* 19, no. 2 (1983): 90–91.

30. Ibid., 85.

31. Ibid., 86.

Chapter 2

1. Quotation from Iris Origo, *The Merchant of Prato: Daily Life in a Medieval Italian City* (London: Penguin Books, 1992), 66.

2. Ibid., 66, 259, 194.

3. Raymond de Roover, *The Rise and Decline of the Medici Bank 1397–1494* (Cambridge, MA: Harvard University Press, 1963), 2–3; Ludovica Sebregondi and Tim Parks, eds., *Money and Beauty: Bankers, Botticelli and the Bonfire of the Vanities* (Florence: Giunti Editore, 2011), 121.

4. Origo, *The Merchant of Prato*, 194; De Roover, *The Rise and Decline of the Medici Bank 1397–1494*, 38, 194.

5. Origo, *The Merchant of Prato*, 259, 276; Tim Parks, *Medici Money: Banking, Metaphysics and Art in Fifteenth-Century Florence* (New York: W. W. Norton, 2006), 32–33.

6. Pierre Jouanique, "Three Medieval Merchants: Francesco di Marco Datini, Jacques Coeur, and Benedetto Cotrugli," *Accounting, Business and Financial History* 6, no. 3 (1996): 263–264.

7. Origo, *The Merchant of Prato*, 149.

8. Ibid., 115–116, 258.

9. Ibid., 257, 280.

10. Ibid., 119.

11. Ibid., 103, 117, 137.

12. Ibid., 115, 137, 122.

13. Basil S. Yamey, *Art and Accounting* (New Haven, CT: Yale University Press, 1989), 16.

14. Richard K. Marshall, *The Local Merchants of Prato: Small Entrepreneurs in the Late Medieval Economy* (Baltimore: Johns Hopkins University Press, 1999), 66–69.

15. Sebregondi and Parks, eds., *Money and Beauty*, 147; Dante, *The Inferno*, trans. Robert Pinsky (New York: Farrar, Straus and Giroux, 1995), Canto XVII, vv. 55–57.

16. Origo, *The Merchant of Prato*, 151.

17. Yamey, *Art and Accounting*, 68.

18. Matthew 25:14–30 (Revised Standard Version).

19. Augustine, *Sermon 30 on the New Testament*, New Advent Catholic Encyclopedia, www.newadvent.org/fathers/160330.htm, stanza 2.

20. Giovanni Boccaccio, "First Day," in *The Decameron*, trans. J. M. Rigg (London: A. H. Bullen, 1903), 12.

21. Dante, "Purgatory," in *The Divine Comedy*, trans. Allen Mandelbaum (Berkeley: University of California Press, 1981), 2:10.105–111.

22. Jean Delumeau, *Sin and Fear: The Emergence of a Western Guilt Culture 13th–18th Centuries*, trans. Eric Nicholson (New York: St. Martin's Press, 1990), 189–197.

23. Robert W. Schaffern, *The Penitent's Treasury: Indulgences in Latin Christendom, 1175–1375* (Scranton, PA: University of Scranton Press, 2007), 45.

24. Ibid., 80–81.

25. Anthony Molho, "Cosimo de' Medici: *Pater Patriae* or *Padrino?*" in *The Italian Renaissance: The Essential Readings*, ed. Paula Findlen (Malden, MA: Wiley-Blackwell, 2002), 69–86.

26. Origo, *The Merchant of Prato*, 154.

27. Ibid., 315, 323.

28. Ibid., 342–346.

Chapter 3

1. Roover, *The Rise and Decline of the Medici Bank 1397–1494*, 47.

2. Quotation from Coluccio Salutati, *Invectiva contra Atonium Luscum*, quoted in Curt S. Gutkind, *Cosimo de' Medici: Pater Patriae, 1389–1464* (Oxford: Clarendon Press, 1938), 1.

3. Ronald Witt, "What Did Giovanni Read and Write? Literacy in Early Renaissance Florence," *I Tatti Studies* 6 (1995): 87–88; Richard Goldthwaite, *The Economy of Renaissance Florence* (Baltimore: Johns Hopkins University Press, 2009), 354.

4. Lauro Martines, *The Social World of the Florentine Humanists 1390–1460* (Princeton, NJ: Princeton University Press, 1963), 320–336.

5. Machiavelli, *The Discourses*, trans. Leslie J. Walker (London: Penguin Books, 1983), 1:192.

6. Anthony Molho, *Firenze nel quattrocento* (Rome: Edizioni di Storia e Letteratura, 2006), 58.

7. De Roover, *The Rise and Decline of the Medici Bank 1397–1494*, 53–76.

8. Ibid., 120.

9. Ibid., 69–70, 227, 265.

10. Nicolai Rubenstein, *The Government of Florence under the Medici 1434–1494* (Oxford: Oxford University Press, 1998); Parks, *Medici Money*, 98.

11. Goldthwaite, *The Economy of Renaissance Florence*, 355; Gutkind, *Cosimo de' Medici*, 196–199; Parks, *Medici Money*, 39.

12. Goldthwaite, *The Economy of Renaissance Florence*, 355.

13. For Cosimo's personal account book, see Cosimo de' Medici, "Calcolo della Fattoria del Mugello," 1448, filza 104, page 6 recto, Mediceo Avanti il Principato, Archivio di Stato di Firenze.

14. Goldthwaite, *The Economy of Renaissance Florence*, 355, 460–461.

15. Raymond de Roover, *Money, Banking and Credit in Medieval Bruges* (Cambridge, MA: Medieval Academy of America, 1948), 35.

16. Ibid., 34, 37.

17. Ibid., 57–58; Federico Arcelli, *Il banchiere del Papa: Antonio della Casa, mercante e banchiere a Roma, 1438–1440* (Soveria Manelli, Italy: Rubbettino Editore, 2001), 79.

18. Plato, *The Republic*, trans. Benjamin Jowett (Oxford: Oxford University Press, 1892), book VII.

19. De Roover, *The Rise and Decline of the Medici Bank 1397–1494*, 75.

20. Francesco Sassetti, "Memorandum of My Last Wishes, 1488," reproduced in Aby Warburg, "Francesco Sassetti's Last Injunctions to His Sons," in *The Renewal of Pagan Antiquity: Contributions to the Cultural History of the European Renaissance*, ed. Gertrude Bing (Los Angeles: Getty Research Institute, 1999), 451–465. Warburg reproduces and translated Marsilio Ficino's *Epistle to Giovanni Rucellai*, 255–258.

21. Giovanni Pico della Mirandola, *On the Dignity of Man*, trans. Charles Glenn Wallis, Paul J. W. Miller, and Douglas Carmichael (Indianapolis, IN: Hackett, 1998), stanza 212.

22. De Roover, *The Rise and Decline of the Medici Bank*, 71; de Roover, *Money, Banking and Credit in Medieval Bruges*, 86; Florence Edler de Roover, "Francesco Sassetti and the Downfall of the Medici Banking House," *Bulletin of the Business Historical Society* 17, no. 4 (1943): 66.

23. De Roover, *The Rise and Decline of the Medici Bank*, 97.

24. Cited in Miles Ungar, *Magnifico: The Brilliant Life and Violent Times of Lorenzo de' Medici* (New York: Simon and Shuster, 2008), 58.

25. Quotation is from Ungar, *Magnifico*, 58; Machiavelli citation is from de Roover, *The Rise and Decline of the Medici Bank*, 364.

26. Giorgio Vasari, *The Lives of the Artists*, trans. Julia Conaway Bonadella and Peter Bonadella (Oxford: Oxford University Press, 1991), 212; Ficino cited by Warburg, "Francesco Sassetti's Last Injunctions to His Sons," 233.

27. Quotation from Warburg, "Francesco Sassetti's Last Injunctions to His Sons," 237–238.

28. Ibid.; de Roover, *Money, Banking and Credit in Medieval Bruges*, 88; de Roover, *The Rise and Decline of the Medici Bank*, 363; Edler de Roover, "Francesco Sassetti and the Downfall of the Medici Banking House," 76.

29. De Roover, *Money, Banking and Credit in Medieval Bruges*, 87; de Roover, *The Rise and Decline of the Medici Bank*, 87, 93.

30. The balance sheet is reproduced and discussed in de Roover, "Francesco Sassetti and the Downfall of the Medici Banking House," 72–74; Warburg, "Francesco Sassetti's Last Injunctions to His Sons," 237.

Chapter 4

1. Grendler, *Schooling in Renaissance Italy*, 321–323.

2. Anthony Grafton, *Leon Battista Alberti: Master Builder of the Renaissance* (London: Allen Lane/Penguin Press, 2000), 154; Yamey, *Art and Accounting*, 130.

3. Yamey, *Art and Accounting*, 130.

4. Quotation from Louis Goldberg in *Journey into Accounting Thought*, ed. Stewart A. Leech (London: Routledge, 2001), 217.

5. Pacioli's text is reproduced in John B. Geijsbeek, *Ancient Double-Entry Bookkeeping: Luca Pacioli's Treatise 1494* (Denver, 1914), 33.

6. Ibid., 39.

7. Ibid.; Brown, *A History of Accounting and Accountants*, 40, 111.

8. Grendler, *Schooling in Renaissance Italy*, 321.

9. Pacioli citations from Geijsbeek, *Ancient Double-Entry Bookkeeping*, 27, 37.

10. Ibid., 41, 51–53.

11. Ibid., 41, 75.

12. Bruce G. Carruthers and Wendy Nelson Espeland, "Accounting for Rationality: Double-Entry Bookkeeping and the Rhetoric of Economic Rationality," *American Journal of Sociology* 97, no. 1 (1991): 30–67; Mary Poovey, *A History of the Modern Fact: Problems of Knowledge in the Sciences of Wealth and Society* (Chicago: University of Chicago Press, 1998), 31.

13. Ingrid D. Rowland, *The Culture of the High Renaissance: Ancients and Moderns in Sixteenth-Century Rome* (Cambridge: Cambridge University Press, 1998), 73–80.

14. Domenico Manzoni, *Quaderno doppio col suo giornale* [Double entry books and their journal] (Venice: Comin de Tridino, 1540); Raymond de Roover, "Aux origines d'une technique intellectuelle: La formation et l'expansion de la comptabilité à partie double," *Annales d'histoire économique et sociale* 9, no. 44 (1937): 279–280; M. F. Bywater and B. S. Yamey, *Historic Accounting Literature: A Companion Guide* (London: Scolar Press, 1982), 41; Basil S. Yamey, "Fifteenth and Sixteenth Century Manuscripts on the Art of Bookkeeping," *Journal of Accounting Research* 5, no. 1 (1967): 53; Bywater and Yamey, *Historic Accounting Literature*, 42.

15. Brown, *A History of Accounting and Accountants*, 120.

16. Baldesar Castiglione, *The Book of the Courtier*, trans. and ed. George Bull (London: Penguin Books, 1976), 10.

17. Ibid., 39.

18. Peter Burke, *The Fortunes of the Courtier: The European Reception of Castiglione's Cortegiano* (Cambridge: Polity Press, 1995), 39.

19. Paolo Quattrone, "Accounting for God: Accounting and Accountability Practices in the Society of Jesus (Italy, XVI–XVII Centuries)," *Accounting Organizations and Society* 29, no. 7 (2004): 664.

20. Philippe Desan, *L'imaginaire économiqe de la Renaissance* (Paris: Presses Université de Paris-Sorbonne, 2002), 85.

21. Yamey, *Art and Accounting*, 45.

22. Ibid., 47.

23. Ibid., 53.

24. A. W. Lovett, "Juan de Ovando and the Council of Finance (1573–1575)," *Historical Journal* 15, no. 1 (1972): 1–2.

25. Rafael Donoso-Anes, *Una Contribución a la Historia de la Contabilidad. Análisis de las Práticas Contables Desarrolladas por la Tesorería de la Casa de la Contratación de la Indias en Sevilla, 1503–1717* (Seville: Universidad de Sevilla, 1996), 122.

26. Rafael Donoso Anes, "The Casa de la Contratación de Indias and the Application of the Double Entry Bookkeeping to the Sale of Precious Metals in

Spain 1557–83," *Accounting, Business and Financial History* 4, no. 1 (1994): 84; Rafael Donoso Anes, "Accounting for the Estates of Deceased Travellers: An Example of Early Spanish Double-Entry Bookkeeping," *Accounting History* 7, no. 1 (2002): 80–81.

27. Donoso Anes, "Accounting for the Estates of Deceased Travellers," 84.

28. Donoso Anes, *Una Contribución a la Historia de la Contabilidad*, 122. See the reproduction of the *Reales Ordenancas y Pragmáticas 1527–1567* (Vallaolid: Editorial Lex Nova, 1987), 176–177.

29. Ramon Carande, *Carlos V y sus banqueros. Los caminos del oro y de la plata (Deuda exterior y tesoros ultramarinos)* (Madrid: Sociedad de Estudios y Publicaciones, 1967), 15f.

30. Geoffrey Parker, *The Grand Strategy of Philip II* (New Haven, CT: Yale University Press, 1998), 21, 50; José Luis Rodríguez de Diego and Francisco Javier Alvarez Pinedo, *Los Archivos de Simancas* (Madrid: Lunwerg Editores, 1993); José Luis Rodríguez de Diego, ed., *Instrucción para el gobierno del archivo de Simancas (año 1588)* (Madrid: Dirección General de Bellas Artes y Archivos, 1989); José Luis Rodríguez de Diego, "La formación del Archivo de Simancas en el siglo xvi. Función y orden interno," in *El libro antiguo español IV*, ed. López Vidriero and Cátedra (Salamanca: Ediciones Universidad de Salamanca, 1998), 519–557; David C. Goodman, *Power and Penury: Government, Technology and Science in Philip II's Spain* (Cambridge: Cambridge University Press, 1988), chap. 4.

31. Quotation from Stafford Poole, *Juan de Ovando: Governing the Spanish Empire in the Reign of Philip II* (Norman: University of Oklahoma Press, 2004), 162.

32. A. W. Lovett, "The Castillian Bankruptcy of 1575," *Historical Journal* 23, no. 4 (1980): 900.

33. Lovett, "Juan de Ovando and the Council of Finance (1573–1575)," 4, 7.

34. Ibid., 9–11.

35. Ibid., 12; Antonio Calabria, *The Cost of Empire: The Finances of the Kingdom of Naples in the Time of the Spanish Rule* (Cambridge: Cambridge University Press, 1991), 44–45.

36. Lovett, "Juan de Ovando and the Council of Finance (1573–1575)," 12, 19.

37. Ibid., 15.

38. Ibid., 17.

39. Ibid., 19.

40. Ibid.

41. Marie-Laure Legay, ed., *Dictionnaire historique de la comptabilité publique 1500–1850* (Rennes: Presses Universitaires de Rennes, 2010), 394–396.

42. Esteban Hernández-Esteve, "The Life of Bartolomé Salvador de Solórzano: Some Further Evidence," *Accounting Historians Journal* 1 (1989): 92.

43. Ibid.; Legay, *Dictionnaire historique de la comptabilité publique 1500–1850*, 395.

44. Esteban Hernández-Esteve, "Pedro Luis de Torregrosa, primer contador del libro de Caxa de Felipe II: Introducción de la contabilidad por partida doble en la Real Hacienda de Castilla (1592)," *Revista de Historia Económica* 3, no. 2 (1985): 237.

45. Quotation from Jack Lynch, *The Hispanic World in Crisis and Change, 1598–1700* (Oxford: Oxford University Press, 1992), 18; Miguel de Cervantes Saavedra, *The History of don Quixote de la Mancha*, trans. anon. (London: James Burns, 1847), 137.

Chapter 5

1. Fernand Braudel, *Civilisation materielle, économie et capitalisme XVe–XVIIIe siècle* (Paris: Armand Colin, 1979), 2:41; Jacob Soll, "Accounting for Government: Holland and the Rise of Political Economy in Seventeenth Century Europe," *Journal of Interdisciplinary History* 40, no. 2 (2009): 215–238.

2. Wantje Fritschy, "Three Centuries of Urban and Provincial Public Debt: Amsterdam and Holland," in *Urban Public Debts: Urban Government and the Market for Annuities in Western Europe (14th–18th Centuries)*, ed. M. Boone, K. Davids and P. Janssens (Turnhout, Belgium: Brepols, 2003), 75; James D. Tracy, *A Financial Revolution in the Habsburg Netherlands: Renten and Renteniers in the County of Holland, 1515–1565* (Berkeley: University of California Press, 1985), 221.

3. Provincial tax collectors paid bond interest (4 percent) at the moment taxes were collected, and the central state never taxed these returns above 1 percent. Wantje Fritschy, "The Efficiency of Taxation in Holland," in *The Political Economy of the Dutch Republic*, ed. Oscar Gelderblom (London: Ashgate, 2009), 56, 88; Wantje Fritschy, "'A Financial Revolution' Reconsidered: Public Finance in Holland During the Dutch Revolt 1568–1648," *Economic History Review* 56, no. 1 (2003): 78.

4. Quotation from Henry Kamen, *Philip of Spain* (New Haven, CT: Yale University Press, 1997), 267.

5. Woodruff D. Smith, "The Function of Commercial Centers in the Modernization of European Capitalism: Amsterdam as an Information Exchange in the Seventeenth Century," *Journal of Economic History* 44, no. 4 (1984): 986.

6. Poem quotation from Robert Colinson, *Idea rationaria, or the Perfect Accomptant* (Edinburgh: David Lindsay, 1683), in B. S. Yamey, "Scientific Bookkeeping and the Rise of Capitalism," *Economic History Review* 1, no. 2–3 (1949): 102; Lodewijk J. Wagenaar, "Les mécanismes de la prospérité," in *Amsterdam XVIIe siècle. Marchands et philosophes: les bénéfices de la tolerance*, ed. Henri Méchoulan (Paris: Editions Autrement, 1993), 59–81; Adam Smith, *An Inquiry into the Nature and Causes of the Wealth of Nations* (Amherst, NY: Prometheus Books, 1991), 4: chap. 3, part 1; Jan de Vries and Ad van der Woude, *The First Modern Economy: Success, Failure, and Perseverance of the Dutch Economy, 1500–1815* (Cambridge: Cambridge University Press, 1997), 129–131.

7. Caspar Barlaeus, *Marie de Medicis entrant dans l'Amsterdam; ou Histoire de la reception faicte à la Reyne Mère du Roy très-Chrestien, par les Bourgmaistres et Bourgeoisie de la Ville d'Amsterdam* (Amsterdam: Jean & Corneille Blaeu, 1638), 57; Simon Schama, *The Embarrassment of Riches: An Interpretation of Dutch Culture in the Golden Age*, 2nd ed. (New York: Vintage, 1997), 301; Clé Lesger, *The Rise of the Amsterdam Market and Information Exchange: Merchants, Commercial Expansion and Change in the Spatial Economy of the Low Countries c. 1550–1630*, trans. J. C. Grayson (London: Ashgate, 2006), 183–214.

8. Michel Morineau, "Or brésilien et gazettes hollandaises," *Revue d'Histoire Moderne et Contemporaine* 25, no. 1 (1978): 3–30; Jan de Vries, "The Economic Crisis of the Seventeenth Century After Fifty Years," *Journal of Interdisciplinary History* 40, no. 2 (2009): 151–194.

9. Oscar Gelderblom, "The Governance of Early Modern Trade: The Case of Hans Thijs, 1556–1611," *Enterprise and Society* 4, no. 4 (2003): 606–639; Harold John Cook, *Matters of Exchange: Commerce, Medicine, and Science in the Dutch Golden Age* (New Haven, CT: Yale University Press, 2007), 20–21; Peter Burke, *A Social History of Knowledge from Gutenberg to Diderot* (Cambridge: Polity Press, 2000), 164.

10. Karel Davids, "The Bookkeepers Tale: Learning Merchant Skills in the Northern Netherlands in the Sixteenth Century," in *Education and Learning in the Netherlands 1400–1600. Essays in Honour of Hilde de Ridder-Symeons*, ed. Koen Goodriaan, Jaap van Moolenbroek, and Ad Tervoort (Leiden: Brill, 2004), 235–241.

11. Raymond de Roover, "Aux origines d'une technique intellectuelle. La formation et l'expansion de la comptabilité à partie double," *Annales d'histoire économique et sociale* 9, no. 45 (1937): 285; M. F. Bywater and B. S. Yamey, *Historic Accounting Literature: A Companion Guide* (London: Scolar Press, 1982), 46; Yamey, "Bookkeeping and the Rise of Capitalism," 106.

12. Yamey, "Bookkeeping and the Rise of Capitalism," 237; Bywater and Yamey, *Historic Accounting Literature*, 54–55, 80.

13. Quotation from Yamey, *Art and Accounting*, 115. It appears that this image derives from a corresponding hieroglyphic in Francesco Colonna's *Hypnerotomachia Poliphili* (Venice: Aldus Manutius, 1499).

14. O. ten Have, "Simon Stevin of Bruges," in *Studies in the History of Accounting*, ed. A. C. Littleton and B. S. Yamey (New York: Arno Press, 1978), 236; J. T. Devreese and G. Vanden Berghe, *"Magic Is No Magic," the Wonderful World of Simon Stevin* (Boston: Southampton, 2008), 201–212.

15. Bywater and Yamey, *Historic Accounting Literature*, 87.

16. Ibid., 16, 120; Ten Have, "Simon Stevin of Bruges," 242, 244; Geijsbeek, *Ancient Double-Entry Bookkeeping*, 114; Kees Zandvliet, *Maurits Prins van Oranje [Exhibition catalogue Rijksmuseum]* (Amsterdam: Rijksmuseum Amsterdam/ Waanders Uitgevers Zwolle, 2000), 276–277.

17. Quotations from Barlaeus, *Marie de Medicis entrant dans l'Amsterdam*, 16, 59–63.

18. J. Matthijs de Jongh, "Shareholder Activism at the Dutch East India Company in 1622: *Redde Rationem Villicationis Tuae! Give an Account of Your Stewardship!*" (paper presented at the Conference on the Origins and History of Shareholder Advocacy, Yale School of Management, Millstein Center for Corporate Governance and Performance, November 6–7, 2009), 1–56; *A Translation of the Charter of the Dutch East India Company (Verenigde Oostindische Compagnie, or VOC)*, trans. Peter Reynders (Canberra: Map Division of the Australasian Hydrographic Society, 2009).

19. *A Translation of the Charter of the Dutch East India Company*, 3.

20. Jeffrey Robertson and Warwick Funnell, "The Dutch East India Company and Accounting for Social Capital at the Dawn of Modern Capitalism 1602–1623," *Accounting Organizations and Society* 37, no. 5 (2012): 342–360.

21. Schama, *The Embarrassment of Riches*, 338–339; De Jongh, "Shareholder Activism at the Dutch East India Company in 1622," 16.

22. Kristof Glamann, *Dutch Asiatic Trade 1620–1740* (The Hague: Martinus Nijhof, 1981), 245.

23. De Jongh, "Shareholder Activism at the Dutch East India Company in 1622," 22.

24. Ibid., 22–23, 31.

25. Glamann, *Dutch Asiatic Trade 1620–1740*, 252.

26. Ibid., 253–254.

27. Quotations from ibid., 253–256.

28. Ibid., 257–261.

29. Pieter de la Court and Jan de Witt, *The True Interest and Political Maxims of the Republic of Holland* (London: John Campbell, 1746), 4–6, 49–50. On new attitudes of merchant virtue, see J. G. A. Pocock, *The Machiavellian Moment: Florentine Political Thought and the Atlantic Republican Tradition* (Princeton, NJ: Princeton University Press, 1975), 478.

30. Antonin Lefèvre Pontalis, *Vingt années de république parlementaire au dix-septième siècle. Jan de Witt, Grand Pensionnaire de Hollande* (Paris: E. Plon, Nourrit & Cie, 1884), 1:313–318; Herbert H. Rowen, *John de Witt, Grand Pensionary of Holland 1625–1672* (Princeton, NJ: Princeton University Press, 1978), 391–398, esp. 393.

31. Pontalis, *Jan de Witt*, 1:88–89; Jan de Witt, *Elementa curvarum linearum liber primus*, trans. and ed. Albert W. Grootendorst and Miente Bakker (New York: Springer Verlag, 2000), 1.

Chapter 6

1. Louis XIV, *Mémoires for the Instruction of the Dauphin*, trans. and ed. Paul Sonnino (New York: Free Press, 1970), 64.

2. Jacob Soll, *The Information Master: Jean-Baptiste Colbert's Secret State Information System* (Ann Arbor: University of Michigan Press, 2009), 3–15; Daniel Dessert, *Colbert ou le serpent venimeux* (Paris: Éditions Complexe, 2000), 44. For biographies of Colbert, see Inès Murat, *Colbert*, trans. Robert Francis Cook and Jeannie Van Asselt (Charlottesville: University Press of Virginia, 1984); and Jean Meyer, *Colbert* (Paris: Hachette, 1981). For the finest work on Colbert's government, see Daniel Dessert and Jean-Louis Journet, "Le lobby Colbert: un Royaume, ou une affaire de famille?" *Annales. Histoire, Sciences sociales* 30, no. 6 (1975): 1303–1336; *Colbert 1619–1683* (Paris: Ministère de la Culture, 1983); Douglas Clark Baxter, *Servants of the Sword: French Intendants of the Army 1630–1670* (Urbana: University of Illinois Press, 1976).

3. Dessert, *Colbert ou le serpent venimeux*, 43.

4. François de Dainville, *L'éducation des jésuites XVI–XVIII siècles*, ed. Marie-Madeleine Compère (Paris: Éditions de Minuit, 1978), 315–322.

5. Dessert, *Colbert ou le serpent venimeux*, 44–45.

6. Pierre Jeannin, *Merchants of the Sixteenth Century*, trans. Paul Fittingoff (New York: Harper and Row, 1972), 91–103.

7. Colbert to Le Tellier, June 23, 1650, in Jean-Baptiste Colbert, *Lettres, instructions et mémoires*, ed. Pierre Clement (Paris: Imprimerie Impériale, 1865), 1:14; David Parrott, *Richelieu's Army: War, Government and Society in France 1624–1642* (Cambridge: Cambridge University Press, 2001), 370–375; Murat, *Colbert*, 8.

8. Jean Villain, *Mazarin, homme d'argent* (Paris: Club du Livre d'Histoire, 1956); Gabriel-Jules, comte de Cosnac, *Mazarin et Colbert* (Paris: Plon, 1892), vol. 1; Murat, *Colbert*, 22–25.

9. Quotations are from Colbert to Mazarin, September 31, 1651, in Colbert, *Lettres*, 1:132–141 at 132; and Colbert to Mazarin, September 14, 1652, in Cosnac, *Mazarin et Colbert*, 1:324. On Mazarin's finances, see Dessert, *Colbert ou le serpent venimeux*, 52; J. A Bergin, "Cardinal Mazarin and His Benefices," *French History* 1, no. 1 (1987): 3–26.

10. Colbert to Mazarin, September 14, 1652, in Cosnac, *Mazarin et Colbert*, 1:324; Daniel Dessert, *Argent, pouvoir, et société au Grand Siècle* (Paris: Fayard, 1984), 294.

11. Mazarin to Colbert, July 27, 1654, in Cosnac, *Mazarin et Colbert*, 1:324.

12. Smith, *Wealth of Nations*, 446.

13. Marie de Rabutin-Chantal de Sévigné, *Lettres*, ed. M. Suard (Paris: Firmin Didot, 1846), 59.

14. Ibid., 63.

15. Dessert, *Argent, pouvoir et société au grand Siècle*, 210–237, 300; Murat, *Colbert*, 61–63; Jean-Baptiste Colbert, "Arrestation de Fouquet; Mésures préparatoires," 1661, in Colbert, *Lettres*, 2:cxcvi.

16. Pierre-Adolphe Chéruel, ed., *Mémoires sur la vie publique et privée de Fouquet, Surintendant des finances. D'après ses lettres et des pièces inédites conservées à la Bibliothèque Impériale* (Paris: Charpentier Éditeur, 1862), 1:489.

17. Dessert, *Colbert ou le serpent venimeux*, 34; Colbert, *Lettres*, 7:cxcvi.

18. Colbert, "Mémoires sur les affaires de finances de France pour servir à l'histoire," 1663, in Colbert, *Lettres*, 2:1, section 2, 17–68. See Dessert's analysis of this text in his *Colbert ou le serpent venimeux*, 17–37.

19. Colbert, "Mémoires sur les affaires de finances de France pour servir à l'histoire," 19–20, 30–32, 50–51.

20. Ibid., 40–45.

21. Ibid., 44–45.

22. Quotations from Louis XIV, *Instructions of the Dauphin*, 29; Louis to Ann of Austria, 1661, cited by Murat, *Colbert*, 69; Colbert, *Lettres*, 2:1, ccxxvi–cclvii; Louis XIV, marginal notes on letter, May 24, 1670, Colbert to Louis XIV, May 22, 1670, ccxxviii; Colbert to Louis XIV, May 24, 1673, with Louis's undated marginal responses in parentheses, ccxxxii. Also see Richard Bonney, "Vindication of the Fronde? The Cost of Louis XIV's Versailles Building Programme," *French History* 21, no. 2 (2006): 212.

23. For Colbert's administrative folios, see Charles de La Roncière and Paul M. Bondois, *Catalogue des Manuscrits de la Collection des Mélanges Colbert* (Paris: Éditions Ernest Leroux, 1920), 1–100.

24. Colbert, "Mémoire pour l'instruction du Dauphin," manuscript in Colbert's hand, 1665, in Colbert, *Lettres*, 2:1, ccvx and ccxvii.

25. Colbert, *Lettres*, Colbert to Louis XIV, "Au Roi. Pour le Conseil Royal," 2:1, cci.

26. Bnf Ms. Fr. 6769-91. The figures from the notebook for the year 1680 are reproduced in the *Lettres*, 2:2, 771–782; "Receuil de Finances de Colbert," Bnf. Ms. Fr. 7753. On the history of the personal agenda and notebook, see Peter Stallybrass, Roger Chartier, J. Franklin Mowrey, and Heather Wolfe, "Hamlet's Tables and the Technologies of Writing in Renaissance England," *Shakespeare Quarterly* 55, no. 4 (2004): 379–419.

27. Jean-Baptiste Colbert, "Abrégé des finances 1665," Bnf. Ms. Fr. 6771, fols. 4-verso–7-recto; "Abrégé des finances 1671," Bnf. Ms. Fr. 6777, final "table." Colbert, *Lettres*, 2:2, 771–783 contains all the figures from the agenda of 1680, yet with no mention of their remarkable decoration.

28. Clément, in Colbert, *Lettres*, 7:xxxviii.

29. Claude Le Pelletier, "Mémoire présenté au Roi par M. Le Pelletier, après avoir quitté les finances, par lequel il rend compte de son administration," June 1691, in Arthur André Gabriel Michel de Boislisle and Pierre de Brotonne, eds., *Correspondance des Contrôleurs Généraux des Finances* (Paris: Imprimérie Nationale, 1874), 1:544; Lionel Rothkrug, *Opposition to Louis XIV: The Political and Social Origins of the French Enlightenment* (Princeton, NJ: Princeton University Press, 1965), 212–213.

Chapter 7

1. J. E. D. Binney, *British Public Finance and Administration 1774–92* (Oxford: Oxford University Press, 1958), 5.

2. Quotations from Paul Seaward, "Parliament and the Idea of Political Accountability in Early Modern Britain," in *Realities of Representation: State Building in Early Modern Europe and European America*, ed. Maija Jansson (New York: Palgrave Macmillan, 2007), 55–56.

3. Samuel Pepys, *Diary*, Thurs 21 December 1665; Sunday 4 March 1665/6; and Friday 2 March 1665/6. The Diary of Samuel Pepys Online: www.pepysdiary .com.

4. Henry Roseveare, *The Treasury, 1660–1870: The Foundations of Control* (London: Allen and Unwin, 1973), 1, 21–28.

5. William Peter Deringer, "Calculated Values: The Politics and Epistemology of Economic Numbers in Britain, 1688–1738" (PhD diss., Princeton University, 2012), 79; Raymond Astbury, "The Renewal of the Licensing Act in 1693 and Its Lapse in 1695," *The Library* 5, no. 4 (1978): 311; Charles Davenant, *Discourses on the Publick Revenues* (London: James Knapton, 1698), 1:266, 14–15.

6. *The Mercator* 36, August 13–15, 1713, quoted in Deringer, "Calculated Values," 222.

7. Angus Vine, "Francis Bacon's Composition Books," *Transactions of the Cambridge Bibliographical Society* 14, no. 1 (2008): 1–31; Margaret C. Jacob, *Scientific Culture and the Making of the Industrial West* (Oxford: Oxford University Press, 1997), 29–33; Thomas Hobbes, *Leviathan*, ed. Richard Tuck (Cambridge: Cambridge University Press, 1996), chap. 4, p. 29; chap 5., p. 31.

8. William Coxe, *Memoirs of the Life and Administration of Sir Robert Walpole* (London: Longman, Hurst, Reese, Orme and Brown, 1816), 1:2.

9. Robert Walpole, *A State of the Five and Thirty Millions Mention'd in the Report of a Committee of the House of Commons* (London: E. Baldwin, 1712), 2.

10. Ibid., 4–5; Hubert Hall, "The Sources for the History of Sir Robert Walpole's Financial Administration," *Transactions of the Royal Historical Society* 4, no. 1 (1910): 34.

11. John Brewer, *The Sinews of Power: War, Money and the English State 1688–1783* (New York: Alfred A. Knopf, 1989), 116–117.

12. Jeremy Black, *Robert Walpole and the Nature of Politics in Early Eighteenth Century England* (New York: St. Martin's Press, 1990), 27.

13. Norris Arthur Brisco, *The Economic Policy of Robert Walpole* (New York: Columbia University Press, 1907), 43–45; Richard Dale, *The First Crash: Lessons from the South Sea Bubble* (Princeton, NJ: Princeton University Press, 2004), 74.

14. Dale, *The First Crash*, 130. For an alternative view on French industrial growth in the eighteenth century, see Jeff Horn, *The Path Not Taken: French Industrialization in the Age of Revolution* (Cambridge, MA: MIT Press, 2008).

15. Dale, *The First Crash*, 82. Deringer, "Calculated Values," 39–47.

16. Quotations from Deringer, "Calculated Values," 85–88; Archibald Hutcheson, *A Collection of Calculations and Remarks Relating to the South Sea Scheme & Stock, Which have been already Published with an Addition of Some Others, which have not been made Publick 'till Now* (London, 1720).

17. Deringer, "Calculated Values," 84.

18. J. H. Plumb, *Sir Robert Walpole: The Making of a Statesman* (Boston: Houghton Mifflin, 1956), 1:306–319.

19. Ibid., 1:302.

20. Deringer, "Calculated Values," 145; Quotations from John Trenchard, *An Examination and Explanation of the South Sea Company's Scheme for Taking in the Publick Debts. Shewing, That it is Not Encouraging to Those Who Shall Become Proprietors of the Company, at Any Advanced Price. And That it is Against the Interest of Those Proprietors Who Shall Remain with Their Stock Till They are Paid Off by the Government, That the Company Should Make Annually Great Dividend Than Their Profits Will Warrant. With Some National Considerations and Useful Observations* (London, 1720), 8, 16–17, 25–26.

21. Edward Pearce, *The Great Man: Sir Robert Walpole: Scoundrel, Genius and Britain's First Prime Minister* (London: Jonathan Cape, 2007), 427.

22. Quotations from Helen Paul, "Limiting the Witch-Hunt: Recovering from the South Sea Bubble," *Past, Present and Policy Conference* 3–4 (2011): 2 and John Richard Edwards, "Teaching 'merchants accompts' in Britain During the Early Modern Period," *Cardiff Business School Working Paper Series in Accounting and Finance* A2009/2 (2009), 20; Deringer, "Calculated Values," 146.

23. Paul, "Limiting the Witch-Hunt," 7; Pearce, *The Great Man*, 95; John Carswell, *The South Sea Bubble* (Stanford, CA: Stanford University Press, 1960), 260–261.

24. Plumb, *Sir Robert Walpole*, 1:332.

25. Deringer, "Calculated Values," 149; Carswell, *The South Sea Bubble*, 237; Paul, "Limiting the Witch-Hunt," 3.

26. Thomas Gordon, *Cato's Letters* (Saturday, January 19, 1723), Liberty Fund, http://oll.libertyfund.org/index, IV: no. 112.

27. Brisco, *The Economic Policy of Robert Walpole*, 61; Black, *Robert Walpole*, 27.

28. Brisco, *The Economic Policy of Robert Walpole*, 62–65; Black, *Robert Walpole*, 29.

29. Samuel Johnson, *London* (1738), ed. Jack Lynch, http://andromeda.rutgers.edu/~jlynch/Texts/london.html; Henry Fielding, *Shamela*, ed. Jack Lynch, http://andromeda.rutgers.edu/~jlynch/Texts/shamela.html.

Chapter 8

1. Eric Hobsbawm, *Industry and Empire: The Birth of the Industrial Revolution* (New York: Free Press, 1998), xi.

2. Roger North, *The Gentleman Accomptant* (London, 1714), i recto–v recto, 1–2; Binney, *British Public Finance and Administration*, 256.

3. Edwards, "Teaching 'merchants accompts' in Britain During the Early Modern Period," 1, 13–17; N. A. Hans, *New Trends in Education in the Eighteenth Century* (London: Routledge & Keegan Paul, 1951), 66–69, 92–93.

4. Edwards, "Teaching 'merchants accompts' in Britain During the Early Modern Period," 25–27.

5. Margaret C. Jacob, "Commerce, Industry and the Laws of Newtonian Science: Weber Revisited and Revised," *Canadian Journal of History* 35, no. 2 (2000): 272–292; Jan de Vries, "The Industrial Revolution and the Industrious Revolution," *Journal of Economic History* 54, no. 2 (1994): 249–270.

6. Edwards, "Teaching 'merchants accompts' in Britain During the Early Modern Period," 19.

7. Quotations from Richard Bentley, *Sermons Preached at Boyle's Lecture*, ed. Alexander Dyce (London: Francis Macpherson, 1838), 227–228; Margaret Jacob, *The Newtonians and the English Revolution 1689–1720* (Ithaca, NY: Cornell University Press, 1976), 160; Deborah Harkness, "Accounting for Science: How a Merchant Kept His Books in Elizabethan London," in *Self-Perception and Early Modern Capitalists*, ed. Margaret Jacob and Catherine Secretan (London: Palgrave Macmillan, 2008), 214–215.

8. Matthew Kadane, *The Watchful Clothier: The Life of an Eighteenth-Century Protestant Capitalist* (New Haven, CT: Yale University Press, 2013), 45; Adam Smyth, *Autobiography in Early Modern Britain* (Cambridge: Cambridge University Press, 2010), chap. 2.

9. Kadane, *The Watchful Clothier*, 162, 169..

10. Wedgwood to Bentley, October 26, 1762, in Josiah Wedgwood, *Correspondence of Josiah Wedgwood*, ed. Katherine Eufemia Farrer (Cambridge: Cambridge University Press, 2010), 1:6.

11. Ibid. Quotations are in the same volume, from Wedgwood to Bentley, October 1, 1769, 1:297; Wedgwood to Bentley, September 3, 1770, 1:375; Wedgwood to John Wedgwood, June 4, 1766, 1:87; Wedgwood to his brother, John Wedgwood, March 1765, 1:39. Also see Sidney Pollard, *The Genesis of Modern Management: A Study of the Industrial Revolution in Great Britain* (London: Edward Arnold, 1965), 211.

12. Yamey, *Art and Accounting*, 36.

13. Pollard, *The Genesis of Modern Management*, 210.

14. Ibid., 222–223.

15. James Watt Papers, James Watt to his father, July 21, 1755, MS 4/11 letters to father, 1754–1774, Birmingham City Library.

16. A. E. Musson and Eric Robinson, *Science and Technology in the Industrial Revolution* (Manchester, UK: Manchester University Press, 1969), 210–211; Pollard, *The Genesis of Modern Management*, 214, 229, 231.

17. Quotation from Josiah Wedgwood to Thomas Bentley, August 2, 1770, in Wedgwood, *Correspondence*, 1:357. Also see Brian Dolan, *Josiah Wedgwood: Entrepreneur to the Enlightenment* (London: Harper Perennial, 2005), 288; Nancy F. Koehn, "Josiah Wedgwood and the First Industrial Revolution," in *Creating Modern Capitalism: How Entrepreneurs, Companies, and Countries Triumphed in Three Industrial Revolutions*, ed. Thomas K. McCraw (Cambridge, MA: Harvard University Press, 1997), 40.

18. Wedgwood to Bentley, September 27, 1769, in Wedgwood, *Correspondence*, 1:291; Koehn, "Josiah Wedgwood and the First Industrial Revolution," 45.

19. Quoted in Neil McKendrick, "Josiah Wedgwood and Cost Accounting in the Industrial Revolution," *Economic History Review* 23, no. 1 (1970): 49. Also see Wedgwood to Bentley, August 23, 1772, in Wedgwood, *Correspondence*, 1:477.

20. McKendrick, "Josiah Wedgwood and Cost Accounting in the Industrial Revolution," 50–54.

21. Ibid., 54–55.

22. Dolan, *Josiah Wedgwood*, 40; McKendrick, "Josiah Wedgwood and Cost Accounting in the Industrial Revolution," 58–59.

23. McKendrick, "Josiah Wedgwood and Cost Accounting in the Industrial Revolution," 60–62.

24. T. S. Ashton, *Economic Fluctuations in England, 1700–1800* (Oxford: Oxford University Press, 1959), 128; McKendrick, "Josiah Wedgwood and Cost Accounting in the Industrial Revolution," 64.

25. Dolan, *Josiah Wedgwood*, 52.

26. Carl B. Cone, "Richard Price and Pitt's Sinking Fund of 1786," *Economic History Review* 4, no. 2 (1951): 243; Peter Dickson, *The Financial Revolution in England: A Study in the Development of Public Credit 1688–1756* (New York: St. Martin's Press, 1967).

27. Binney, *British Public Finance and Administration*, 254, 207–208, 254.

28. Ibid., 254.

29. Ibid.

30. In Wedgwood, *Correspondence*, Wedgwood to Bentley, June 1, 1780, 2:466; Wedgwood to Bentley, June 10, 1780, 2:469; Wedgwood to Bentley, June 5, 1780, 2:468; Josiah Wedgwood Jr. to Wedgwood, July 5, 1790, 3:149; Josiah Wedgwood Jr. to Wedgwood, July 28, 1789, 3:95.

31. Wedgwood to Priestley, November 30, 1791, in Wedgwood, *Correspondence*, 3:178.

32. Dolan, *Josiah Wedgwood*, 368.

33. Ibid., 380.

34. Adam Smith, *Wealth of Nations*, 3:3, 2; 4:5, 34.

35. Jeremy Bentham, *An Introduction to the Principles of Morals and Legislation* (1789), 1–13.

Chapter 9

1. On France's role as the center of Enlightenment and financial debate, see Robert Darnton, "Trends in Radical Propaganda on the Eve of the French Revolution (1782–1788)" (DPhil diss., Oxford University, 1964), 196–232; John Shovlin, *The Political Economy of Virtue: Luxury, Patriotism, and the Origins of the French Revolution* (Ithaca, NY: Cornell University Press, 2006), 148.

2. Marc Nikitin, "The Birth of a Modern Public Sector Accounting System in France and Britain and the Influence of Count Mollien," *Accounting History* 6, no. 1 (2001): 75–101; Yannick Lemarchand, "Accounting, the State and Democracy: A Long-Term Perspective on the French Experiment, 1716–1967," *LEMNA* WP 2010 43 (2010): 1–26; Seaward, "Parliament and the Idea of Political Accountability in Early Modern Britain," 59. In English, this clearly meant both financial and political accountability. In Romance languages, *accountability* is still translated as "responsibility." Also see "Accountability" in the OED. On English public accounting, see William F. Willoughby, Westel W. Willoughby, and Samuel McCune Lindsay, *The System of Financial Administration of Great Britain: A Report* (New York: D. Appleton, 1917); P. G. M. Dickson, *The Financial Revolution in England*, 81; John Torrance, "Social Class and Bureaucratic Innovation: The Commissioners for Examining the Public Accounts 1780–1787," *Past and Present* 78 (1978): 65; Henry Roseveare, *The Treasury, 1660–1870*, 1.

3. Yannick Lemarchand, "Introducing Double-Entry Bookkeeping in Public Finance," *Accounting, Business, and Financial History* 9 (1999): 228–229. For the posters, see "Modelles des Registres Journaux que le Roy, en son Conseil, Veut et ordonne estre tenus par les Receveurs Généraux des Finances, Caissier de leur Caisse commune, Commis aux Recettes générales, Receveurs des Tailles, Et autres Receveurs des Impositions (. . .). Execution de l'Edit du mois du juin 1716. des Déclarations des 10 Juin 1716. 4 Octobre & 7 Décembre 1723. Et de l'Arrest du Conseil du 15 Mars 1724 portant Réglement pour la tenuë desdits Registres-Journaux (1724)."

4. Yannick Lemarchand, "Comptabilité, discipline, et finances publiques: Un expérience d'introduction de la partie double sous la Régence," *Politiques et Management Public* 18, no. 2 (2000): 93–118.

5. Claude Pâris La Montagne, "Traitté des Administrations des Recettes et des Dépenses du Royaume," (1733) AN 1005, II: 3–8, 48–49, 55, 66, 336. It is not clear if this treatise was earlier than the 1733 date on the manuscript. On the Pâris brothers' accounting reforms of the 1720s, see *Declaration du Roy concernant la tenue des Registres Journaux* (Versailles: October 4, 1723), 1, which codified in law the practice that all "Accountants, Treasurers, Receivers, Cashiers, Accountant's Apprentices in our Finances, Tax Farms and depositories of public funds" would have to follow a strict law of daily double-entry accounting by keeping a "Daily Register."

6. Pâris La Montagne, "Traitté des Administrations des Recettes et des Dépenses du Royaume," 128.

7. Jean-Claude Perrot, *Une histoire intellectuelle de l'économie politique XVIIe–XVIIIe siècle* (Paris: Éditions de l'EHESS, 1992), 162; Sophus Reinert, *Translating Empire: Emulation and the Origins of Political Economy* (Cambridge, MA: Harvard University Press, 2011), 177; Steven L. Kaplan, *Bread, Politics, and Political Economy in the Reign of Louis XIV* (The Hague: Martinus Nijhof, 1976), 2:660–675.

8. David Hume, "Of Public Credit," in *Essays, Moral, Political and Literary*, 2:ix, 2, and 2:x, 28; J. G. A. Pocock, *The Machiavellian Moment*, 496–497; Istvan Hont, "The Rhapsody of Public Debt: David Hume and Voluntary State Bankruptcy," in *Jealousy of Trade: International Competition and the Nation-State in Historical Perspective*, ed. Istvan Hont (Cambridge, MA: Belknap Press of Harvard Press, 2005), 326; Eugene Nelson White, "The French Revolution and the Politics of Government Finance, 1770–1815," *Journal of Economic History* 55, no. 2 (1995): 229; Michael Sonenscher, *Before the Deluge: Public Debt, Inequality, and the Intellectual Origins of the French Revolution* (Princeton, NJ: Princeton University Press, 2007), 1–3; Dan Edelstein, *The Terror of Natural Right: Republicanism, the State of Nature and the French Revolution* (Chicago: University of Chicago Press, 2009), 102; Edmund Burke, *Reflections on the French Revolution*, in *Readings in Western Civilization: The Old Regime and the French Revolution*, ed. Keith Michael Baker (Chicago: University of Chicago Press, 1987), 432.

9. White, "The French Revolution and the Politics of Government Finance," 230–231; Léonard Burnand, *Les Pamphlets contre Necker. Médias et imginaire politique au XVIIIe siècle* (Paris: Éditions Classiques Garnier, 2009), 81; René Stourm, *Les finances de l'Ancien Régime et de la Révolution. Origins du système actuel* (first printing 1885; New York: Burt Franklin, 1968), 2:188.

10. J. F. Bosher, *French Finances 1770–1795: From Business to Bureaucracy* (Cambridge: Cambridge University Press, 1970), 23–25; Joël Félix, *Finances et politiques au siècle des Lumières. Le ministère L'Averdy, 1763–1768* (Paris: Comité pour l'Histoire Économique et Financière de la France, 1999), 144–145.

11. Jean Egret, *Necker, ministre de Louis XVI 1776–1790* (Paris: Honoré Champion, 1975), 123, 170; Michel Antoine, *Le coeur de l'État* (Paris: Fayard, 2003), 506–519; Burnand, *Les pamphlets*, 80–81; Jean Egret, *Parlement de Dauphiné et les affaires publiques dans la deuxième moitié du XVIIIe siècle* (Paris: B. Arthuad, 1942), 2:133–140; Marie-Laure Legay, "The Beginnings of Public Management: Administrative Science and Political Choices in the Eighteenth Century in France, Austria, and the Austrian Netherlands," *Journal of Modern History* 81, no. 2 (2009): 280; Shovlin, *The Political Economy of Virtue*, 148.

12. Charles Alexandre, vicomte de Vergennes, "Lettre de M. le marquis de Caraccioli à M. d'Alembert," in *Collection complette de tous les ouvrages pour et contre M. Necker, avec des notes critiques, politiques et secretes* (Utrecht, 1782), 3:63; Louis-Petit de Bachaumont et al., *Mémoires secrets pour servir à l'histoire de la République des lettres en France* (London: John Adamson, 1784), 15:56.

13. Egret, *Necker*, 61. Burnand, *Les Pamphlets contre Necker*, 95; Augéard was the author of a number of seditious pamphlets. Bachaumont, *Mémoires secrets pour servir à l'histoire de la République des lettres en France*, 15:152. Quotations from "Lettre de M. Turgot à M. Necker," in *Collection Complette*, 1:8.

14. "Lettre de M. Turgot à M. Necker," in *Collection Complette*, 1:8; Jacques-Mathieu Augéard, *Mémoires Sécrets* (Paris: Plon, 1866), 136. Also see Burnand, *Les Pamphlets contre Necker*, 96, 108–110.

15. Michel Antoine, *Le coeur de l'État*, 506–519; Burnand, *Les Pamphlets contre Necker*, 80–81; Jacques Necker, *Sur le Compte Rendu au Roi en 1781. Nouveaux éclaircissemens par M. Necker* (Paris: Hôtel de Thou, 1788), 7–8; Stourm, *Les finances de l'Ancien Régime et de la Révolution*, 2:194–197; Robert D. Harris, "Necker's Compte Rendu of 1781: A Reconsideration," *Journal of Modern History* 42, no. 2 (1970): 161–183; Robert Darnton, "The Memoirs of Lenoir, Lieutenant of Police of Paris, 1774–1785," *English Historical Review* 85, no. 336 (1970): 536; Egret, *Necker*, 170; Jeremy Popkin, "Pamphlet Journalism at the End of the Old Regime," *Eighteenth-Century Studies* 22, no. 3 (1989): 359. For Necker's surplus number see Jacques Necker, *Compte rendu au roi* (Paris: Imprimerie du Cabinet du Roi, 1781), 3. 1 livre = 0.29 grams of pure gold; 1 livre = 20 sols, or sous; 1 sou = 12 deniers.

16. On the rise of mathematics and the social sciences in political culture, see Keith Michael Baker, "Politics and Social Science in Eighteenth-Century France: The 'Société de 1789,'" in *French Government and Society 1500–1850: Essays in Memory of Alfred Cobban*, ed. J. F. Bosher (London: Athlone Press, 1973), 225.

17. Necker, *Compte rendu au roi*, 2–4; Munro Price, *Preserving the Monarchy: The Comte de Vergennes 1784–1787* (Cambridge: Cambridge University Press, 1995), 55–56.

18. Necker, *Compte rendu au roi*, 3–5, 104.

19. Ibid., 45.

20. Ibid., 10, 116; Egret, *Necker*, 200.

21. Burnand, *Les Pamphlets contre Necker*, 96; Jean-Claude Perrot, "Nouveautés: L'économie politique et ses livres," in *L'Histoire de l'édition française*, ed. Roger Chartier et Henri-Jean Martin (Paris: Fayard/Promodis, 1984), 2:322; Stourm, *Les finances de l'Ancien Régime et de la Révolution*, 191; Charles-Joseph Mathon de la Cour, *Collection de Compte-Rendu, pièces authentiques, états et tableaux, concernant les finances de France depuis 1758 jusqu'en 1787* (Paris: Chez Cuchet, Chez Gatteu, 1788), iii–iv.

22. Bosher, *French Finances*, 126; Legay, "Beginnings of Public Management," 285. "In the introduction to the Declaration on Accounting of October 17, 1779, Necker had pointed out how the flaws in the Royal Treasury's system of accounting made it impossible to manage government accounts. Necker noted that the Treasury had 'incomplete information' and that many expenditures left

'no traces.' In order to obtain accurate results, Necker warned, it would take 'an immense amount of work.'" Text cited in Stourm, *Les finances de l'Ancien Régime et de la Révolution*, 2:189; M. A. Bailly, *Histoire financière de la France depuis l'origine de la Monarchie jusqu'à la fin de 1786. Un tableau général des anciennes impositions et un état des recettes et des dépenses du trésor royal à la même époque* (Paris: Moutardier, 1830), 1:238; Egret, *Necker*, 177. Quotation from Vergennes to Louis XVI, May 3, 1781, in Jean-Louis Soulavie, *Mémoires historiques et politiques du règne de Louis XIV* (Paris: Treuttel et Würtz, 1801), 4:149–159.

23. Renée-Caroline, marquise de Créquy, *Souvenirs de 1710 à 1803* (Paris: Garnier Frères, 1873), 7:33–36.

24. "Les pourquoi, ou la réponse verte," in *Collection complette*, 3:141.

25. Charles Alexandre, vicomte de Calonne, *Réponse de M. de Calonne à l'Écrit de M. Necker; contenant l'Examen des comptes de la situation des Finances Rendus en 1774, 1776, 1781, 1783 & 1787 avec des Observations sur les Résultats de l'Assemblée des Notables* (London: T. Spilsbury, 1788), 6, 51. A copy in the Rare Books Collection at Princeton University is bound with the separate "Pièces justificative ou accessoires," which contains numerous tables prepared by Calonne.

26. Desrosières, *The Politics of Large Numbers*, 31.

27. *Courrier d'Avignon*, April 22, 1788, 134–135.

28. François-Auguste-Marie-Alexis Mignet, *History of the French Revolution, from 1789–1814* (London: George Bell and Sons, 1891), 36.

29. Seaward, "Parliament and the Idea of Political Accountability in Early Modern Britain," 59; "Of Accountability," *Authentic Copy of the New Constitution of France, Adopted by the National Convention, June 23, 1793* (London: J. Debrett, 1793), 15, clauses 105–106. The OED traces the first English appearance of the word to 1794; *Constitution of 1791*: "Detailed accounts of the expenditure of ministerial departments, signed and certified by the ministers or general managers, shall be rendered public by being printed at the beginning of the sessions of every legislature. {260}

The same shall apply to statements of receipts from divers taxes; and from all public revenues.

The statements of such expenditures and receipts shall be differentiated according to their nature, and shall indicate the sums received and expended from year to year in each and every district.

The special expenditures of each and every department relative to courts, administrative bodies, and other establishments likewise shall be rendered public (5, 3)."

30. *Convention Nationale: Projet d'organisation du Bureau de Comptabilité* (Paris: Par Ordre de la Convention Nationale, 1792), 25, 28, Maclure Collection, 1156:1, University of Pennsylvania, Special Collections Library; Antoine Burté, "Pour L'Assemblée Nationale. Observations rapides sur les conditions d'eligibilité des Commissaires de la Comptabilité" (Paris: Imprimérie Nationale,

1792), 5–13, Maclure Collection, 735:5, University of Pennsylvania, Special Collections Library.

31. Isser Woloch, *The New Régime: Transformations of the French Civic Order, 1789–1820s* (New York: W. W. Norton, 1994), 40; "Compte rendu par le Ministre de la Marine à l'Assemblée Nationale 31 Oct. 1791" (Paris: Imprimérie Nationale, 1791), Maclure 974:19, University of Pennsylvania, Special Collections Library.

Chapter 10

1. Quotations from Previts and Merino, *A History of Accountancy in the United States*, 15–17; Bernard Bailyn, *The New England Merchants in the Seventeenth Century* (New York: Harper Torchbook, 1964), 170.

2. W. T. Baxter, "Accounting in Colonial America," in *Studies in the History of Accounting*, ed. Littleton and Yamey, 278.

3. Quotations from Previts and Merino, *A History of Accountancy in the United States*, 17, 21.

4. John Mair, frontispiece and page 4 of preface to *Book-Keeping Methodiz'd; or A methodical treatise of MERCHANT-ACCOMPTS, according to the Italian Form* (Edinburgh: W. Sands, A. Murray, and J. Cochran, 1765). Library Company of Philadelphia: Am 1765 Mai Dj.8705.M228 1765.

5. Baxter, "Accounting in Colonial America," 279.

6. Ibid.

7. Max Weber, *The Protestant Ethic and the Spirit of Capitalism*, 50–67.

8. Benjamin Franklin, *The Autobiography and Other Writings on Politics, Economics and Virtue*, ed. Alan Houston (Cambridge: Cambridge University Press, 2004), 34–35.

9. Benjamin Franklin, *Papers of Franklin*, ed. by Leonard W. Lebaree and Whitfield Bell Jr. (New Haven, CT: Yale University Press, 1960), 1:128; Franklin, *Autobiography*, 81.

10. Franklin, *Papers of Benjamin Franklin*, 5:165–167.

11. Ibid., 5:174–175.

12. Benjamin Franklin, *DIRECTIONS to the DEPUTY POST-MASTERS, for keeping their ACCOUNTS* (Broadside, Philadelphia, 1753), Pennsylvania Historical Society, Ab [1775]–35, 61×48 cm; *The Ledger of Doctor Benjamin Franklin, Postmaster General, 1776. A Facsimile of the Original Manuscript Now on File on the Records of the Post Office Department of the United States* (Washington, DC, 1865).

13. *The Ledger of Doctor Benjamin Franklin*, 127, 172–173.

14. Benjamin Franklin and George Simpson Eddy, "Account Book of Benjamin Franklin Kept by Him During His First Mission to England as Provincial Agent 1757–1762," *Pennsylvania Magazine of History and Biography* 55, no. 2 (1931): 97–133; Ellen R. Cohn, "The Printer at Passy," in *Benjamin Franklin in*

Search of a Better World, ed. Page Talbott (New Haven, CT: Yale University Press, 2005), 246–250.

15. Stacy Schiff, *A Great Improvisation: Franklin, France, and the Birth of America* (New York: Henry Holt, 2005), 87, 268; Franklin and Necker corresponded February 21, 1780, and April 10, 1781. Quotations from Benjamin Franklin, *The Writings of Benjamin Franklin*, ed. Albert Henry Smyth (New York: Macmillan, 1907), 8:581–583.

16. Stephanie E. Smallwood, *Saltwater Slavery: A Middle Passage from Africa to American Diaspora* (Cambridge, MA: Harvard University Press, 2008), 98.

17. William Peden, "Thomas Jefferson: The Man as Reflected in His Account Books" *Virginia Quarterly Review* 64, no. 4 (1988): 686–694; Thomas Jefferson, *The Works of Thomas Jefferson*, Federal Edition (New York: G. P. Putnam's Sons, 1904–1905). II "inscription for an african slave": 1.

18. All of Washington's accounts are online: http://memory.loc.gov/ammem /gwhtml/gwseries5.html.

19. Previts and Merino, *A History of Accountancy in the United States*, 46; Jack Rakove, *Revolutionaries: A New History of the Invention of America* (New York: Houghton Mifflin Harcourt, 2010), 233.

20. Marvin Kitman, *George Washington's Expense Account* (New York: Grove Press, 1970), 15.

21. Facsimile of the *Accounts of G. Washington with the United States, Commencing June 1775, and Ending June 1783, Comprehending a Space of 8 Years* (Washington, DC: Treasury Department, 1833), 65–66.

22. Ibid., 5–6; Kitman, *George Washington's Expense Account*, 127–129, 276.

23. Thomas K. McCraw, *The Founders and Finance: How Hamilton, Gallatin, and Other Immigrants Forged a New Economy* (Cambridge, MA: Harvard University Press, 2012), 65–66.

24. Michael P. Schoderbek, "Robert Morris and Reporting for the Treasury Under the U.S. Continental Congress," *Accounting Historians Journal* 26, no. 2 (1999): 5–7.

25. Ibid., 7–8; Charles Rappleye, *Robert Morris: Financier of the American Revolution* (New York: Simon and Schuster, 2010), 231.

26. Rappleye, *Robert Morris*, 234; Schoderbek, "Robert Morris and Reporting for the Treasury Under the U.S. Continental Congress," 10–11.

27. Schoderbek, "Robert Morris and Reporting for the Treasury Under the U.S. Continental Congress," 12.

28. Ibid., 16–17.

29. Robert Morris, *A State of the Receipts and Expenditures of Public Monies upon Warrants from the Superintendent of Finance, from the 1st of January, 1782, to the 1st of January 1783*. Cited in Schoderbek, "Robert Morris and Reporting for the Treasury Under the U.S. Continental Congress," 18, 28.

30. Quotations from McCraw, *The Founders and Finance*, 16.

31. Ibid., 17–18.

32. Ibid., 24, 54.

33. Jack Rackove, *Original Meanings: Politics and Ideas in the Making of the Constitution* (New York: Vintage Books, 1997), 236.

34. Ron Chernow, *Alexander Hamilton* (New York: Penguin Books, 2004), 249.

35. Albert Gallatin, the Genevan one-time French tutor at Harvard and longest serving secretary of the Treasury in U.S. history wrote his own detailed *Sketch of the Finances of the United States* in 1796; *Journal of the First Session of the Second House of Representatives of the Commonwealth of Pennsylvania* (Philadelphia: Francis Bailey and Thomas Lang, 1791), last two pages of "Appendix"; John Nicholson, *Accounts of Pennsylvania* (Philadelphia: Comptroller-General's Office, 1785), 1 of the "Advertisement."

Chapter 11

1. Lady Holland, *A Memoir of the Reverend Sydney Smith* (London: Longman, Brown, Green and Longmans, 1855) 2:215.

2. Hugh Coombs, John Edwards, and Hugh Greener, eds., *Double-Entry Bookkeeping in British Central Government, 1822–1856* (London: Routledge, 1997), 3–5.

3. John Bowring, *Report on the Public Accounts of the Netherlands* (London: House of Commons, 1832); Nikitin, "The Birth of a Modern Public Sector Accounting System in France and Britain, 90. Quotations from John Bowring, *Report of the Public Accounts of France to the Right Honorable the Lords Commissioners of His Majesty's Treasury* (London: House of Commons, 1831), 3–7.

4. Oliver Evans, "Steamboats and Steam Wagons," *Hazard's Register of Pennsylvania* 16 (July–January 1836): 12.

5. Hobsbawm, *Industry and Empire*, 88, 93.

6. Previts and Merino, *A History of Accountancy in the United States*, 69, 110, 134; Alfred D. Chandler, *The Visible Hand: The Managerial Revolution in American Business* (Cambridge, MA: Harvard University Press, 1977), 122.

7. Theodore M. Porter, *Trust in Numbers: The Pursuit of Objectivity in Science and Public Life* (Princeton, NJ: Princeton University Press, 1995), 60.

8. Ibid., 87–88.

9. Chandler, *The Visible Hand*, 11, 110; Vanessa Ogle, *Contesting Time: The Global Struggle for Uniformity and Its Unintended Consequences, 1870s–1940s* (Cambridge, MA: Harvard University Press, forthcoming).

10. Chandler, *The Visible Hand*, 110–112; Previts and Merino, *A History of Accountancy in the United States*, 99.

11. Drew quotation from Previts and Merino, *A History of Accountancy in the United States*, 112; Mark Twain, Letter to *The San Francisco Alta California*, May 26, 1867.

12. "Reports of Cases Decided on All the Courts of Equity and Common Law in Ireland for the Year 1855," *The Irish Jurist* 1 (1856): 386–387; *Times of London*, February 18, 1856; Dickens quotation from *The Dictionary of National Biography*, ed. Sydney Lee (New York: Macmillan, 1897), 50:103.

13. Brown, *A History of Accounting and Accountants*, chaps. 3–4; Previts and Merino, *A History of Accountancy in the United States*, 69.

14. Brown, *A History of Accounting and Accountants*, 285.

15. David Grayson Allen and Kathleen McDermott, *Accounting for Success: A History of Price Waterhouse in America 1890–1990* (Cambridge, MA: Harvard Business School Press, 1993), 4; Previts and Merino, *A History of Accountancy in the United States*, 99; Porter, *Trust in Numbers*, 91, 103.

16. Allen and McDermott, *Accounting for Success*, 14, 34.

17. John Moody, *How to Analyze Railroad Reports* (New York: Analyses, 1912), 18–21; Previts and Merino, *A History of Accountancy in the United States*, 216.

18. Previts and Merino, *A History of Accountancy in the United States*, 157.

19. Ibid., 116–117.

20. Ibid., 98.

21. Ibid., 132; D. A. Keister, "The Public Accountant," *The Book-Keeper* 8, no. 6 (1896): 21–23.

22. Charles Waldo Haskins, *Business Education and Accountancy* (New York: Harper & Brothers, 1904), 32, 54.

23. Charles Waldo Haskins, *How to Keep Household Accounts: A Manual of Family Accounts* (New York: Harper & Brothers, 1903), v, 13–14.

Chapter 12

1. Honoré de Balzac, *L'Interdiction* (Paris: Éditions Garnier Frères, 1964), 37.

2. Charles Dickens, *A Christmas Carol* (Clayton, DE: Prestwick House, 2010), 21.

3. Charles Dickens, *Little Dorrit*, ed. by Peter Preston (Ware, UK: Wordsworth Editions, 1996), 102.

4. Henry David Thoreau, *Walden or Life in the Woods* (Mansfield Centre, CT: Martino, 2009), 26.

5. Ibid., 17, 28.

6. Amanda Vickerey, "His and Hers: Gender, Consumption and Household Accounting in Eighteenth-Century England," *Past and Present* 1, Supplement 1 (2006): 12–38.

7. Porter, *Trust in Numbers*, 17–30.

8. Thomas Malthus, *An Essay on the Principle of Population* (New York: Oxford University Press, 1999), 61.

9. Janet Browne, "The Natural Economy of Households: Charles Darwin's Account Books," in *Aurora Torealis: Studies in the History of Science and Ideas in the Honor Tore Frängsmyr*, ed. Marco Beretta, Karl Grandin, and Svante Lindqvist (Sagamore Beach, MA: Watson, 2008), 104.

10. The questionnaire is reproduced in Francis Darwin, ed., *The Life and Letters of Charles Darwin* (London, 1887), 3:178–179. All citations come from it.

11. Browne, "The Natural Economy of Households," 88–99.

12. Ibid., 92–94.

13. Ibid., 97; Charles Darwin, *The Descent of Man, and Selection in Relation to Sex* (London: John Murray, 1871), 1:167–182.

14. Joseph Conrad, *Heart of Darkness*, ed. Ross C. Murfin (Boston: Bedford/St. Martin's, 1989), 33.

15. Rosita S. Chen and Sheng-Der Pan, "Frederick Winslow Taylor's Contributions to Cost Accounting," *Accounting Historians Journal* 7, no. 2 (1980): 2.

16. Daniel J. Boorstin, *The Americans: The Democratic Experience* (New York: Vintage Books, 1973).

17. Cited by John Huer, *Auschwitz USA* (Lanham, MD: Hamilton Books, 2010), 31.

18. Alfred C. Mierzejewski, *Most Valuable Asset of the Reich: A History of the German National Railway* (Chapel Hill: University of North Carolina Press, 2000), 2:20–21.

Chapter 13

1. Allen and McDermott, *Accounting for Success*, 32–37.

2. Ibid., 31.

3. Ibid., 45, 61.

4. William Z. Ripley, "Stop, Look, Listen! The Shareholder's Right to Adequate Information," *Atlantic Monthly*, January 1, 1926.

5. Allen and McDermott, *Accounting for Success*, 67.

6. Ibid., 64; John Kenneth Galbraith, *The Great Crash of 1929* (New York: Houghton Mifflin Harcourt, 2000), 64.

7. Previts and Merino, *A History of Accountancy in the United States*, 275.

8. Securities Act of 1933, www.sec.gov/about/laws/sa33.pdf, section 19; Stephen A. Zeff, "The SEC Rules Historical Cost Accounting: 1934 to the 1970s," *Accounting and Business Research* 37, suppl. 1 (2007): 1; Mike Brewster, *Unaccountable: How the Accounting Profession Forfeited a Public Trust* (Hoboken, NJ: John Wiley & Sons, 2003), 81.

9. Allen and McDermott, *Accounting for Success*, 71; Previts and Merino, *A History of Accountancy in the United States*, 70, 270.

10. Kees Camfferman and Stephen A. Zeff, *Financial Reporting and Global Capital Markets: A History of the International Accounting Standards Committee 1973–2000* (Oxford: Oxford University Press, 2006), 21–24; "The Norwalk Agreement," www.fasb.org/news/memorandum.pdf.

11. Barbara Ley Toffler, *Final Accounting: Ambition, Greed and the Fall of Arthur Andersen* (New York: Crown, 2003), 18; Robert A. G. Monks and Nell Minow, *Corporate Governance* (New York: John Wiley & Sons, 2008), 563.

12. Toffler, *Final Accounting*, 28, 41.

13. Ibid., 14.

14. Allen and McDermott, *Accounting for Success*, 171–172.

15. Ibid., 173.

16. Ibid., 175–181.

17. Philip G. Joyce, *Congressional Budget Office: Honest Numbers, Power, and Policymaking* (Washington, DC: Georgetown University Press, 2011), 16–17.

18. Richard Cantor and Frank Packer, "Sovereign Credit Ratings," *Current Issues in Economics and Finance of the Federal Reserve Board of New York* 1, no. 3 (1995): 41.

19. Allen and McDermott, *Accounting for Success*, 181.

20. Mark Stevens, *The Big Six: The Selling Out of America's Accounting Firms* (New York: Simon and Schuster, 19991), 28.

21. Richard Melcher, "Where Are the Accountants?" *BusinessWeek*, October 5, 1998.

22. Toffler, *Final Accounting*, 203.

23. Ibid., 138.

24. William Jefferson Clinton, "Statement on Signing the Gramm-Leach-Bliley, Act November 12, 1999," www.presidency.ucsb.edu/ws/?pid=56922.

25. For the SEC's charges against Andersen in relation to WorldCom and Waste Management, see www.sec.gov/litigation/complaints/comp17753.htm and www.sec.gov/litigation/litreleases/lr17039.htm.

26. Toffler, *Final Accounting*, 217.

27. Ibid., 213.

28. Elizabeth Bumiller, "Bush Signs Bill Aimed at Fraud in Corporations," *New York Times*, July 31, 2002. Note also that in 2002, President Bush cut SEC funding by 27 percent, causing its chairman, Harvey Pitt, to publicly warn that "the administration's level of financing will not allow it to undertake important initiatives": Stephen Labaton, "Bush Tries to Shrink S.E.C. Raise Intended for Corporate Cleanup," *New York Times*, October 19, 2002.

29. Adam Jones, "Auditors Criticized for Role in Financial Crisis," *Financial Times*, March 30, 2011; Adam Jones, "Big Four Rivals Welcome Audit Shake-up," *Financial Times*, February 2, 2013.

30. Andrew Ross Sorkin, "Realities Behind Prosecuting Big Banks," *New York Times*, March 11, 2013.

31. Matt Taibbi, "The People vs. Goldman Sachs," *Rolling Stone*, May 11, 2011; "Government Accounting Book-Cooking Guide: The Public Sector Has Too Much Freedom to Dress Up the Accounts," *Economist*, April 7, 2012; Peter J. Henning, "Justice Department Again Signals Interest to Pursue Financial Crisis Cases," *New York Times*, August 26, 2013.

Conclusion

1. Dickens, *Little Dorrit*, 107.

2. "Government Accounting Book-Cooking Guide: The Public Sector Has Too Much Freedom to Dress Up the Accounts," *Economist*, April 7, 2012.

3. "An Aberrant Abacus: Coming to Terms with China's Untrustworthy Numbers," *Economist*, May 1, 2008; Timothy Irwin, "Accounting Devices and Fiscal Illusions," *IMF Staff Discussion Note*, March 28, 2012, www.imf.org /external/pubs/ft/sdn/2012/sdn1202.pdf; Alan J. Blinder, "Financial Collapse: A Ten-Step Recovery Plan," *New York Times*, January 19, 2013.

4. Jean-Baptiste Say, *Traité d'économie politique ou simple exposition de la manière dont se forment, se distribuent et se composent les richesses* (Paris: Crapalet, 1803).

BIBLIOGRAPHY

Aho, J. A. *Confession and Bookkeeping: The Religious, Moral, and Rhetorical Roots of Modern Accounting.* Albany: State University of New York Press, 2005.

Alberti, Leon Battista. *The Family in Renaissance Florence.* Book 3. Translated by Renée Neu Watkins. Long Grove, IL: Waveland Press, 1994.

Alcott, Louisa May. *Little Women.* Boston: Roberts Brothers, 1868.

Allen, David Grayson, and Kathleen McDermott. *Accounting for Success: A History of Price Waterhouse in America 1890–1990.* Cambridge, MA: Harvard Business School Press, 1993.

Antoine, Michel. *Le coeur de l'État.* Paris: Fayard, 2003.

Arcelli, Federico. *Il banchiere del Papa: Antonio della Casa, mercante e banchiere a Roma, 1438–1440.* Soveria Manelli, Italy: Rubbettino Editore, 2001.

Aristotle. *The Athenian Constitution.* Translated by P. J. Rhodes. London: Penguin Books, 1984.

———. *Nichomachean Ethics.* Translated by H. Rackham. Cambridge, MA: Loeb Classical Library, 1926.

Ashton, T. S. *Economic Fluctuations in England, 1700–1800.* Oxford: Oxford University Press, 1959.

Astbury, Raymond. "The Renewal of the Licensing Act in 1693 and Its Lapse in 1695." *The Library* 5, no. 4 (1978): 296–322.

Augéard, Jacques-Mathieu. *Letter from Monsieur Turgot to Monsieur Necker.* 1780.

———. *Mémoires Sécrets.* Paris: Plon, 1866.

Augustus. *Res gestae divi Augusti.* Translated by P. A. Brunt and J. M. Moore. Oxford: Oxford University Press, 1973.

Authentic Copy of the New Constitution of France, Adopted by the National Convention, June 23, 1793. London: J. Debrett, 1793.

Bachaumont, Louis-Petit de. *Mémoires secrets pour servir à l'histoire de la République des lettres en France.* 36 vols. London: John Adamson, 1777–1787.

Bailly, M. A. *Histoire financière de la France depuis l'origine de la Monarchie jusqu'à la fin de 1786. Un tableau général des anciennes impositions et un état des recettes et des dépenses du trésor royal à la même époque.* 2 vols. Paris: Moutardier, 1830.

Bailyn, Bernard. *The New England Merchants in the Seventeenth Century.* New York: Harper Torchbook, 1964.

Baker, Keith Michael. "Politics and Social Science in Eighteenth-Century France: The 'Société de 1789.'" In *French Government and Society 1500–1850: Essays in Memory of Alfred Cobban*, edited by J. F. Bosher, 208–230. London: Athlone Press, 1973.

Balzac, Honoré de. *L'Interdiction.* Paris: Éditions Garnier Frères, 1964.

Barlaeus, Caspar. *Marie de Medicis entrant dans l'Amsterdam; ou Histoire de la reception faicte à la Reyne Mère du Roy très-Chrestien, par les Bourgmaistres et Bourgeoisie de la Ville d'Amsterdam.* Amsterdam: Jean & Corneille Blaeu, 1638.

Bautier, Robert-Henri. "Chancellerie et culture au moyen age." In vol. 1 of *Chartes, sceaux et chancelleries: Études de diplomatique et de sigillographie médiévales*, edited by Robert-Henri Bautier, 47–75. Paris: École des Chartes, 1990.

Baxter, Douglas Clark. *Servants of the Sword: French Intendants of the Army 1630–1670.* Urbana: University of Illinois Press, 1976.

Baxter, W. T. "Accounting in Colonial America." In *Studies in the History of Accounting*, edited by Charles Littleton and Basil S. Yamey, 272–287. New York: Arno Press, 1978.

Bentham, Jeremy. *An Introduction to the Principles of Morals and Legislation.* 1789.

Bentley, Richard. *Sermons Preached at Boyle's Lecture.* Edited by Alexander Dyce. London: Francis Macpherson, 1838.

Bergin, J. A. "Cardinal Mazarin and His Benefices." *French History* 1, no. 1 (1987): 3–26.

Binney, J. E. D. *British Public Finance and Administration 1774–92.* Oxford: Oxford University Press, 1958.

Black, Jeremy. *Robert Walpole and the Nature of Politics in Early Eighteenth Century England.* New York: St. Martin's Press, 1990.

Blinder, Alan J. "Financial Collapse: A Ten-Step Recovery Plan." *New York Times*, January 19, 2013.

Bocaccio, Giovanni. *The Decameron.* Translated by J. M. Rigg. London: A. H. Bullen, 1903.

Boeckh, Augustus. *The Public Economy of Athens.* London: John W. Parker, 1842.

Boislisle, Arthur André Gabriel Michel de, and Pierre de Brotonne, eds. *Correspondance des Contrôleurs Généraux des Finances.* 3 vols. Paris: Imprimérie Nationale, 1874.

Bondi, Yuri. "Schumpeter's Economic Theory and the Dynamic Accounting View of the Firm: Neglected Pages from the *Theory of Economic Development*." *Economy and Society* 37, no. 4 (2008): 525–547.

Bonney, Richard. "Vindication of the Fronde? The Cost of Louis XIV's Versailles Building Programme." *French History* 21, no. 2 (2006): 205–225.

Boorstin, Daniel J. *The Americans: The Democratic Experience.* New York: Vintage Books, 1973.

Bosher, J. F. *French Finances 1770–1795: From Business to Bureaucracy.* Cambridge: Cambridge University Press, 1970.

Bowring, John. *Report of the Public Accounts of France to the Right Honorable the Lords Commissioners of His Majesty's Treasury.* London: House of Commons, 1831.

———. *Report on the Public Accounts of the Netherlands.* London: House of Commons, 1832.

Braudel, Fernand. *Civilisation materielle, économie et capitalisme XVe–XVIIIe siècle.* 2 vols. Paris: Armand Colin, 1979.

Brewer, John. *The Sinews of Power: War, Money and the English State 1688–1783.* New York: Alfred A. Knopf, 1989.

Brewster, Mike. *Unaccountable: How the Accounting Profession Forfeited a Public Trust.* Hoboken, NJ: John Wiley & Sons, 2003.

Brisco, Norris Arthur. *The Economic Policy of Robert Walpole.* New York: Columbia University Press, 1907.

Brown, Richard. *A History of Accounting and Accountants.* Edinburgh: T. C. & E. C. Jack, 1905.

Browne, Janet. "The Natural Economy of Households: Charles Darwin's Account Books." In *Aurora Torealis: Studies in the History of Science and Ideas in the Honor Tore Frängsmyr,* edited by Marco Beretta, Karl Grandin, and Svante Lindqvist, 87–110. Sagamore Beach, MA: Watson, 2008.

Bumiller, Elizabeth. "Bush Signs Bill Aimed at Fraud in Corporations." *New York Times,* July 31, 2002.

Burke, Edmund. *Reflections on the French Revolution.* In *Readings in Western Civilization: The Old Regime and the French Revolution,* edited by Keith Michael Baker. Chicago: University of Chicago Press, 1987.

Burke, Peter. *The Fortunes of the Courtier: The European Reception of Castiglione's Cortegiano.* Cambridge: Polity Press, 1995.

———. *A Social History of Knowledge from Gutenberg to Diderot.* Cambridge: Polity Press, 2000.

Burnand, Léonard. *Les Pamphlets contre Necker. Médias et imginaire politique au XVIIIe siècle.* Paris: Éditions Classiques Garnier, 2009.

Burté, Antoine. *Pour L'Assemblée Nationale. Observations rapides sur les conditions d'eligibilité des Commissaires de la Comptabilité.* Paris: Imprimérie Nationale, 1792.

———. "Rapid Observations on the Conditions of Eligibility of the Commissars of Accountability." 1792. University of Pennsylvania, Special Collections Library, Maclure 735:5.

Bywater, M. F., and B. S. Yamey. *Historic Accounting Literature: A Companion Guide.* London: Scholar Press, 1982.

Calabria, Antonio. *The Cost of Empire: The Finances of the Kingdom of Naples in the Time of the Spanish Rule.* Cambridge: Cambridge University Press, 1991.

Camfferman, Kees, and Stephen A. Zeff. *Financial Reporting and Global Capital Markets: A History of the International Accounting Standards Committee 1973–2000.* Oxford: Oxford University Press, 2006.

Cantor, Richard, and Frank Packer. "Sovereign Credit Ratings." *Current Issues in Economics and Finance of the Federal Reserve Board of New York* 1, no. 3 (1995): 37–54.

Carande, Ramon. *Carlos V y sus banqueros. Los caminos del oro y de la plata (Deuda exterior y tesoros ultramarinos).* Madrid: Sociedad de Estudios y Publicaciones, 1967.

Carmona, Salvador, and Mahmous Ezzamel. "Ancient Accounting." In *The Routledge Companion to Accounting History*, edited by John Richard Edwards and Stephen P. Walker. Oxford: Routledge, 2009.

Carruthers, Bruce G., and Wendy Nelson Espeland. "Accounting for Rationality: Double-Entry Bookkeeping and the Rhetoric of Economic Rationality." *American Journal of Sociology* 97, no. 1 (1991): 30–67.

Carswell, John. *The South Sea Bubble.* Stanford, CA: Stanford University Press, 1960.

Carter, F. E. L., and D. E. Greenway. *Dialogus de Scaccario (the Course of the Exchequer), and Constitutio Domus Regis (The Establishment of the Royal Household).* London: Charles Johnson, 1950.

Castiglione, Baldesar. *The Book of the Courtier.* Translated and edited by George Bull. London: Penguin Books, 1976.

Cervantes Saavedra, Miguel de. *The History of don Quixote de la Mancha.* London: James Burns, 1847.

Chandler, Alfred D. *The Visible Hand: The Managerial Revolution in American Business.* Cambridge, MA: Harvard University Press, 1977.

Chatfield, Michael. *A History of Accounting Thought.* Hisdale, IL: Dryden Press, 1974.

Chen, Rosita S., and Sheng-Der Pan. "Frederick Winslow Taylor's Contributions to Cost Accounting." *The Accounting Historians Journal* 7, no. 2 (1980): 1–22.

Chernow, Ron. *Alexander Hamilton.* New York: Penguin Books, 2004.

Chéruel, Pierre-Adolphe, ed. *Mémoires sur la vie publique et privée de Fouquet, Surintendant des finances. D'après ses lettres et des pièces inédites conservées à la Bibliothèque Impériale.* 2 vols. Paris: Charpentier Éditeur, 1862.

Cicero. *The Orations of Marcus Tullius Cicero (Philippics).* Translated by C. D. Yonge. London: Henry J. Bohn, 1852.

Clanchy, M. T. *From Memory to Written Record: England 1066–1307.* London: Blackwell, 1979.

Clinton, William Jefferson. *Statement on Signing the Gramm–Leach–Bliley Act.* November 12, 1999. www.presidency.ucsb.edu/ws/?pid=56922.

Cohen, Patricia Cline. *A Calculating People: The Spread of Numeracy in Early America*. Chicago: University of Chicago Press, 1982.

Cohn, Ellen R. "The Printer at Passy." In *Benjamin Franklin in Search of a Better World*, edited by Page Talbott, 236–259. New Haven, CT: Yale University Press, 2005.

Colbert, Jean-Baptiste. *Abrégé des finances 1665*. Bnf. Ms. Fr. 6771, fols. 4 verso–7 recto.

———. *Abrégé des finances 1671*. Bnf. Ms. Fr. 6777, final "table."

———. *Lettres, instructions et mémoires*. Edited by Pierre Clement. 7 vols. Paris: Imprimerie Impériale, 1865.

———. *Receuil de Finances de Colbert*. Bnf. Ms. Fr. 7753.

Colbert 1619–1683. Paris: Ministère de la Culture, 1983.

Colinson, Robert. *Idea rationaria, or the Perfect Accomptant*. Edinburgh: David Lindsay, 1683.

Collection complette de tous les ouvrages pour et contre M. Necker, avec des notes critiques, politiques et secretes. 3 vols. Utrecht, 1782.

Colonna, Francesco. *Hypnerotomachia Poliphili*. Venice: Aldus Manutius, 1499.

Compte rendu par le Ministre de la Marine à l'Assemblée Nationale 31 Oct. 1791. Paris: Imprimérie Nationale, 1791. University of Pennsylvania, Special Collections Library, Maclure 974:19.

Cone, Carl B. "Richard Price and Pitt's Sinking Fund of 1786." *Economic History Review* 4, no. 2 (1951): 243–251.

Conrad, Joseph. *Heart of Darkness*. Edited by Ross C. Murfin. Boston: Bedford/St. Martin's, 1989.

Convention Nationale: Projet d'organisation du Bureau de Comptabilité. Paris: Par Ordre de la Convention Nationale, 1792. University of Pennsylvania, Special Collections Library, Maclure 1156:1.

Cook, Harold John. *Matters of Exchange: Commerce, Medicine, and Science in the Dutch Golden Age*. New Haven, CT: Yale University Press, 2007.

Coombs, Hugh, John Edwards, and Hugh Greener, eds. *Double-Entry Bookkeeping in British Central Government, 1822–1856*. London: Routledge, 1997.

Cosnac, Gabriel-Jules, comte de. *Mazarin et Colbert*. 2 vols. Paris: Plon, 1892.

Coxe, William. *Memoires of the Life and Administration of Sir Robert Walpole*. 4 vols. London: Longman, Hurst, Reese, Orme and Brown, 1816.

Dainville, François de. *L'éducation des jésuites XVI–XVIII siècles*. Edited by Marie-Madeleine Compère. Paris: Éditions de Minuit, 1978.

Dale, Richard. *The First Crash: Lessons from the South Sea Bubble*. Princeton, NJ: Princeton University Press, 2004.

Dante. *The Divine Comedy*. Translated by Allen Mandelbaum. 3 vols. Berkeley: University of California Press, 1981.

———. *The Inferno*. Translated by Robert Pinsky. New York: Farrar, Straus and Giroux, 1995.

Darnton, Robert. "The Memoirs of Lenoir, Lieutenant of Police of Paris, 1774–1785." *English Historical Review* 85, no. 336 (1970): 532–559.

———. "Trends in Radical Propaganda on the Eve of the French Revolution (1782–1788)." DPhil diss., Oxford University, 1964.

Darwin, Charles. *The Descent of Man, and Selection in Relation to Sex.* Vol. 1. London: John Murray, 1871.

———. *On the Origin of the Species.* London, 1859.

Darwin, Francis, ed. *The Life and Letters of Charles Darwin.* Vol. 3. London, 1887.

Davenant, Charles. *Discourses on the Publick Revenues.* 2 vols. London: James Knapton, 1698.

Davids, Karel. "The Bookkeepers Tale: Learning Merchant Skills in the Northern Netherlands in the Sixteenth Century." In *Education and Learning in the Netherlands 1400–1600. Essays in Honour of Hilde de Ridder-Symeons*, edited by Koen Goodriaan, Jaap van Moolenbroek, and Ad Tervoort, 235–251. Leiden: Brill, 2004.

De Calonne, Vicomte, Charles Alexandre. *Réponse de M. de Calonne à l'Écrit de M. Necker; contenant l'Examen des comptes de la situation des Finances Rendus en 1774, 1776, 1781, 1783 & 1787 avec des Observations sur les Résultats de l'Assemblée des Notables.* London: T. Spilsbury, 1788.

Declaration du Roy concernant la tenue des Registres Journaux. Versailles: October 4, 1723.

De Cosnac, Comte, Gabriel-Jules. *Mazarin et Colbert.* 2 vols. Paris: Plon, 1892.

De Créquy, Marquise, Renée-Caroline. *Souvenirs de 1710 à 1803.* 10 vols. Paris: Garnier Frères, 1873.

De Diego, José Luis Rodríguez, ed. *Instrucción para el gobierno del archivo de Simancas (año 1588).* Madrid: Dirección General de Bellas Artes y Archivos, 1989.

———. "La formación del Archivo de Simancas en el siglo xvi. Función y orden interno." In *El libro antiguo español IV*, edited by Maria Luisa López Vidriero and Pedro M. Cátedra. Salamanca: Ediciones Universidad de Salamanca, 1998.

De Diego, José Luis Rodríguez, and Francisco Javier Alvarez Pinedo. *Los Archivos de Simancas.* Madrid: Lunwerg Editores, 1993.

Defoe, Daniel. *The Complete English Tradesman.* Edinburgh, 1839.

———. *The Life and Strange Surprizing Adventures of Robinson Crusoe.* London: Taylor, 1719.

De Jongh, J. Matthijs. "Shareholder Activism at the Dutch East India Company in 1622: *Redde Rationem Villicationis Tuae! Give an Account of Your Stewardship!*" Paper presented at the Conference on the Origins and History of Shareholder Advocacy, Yale School of Management, Millstein

Center for Corporate Governance and Performance, November 6 and 7, 2009.

De la Court, Pieter, and Jan de Witt. *The True Interest and Political Maxims of the Republic of Holland*. London: John Campbell, 1746.

Della Mirandola, Giovanni Pico. *On The Dignity of Man*. Translated by Charles Glenn Wallis, Paul J. W. Miller, and Douglas Carmichael. Indianapolis: Hackett, 1998.

Delumeau, Jean. *Sin and Fear: The Emergence of a Western Guilt Culture 13th–18th Centuries*. Translated by Eric Nicholson. New York: St. Martin's Press, 1990.

Deringer, William Peter. "Calculated Values: The Politics and Epistemology of Economic Numbers in Britain, 1688–1738." PhD diss., Princeton University, 2012.

De Roover, Florence Edler. "Francesco Sassetti and the Downfall of the Medici Banking House." *Bulletin of the Business Historical Society* 17, no. 4 (1943): 65–80.

De Roover, Raymond. "Aux origines d'une technique intellectuelle. La formation et l'expansion de la comptabilité à partie double." *Annales d'histoire économique et sociale* 9, no. 45 (1937): 270–298.

―――. "The Development of Accounting Prior to Luca Pacioli." In *Business, Banking and Economic Thought in Late Medieval and Early Modern Europe: Selected Studies of Raymond de Roover*, edited by Julius Kirschner, 119–180. Chicago: University of Chicago Press, 1974.

―――. "The Development of Accounting Prior to Luca Pacioli According to the Account-Books of Medieval Merchants." In *Studies in the History of Accounting*, edited by A. C. Littleton and B. S. Yamey, 114–174. London: Richard D. Irwin, 1956.

―――. *Money, Banking and Credit in Medieval Bruges*. Cambridge, MA: The Medieval Academy of America, 1948.

―――. *The Rise and Decline of the Medici Bank 1397–1494*. Cambridge, MA: Harvard University Press, 1963.

Desan, Philippe. *L'imaginaire économiqe de la Renaissance*. Paris: Presses Université de Paris-Sorbonne, 2002.

De Solórzano, Bartolomé Salvador. *Libro de Caxa y Manual de cuentas de Mercaderes, y otras personas, con la declaracion dellos*. Madrid: Pedro Madrigal, 1590.

Desrosières, Alain. *The Politics of Large Numbers: A History of Statistical Reasoning*. Translated by Camille Nash. Cambridge, MA: Harvard University Press, 1998.

Dessert, Daniel. *Argent, pouvoir, et société au Grand Siècle*. Paris: Fayard, 1984.

―――. *Colbert ou le serpent venimeux*. Paris: Éditions Complexe, 2000.

Dessert, Daniel, and Jean-Louis Journet. "Le lobby Colbert." *Annales* 30, no. 6 (1975): 1303–1329.

De Vergennes, Vicomte, Charles Alexandre. "Lettre de M. le marquis de Caraccioli à M. d'Alembert." In *Collection complette de tous les ouvrages pour et contre M. Necker, avec des notes critiques, politiques et secretes*. Vol. 3, 42–64. Utrecht, 1782.

Devreese, J. T., and G. Vanden Berghe, *"Magic Is No Magic," The Wonderful World of Simon Stevin*. Boston: WIT Press, 2008.

De Vries, Jan. "The Economic Crisis of the Seventeenth Century After Fifty Years." *Journal of Interdisciplinary History* 40, no. 2 (2009): 151–194.

———. "The Industrial Revolution and the Industrious Revolution." *Journal of Economic History* 54, no. 2 (1994): 249–270.

De Vries, Jan, and Ad van der Woude. *The First Modern Economy: Success, Failure, and Perseverance of the Dutch Economy, 1500–1815*. Cambridge: Cambridge University Press, 1997.

De Witt, Jan. *Elementa curvarum linearum liber primus*. Translated and edited by Albert W. Grootendorst and Miente Bakker. New York: Springer Verlag, 2000.

De Witt, Johan. *Treatise on Life Annuities*. 1671. www.stat.ucla.edu/history/dewitt.pdf.

Dickens, Charles. *A Christmas Carol*. Clayton, DE: Prestwick House, 2010.

———. *Little Dorrit*. Edited by Peter Preston. Ware, UK: Wordsworth Editions, 1996.

Dickinson, Arthur Lowes. *Accounting Practice and Procedure*. New York: Ronald Press, 1918.

Dickson, Peter G. M. *The Financial Revolution in England: A Study in the Development of Public Credit 1688–1756*. London: Macmillan, 1967.

Dictionary of National Biography. Edited by Sydney Lee. Vol. 50. London: Smith, Elder, 1897.

Dobija, Dorota. *Early Evolution of Corporate Control and Auditing: The British East India Company (1600–1643 CE)*. July 16, 2011. http://ssrn.com/abstract=1886945.

Dolan, Brian. *Josiah Wedgwood: Entrepreneur to the Enlightenment*. London: Harper Perennial, 2005.

Donoso Anes, Rafael. "Accounting for the Estates of Deceased Travellers: An Example of Early Spanish Double-Entry Bookkeeping." *Accounting History* 7, no. 1 (2002): 80–99.

———. "The Casa de la Contratación de Indias and the Application of the Double Entry Bookkeeping to the Sale of Precious Metals in Spain 1557–83." *Accounting, Business and Financial History* 4, no. 1 (1994): 83–98.

———. *Una Contribución a la Historia de la Contabilidad. Análisis de las Práticas Contables Desarrolladas por la Tesorería de la Casa de la Contratación de la Indias en Sevilla, 1503–1717*. Seville: Universidad de Sevilla, 1996.

Durham, John W. "The Introduction of 'Arabic' Numerals in European Accounting." *Accounting Historians Journal* 19, no. 2 (1992): 25–55.

The Economist. "An Aberrant Abacus: Coming to Terms with China's Untrustworthy Numbers," May 1, 2008.

———. "Government Accounting Book-Cooking Guide: The Public Sector Has Too Much Freedom to Dress Up the Accounts," April 7, 2012.

Edelstein, Dan. *The Terror of Natural Right: Republicanism, the State of Nature and the French Revolution.* Chicago: University of Chicago Press, 2009.

Edwards, John Richard. "Teaching 'Merchants Accompts' in Britain During the Early Modern Period." *Cardiff Business School Working Paper Series in Accounting and Finance* A2009/2 (2009): 1–38.

Edwards, John Richard, and Stephen P. Walker, eds. *The Routledge Companion to Accounting History.* London: Routledge, 2009.

Egret, Jean. *Necker, ministre de Louis XVI 1776–1790.* Paris: Honoré Champion, 1975.

———. *Parlement de Dauphiné et les affaires publiques dans la deuxième moitié du XVIIIe siècle.* 2 vols. Paris: B. Arthaud, 1942.

Erasmus, Desiderius. *The Education of a Christian Prince.* Edited and translated by Lisa Jardine. Cambridge: Cambridge University Press, 1997.

Evans, Oliver. "Steamboats and Steam Wagons." *Hazard's Register of Pennsylvania* 16 (July–January 1836): 12.

The Federalist (The Gideon Edition). Edited by George W. Carey and James McClellan. Indianapolis, IN: Liberty Fund, 2001.

Félix, Joël. *Finances et politiques au siècle des Lumières. Le ministère L'Averdy, 1763–1768.* Paris: Comité pour l'Histoire Économique et Financière de la France, 1999.

Ficino, Marsilio. *Epistle to Giovanni Rucellai.* In *The Renewal of Pagan Antiquity: Contributions to the Cultural History of the European Renaissance*, edited by Aby Warburg and translated by David Britt, 222–264. Los Angeles: Getty Research Institute, 1999.

Fielding, Henry. *Shamela.* Edited by Jack Lynch. http://andromeda.rutgers.edu/~jlynch/Texts/shamela.html.

Financial Accounting Standards Board and the International Accounting Standards Board. *The Norwalk Agreement.* Norwalk, CT, 2002. www.fasb.org/news/memorandum.pdf.

Finley, Moses I. *The Ancient Economy.* Berkeley: University of California Press, 1973.

Franklin, Benjamin. *The Autobiography and Other Writings on Politics, Economics and Virtue.* Edited by Alan Houston. Cambridge: Cambridge University Press, 2004.

———. *Directions to the Deputy Post-Masters, for Keeping Their Accounts.* Broadside, Philadelphia, 1753. Pennsylvania Historical Society, Ab [1775].

———. *Instructions Given by Benjamin Franklin, and William Hunter, Esquires, His Majesty's Deputy Post-Masters General of All his Dominions on the Continent of North America.* University of Pennsylvania Library, 1753.

————. *The Ledger of Doctor Benjamin Franklin, Postmaster General, 1776. A Facsimile of the Original Manuscript Now on File on the Records of the Post Office Department of the United States.* Washington, DC, 1865.

————. *Papers of Franklin.* Edited by Leonard W. Lebaree and Whitfield Bell Jr. 40 vols. New Haven, CT: Yale University Press, 1960.

————. *The Writings of Benjamin Franklin.* Edited by Albert Henry Smyth. 10 vols. New York: Macmillan, 1907.

Franklin, Benjamin, and George Simpson Eddy. "Account Book of Benjamin Franklin Kept by Him During His First Mission to England as Provincial Agent 1757–1762." *Pennsylvania Magazine of History and Biography* 55, no. 2 (1931): 97–133.

Fritschy, Wantje. "The Efficiency of Taxation in Holland." In *The Political Economy of the Dutch Republic*, edited by Oscar Gelderblom. London: Ashgate, 2009.

————. "'A Financial Revolution' Reconsidered: Public Finance in Holland During the Dutch Revolt 1568–1648." *Economic History Review* 56, no. 1 (2003): 57–89.

————. "Three Centuries of Urban and Provincial Public Debt: Amsterdam and Holland." In *Urban Public Debts: Urban Government and the Market for Annuities in Western Europe (14th–18th Centuries)*, edited by M. Boone, K. Davids, and P. Janssens, 75–92. Turnhout: Brepols, 2003.

Galbraith, John Kenneth. *The Great Crash of 1929.* New York: Houghton, Mifflin, Harcourt, 2000.

Gallatin, Albert. *Sketch of the Finances of the United States.* New York, 1796.

Geijsbeek, John B. *Ancient Double-Entry Bookkeeping: Luca Pacioli's Treatise 1494.* Denver, 1914.

Gelderblom, Oscar. "The Governance of Early Modern Trade: The Case of Hans Thijs, 1556–1611." *Enterprise and Society* 4, no. 4 (2003): 606–639.

Gibbon, Edward. *History of the Decline and Fall of the Roman Empire.* 4th ed. 6 vols. London: W. and T. Cadell, 1781–1788.

Glamann, Kristof. *Dutch Asiatic Trade 1620–1740.* The Hague: Martinus Nijhof, 1981.

Goldberg, Louis. *Journey into Accounting Thought.* Edited by Stewart A. Leech. London: Routledge, 2001.

Goodman, David C. *Power and Penury: Government, Technology and Science in Philip II's Spain.* Cambridge: Cambridge University Press, 1988.

Grafton, Anthony. *Leon Battista Alberti: Master Builder of the Renaissance.* London: Allen Lane/Penguin Press, 2000.

Graves, Robert. *I Claudius.* London: Arthur Barker, 1934.

Grendler, Paul F. *Schooling in Renaissance Italy: Literacy and Learning 130–1600.* Baltimore: Johns Hopkins University Press, 1989.

Gutkind, Curt S. *Cosimo de' Medici: Pater Patriae, 1389–1464.* Oxford: Clarendon Press, 1938.

Hall, Hubert. "The Sources for the History of Sir Robert Walpole's Financial Administration." *Transactions of the Royal Historical Society* 4, no. 1 (1910): 33–45.

Hamilton, Alexander. *The Papers of Alexander Hamilton*. Edited by Harold C. Syrett et al. 26 vols. New York: Columbia University Press, 1961–1979.

Hans, N. A. *New Trends in Education in the Eighteenth Century*. London: Routledge & Keegan Paul, 1951.

Harkness, Deborah. "Accounting for Science: How a Merchant Kept His Books in Elizabethan London." In *Self-Perception and Early Modern Capitalists*, edited by Margaret Jacob and Catherine Secretan, 205–228. London: Palgrave Macmillan, 2008.

Harris, Robert D. "Necker's Compte Rendu of 1781: A Reconsideration." *Journal of Modern History* 42, no. 2 (1970): 161–183.

Haskins, Charles Waldo. *Business Education and Accountancy*. New York: Harper & Brothers, 1904.

———. *How to Keep Household Accounts: A Manual of Family Accounts*. New York: Harper & Brothers, 1903.

Henning, Peter J. "Justice Department Again Signals Interest to Pursue Financial Crisis Cases." *New York Times*, August 26, 2013.

Hernández-Esteve, Esteban. "The Life of Bartolomé Salvador de Solórzano: Some Further Evidence." *Accounting Historians Journal* 1 (1989): 87–99.

———. "Pedro Luis de Torregrosa, primer contador del libro de Caxa de Felipe II: Introducción de la contabilidad por partida doble en la Real Hacienda de Castilla (1592)." *Revista de Historia Económica* 3, no. 2 (1985): 221–245.

Hobbes, Thomas. *Leviathan*. Edited by Richard Tuck. Cambridge: Cambridge University Press, 1996.

Hobsbawm, Eric. *Industry and Empire: The Birth of the Industrial Revolution*. New York: Free Press, 1998.

Holland, Saba, Lady. *A Memoir of the Reverend Sydney Smith*. 2 vols. London: Longman, Brown, Green and Longmans, 1855.

Hont, Istvan. "The Rhapsody of Public Debt: David Hume and Voluntary State Bankruptcy." In *Jealousy of Trade: International Competition and the Nation-State in Historical Perspective*, edited by Istvan Hont, 325–253. Cambridge, MA: Belknap Press of Harvard University Press, 2005.

Horn, Jeff. *The Path Not Taken: French Industrialization in the Age of Revolution*. Cambridge, MA: MIT Press, 2008.

Huer, John. *Auschwitz USA*. Lanham, MD: Hamilton Books, 2010.

Hume, David. "Of Public Credit." In *Essays, Moral, Political and Literary*. Vol. 2, *Political Discourses*. Edinburgh: Fleming, 1752.

Hutcheson, Archibald. *A Collection of Calculations and Remarks Relating to the South Sea Scheme & Stock, Which have been already Published with an Addition of Some Others, which have not been made Publick 'till Now*. London, 1720.

————. *Some Calculations and Remarks Relating to the Present State of the Public Debts and Funds*. London, 1718.

————. *Some Calculations Relating to the Proposals Made by the South Sea Company and the Bank of England, to the House of Commons*. London: Morphew, 1720.

The Irish Jurist: Reports of Cases Decided on All the Courts of Equity and Common Law in Ireland for the Year 1855. Dublin, 1849–1855.

Irwin, Timothy. "Accounting Devices and Fiscal Illusions." *IMF Staff Discussion Note*, March 28, 2012. www.imf.org/external/pubs/ft/sdn/2012/sdn1202 .pdf.

Jacob, Margaret C. "Commerce, Industry and the Laws of Newtonian Science: Weber Revisited and Revised." *Canadian Journal of History* 35, no. 2 (2000): 272–292.

————. *The Newtonians and the English Revolution 1689–1720*. Ithaca, NY: Cornell University Press, 1976.

————. *Scientific Culture and the Making of the Industrial West*. Oxford: Oxford University Press, 1997.

Jeannin, Pierre. *Merchants of the Sixteenth Century*. Translated by Paul Fittingoff. New York: Harper and Row, 1972.

Jefferson, Thomas. "Inscription for an African Slave." In *The Works of Thomas Jefferson*, Federal Edition, vol. 2. New York: G. P. Putnam's Sons, 1904–1905.

Johnson, Samuel. *London: A Poem*. London: R. Dodsley, 1738. Edited by Jack Lynch. http://andromeda.rutgers.edu/~jlynch/Texts/london.html.

Jones, Adam. "Auditors Criticized for Role in Financial Crisis." *Financial Times*, March 30, 2011.

————. "Big Four Rivals Welcome Audit Shake-Up." *Financial Times*, February 2, 2013.

Jouanique, Pierre. "Three Medieval Merchants: Francesco di Marco Datini, Jacques Coeur, and Benedetto Cotrugli." *Accounting, Business and Financial History* 6, no. 3 (1996): 261–275.

Journal of the First Session of the Second House of Representatives of the Commonwealth of Pennsylvania. Philadelphia: Francis Bailey and Thomas Lang, 1791.

Joyce, Philip G. *Congressional Budget Office: Honest Numbers, Power, and Policymaking*. Washington, DC: Georgetown University Press, 2011.

Kadane, Matthew. *The Watchful Clothier: The Life of an Eighteenth-Century Protestant Capitalist*. New Haven, CT: Yale University Press, 2013.

Kamen, Henry. *Philip of Spain*. New Haven, CT: Yale University Press, 1997.

Kaplan, Steven L. *Bread, Politics, and Political Economy in the Reign of Louis XIV*. 2 vols. The Hague: Martinus Nijhof, 1976.

Keister, D. A. "The Public Accountant." *The Book-Keeper* 8, no. 6 (1896): 21–23.

Kitman, Marvin. *George Washington's Expense Account*. New York: Grove Press, 1970.

Koehn, Nancy F. "Josiah Wedgwood and the First Industrial Revolution." In *Creating Modern Capitalism: How Entrepreneurs, Companies, and Countries Triumphed in Three Industrial Revolutions*, edited by Thomas K. McCraw, 19–48. Cambridge, MA: Harvard University Press, 1997.

Labaton, Stephen. "Bush Tries to Shrink S.E.C. Raise Intended for Corporate Cleanup." *New York Times*, October 19, 2002.

Landes, David. *The Wealth and Poverty of Nations: Why Some Are Rich and Some Are Poor*. New York: W. W. Norton, 1998.

La Roncière, Charles de, and Paul M. Bondois. *Catalogue des Manuscrits de la Collection des Mélanges Colbert*. Paris: Éditions Ernest Leroux, 1920.

Lee, Geoffrey Alan. "The Coming of Age of Double Entry: The Giovanni Farolfi Ledger of 1299–1300." *Accounting Historians Journal* 4, no. 2 (1977): 79–95.

———. "The Development of Italian Bookkeeping 1211–1300." *Abacus* 9, no. 2 (1973): 137–155.

———. "The Oldest European Account Book: A Florentine Bank Ledger of 1211." *Nottingham Medieval Studies* 16, no. 1 (1972): 28–60.

Legay, Marie-Laure. "The Beginnings of Public Management: Administrative Science and Political Choices in the Eighteenth Century in France, Austria, and the Austrian Netherlands." *Journal of Modern History* 81, no. 2 (2009): 253–293.

———, ed. *Dictionnaire historique de la comptabilité publique 1500–1850*. Rennes: Presses Universitaires de Rennes, 2010.

Lemarchand, Yannick. "Accounting, the State and Democracy: A Long-Term Perspective on the French Experiment, 1716–1967," *LEMNA* WP 2010 43 (2010): 1–26

———."Comptabilité, discipline, et finances publiques: Une expérience d'introduction de la partie double sous la Régence." *Politiques et Management Public* 18, no. 2 (2000): 93–118.

———. "Introducing Double-Entry Bookkeeping in Public Finance." *Accounting, Business, and Financial History* 9 (1999): 225–254.

Lesger, Clé. *The Rise of the Amsterdam Market and Information Exchange: Merchants, Commercial Expansion and Change in the Spatial Economy of the Low Countries c.1550–1630*. Translated by J. C. Grayson. London: Ashgate, 2006.

Littleton, A. C. *Accounting Evolution to 1900*. New York: American Institute, 1933.

Littleton, Charles, and Basil S. Yamey, eds. *Studies in the History of Accounting*. New York: Arno Press, 1978.

Littleton, Charles, and V. K. Zimmerman. *Accounting Theory: Continuity and Change*. Englewood Cliffs, NJ: Prentice Hall, 1962.

Locke, John. *Two Treatises of Government*. Edited by Peter Laslett. Cambridge: Cambridge University Press, 1988.

Louis XIV. *Mémoires for the Instruction of the Dauphin*. Translated and edited by Paul Sonnino. New York: Free Press, 1970.

Lovett, A. W. "The Castillian Bankruptcy of 1575." *Historical Journal* 23, no. 4 (1980): 899–911.

———. "Juan de Ovando and the Council of Finance (1573–1575)." *Historical Journal* 15, no. 1 (1972): 1–21.

Lynch, Jack. *The Hispanic World in Crisis and Change, 1598–1700*. Oxford: Oxford University Press, 1992.

Machiavelli. *The Discourses*. Translated by Leslie J. Walker. London: Penguin Books, 1983.

Madox, Thomas. *The Anqituities and the History of the Exchequer of the Kings of England*. London: Matthews and Knaplock, 1711.

Mair, John. *Book-Keeping Methodiz'd; or A Methodical Treatise of Merchant-Accompts, According to the Italian Form*. Edinburgh: W. Sands, A. Murray, and J. Cochran, 1765.

Malthus, Thomas. *An Essay on the Principle of Population*. New York: Oxford University Press, 1999.

Manzoni, Domenico. *Quaderno doppio col suo giornale*. Venice: Comin de Tridino, 1540.

Marshall, Richard K. *The Local Merchants of Prato: Small Entrepreneurs in the Late Medieval Economy*. Baltimore: Johns Hopkins University Press, 1999.

Martinelli, Alvaro. "The Ledger of Cristianus Lomellinus and Dominicus De Garibaldo, Stewards of the City of Genoa (1340–41)." *Abacus* 19, no. 2 (1983): 83–118.

Martines, Lauro. *The Social World of the Florentine Humanists 1390–1460*. Princeton, NJ: Princeton University Press, 1963.

Mathon de la Cour, Charles-Joseph. *Collection de Compte-Rendu, pièces authentiques, états et tableaux, concernant les finances de France depuis 1758 jusqu'en 1787*. Paris: Chez Cuchet, Chez Gatteu, 1788.

Maynwaring, Arthur. *A Letter to a Friend Concerning the Publick Debts, particularly that of the Navy*. London, 1711.

McCraw, Thomas K. *The Founders and Finance: How Hamilton, Gallatin, and Other Immigrants Forged a New Economy*. Cambridge, MA: Harvard University Press, 2012.

McKendrick, Neil. "Josiah Wedgwood and Cost Accounting in the Industrial Revolution." *Economic History Review* 23, no. 1 (1970): 45–67.

Melcher, Richard. "Where Are the Accountants?" *BusinessWeek*, October 5, 1998.

Melis, Federigo. *Documenti per la storia economica dei secoli XIII–XVI*. Firenze: Olschki, 1972.

———. *Storia della ragioneria*. Bologna: Cesare Zuffi, 1950.

Meyer, Jean. *Colbert*. Paris: Hachette, 1981.

Mierzejewski, Alfred C. *Most Valuable Asset of the Reich: A History of the German National Railway.* 2 vols. Chapel Hill: University of North Carolina Press, 2000.

Mignet, François-Auguste-Marie-Alexis. *History of the French Revolution, from 1789–1814.* London: George Bell and Sons, 1891.

Modelles des Registres Journaux que le Roy, en son Conseil, Veut et ordonne estre tenus par les Receveurs Généraux des Finances, Caissier de leur Caisse commune, Commis aux Recettes générales, Receveurs des Tailles, Et autres Receveurs des Impositions ... Execution de l'Edit du mois du juin 1716. des Déclarations des 10 Juin 1716. 4 Octobre & 7 Décembre 1723. Et de l'Arrest du Conseil du 15 Mars 1724 portant Réglement pour la tenuë desdits Registres-Journaux. 1724.

Molho, Anthony. "Cosimo de' Medici: *Pater Patriae* or *Padrino?*" In *The Italian Renaissance: The Essential Readings,* edited by Paula Findlen, 64–90. Malden, MA: Wiley-Blackwell, 2002.

———. *Firenze nel quattrocento.* Rome: Edizioni di Storia e Letteratura, 2006.

Monks, Robert A. G., and Nell Minow. *Corporate Governance.* New York: John Wiley & Sons, 2008.

Montaigne, Michel de. *The Complete Essays.* Translated by M. A. Screech. London: Penguin, 2003.

Moody, John. *How to Analyze Railroad Reports.* New York: Analyses, 1912.

Morineau, Michel. "Or brésilien et gazettes hollandaises." *Revue d'Histoire Moderne et Contemporaine* 25, no. 1 (1978): 3–30.

Morris, Robert. *A general View of Receipts and Expenditures of Public Monies, by Authority from the Superintendent of Finance, from the Time of his entering on the Administration of the Finances, to the 31st December, 1781.* Philadelphia: Register's Office, 1782.

———. *A State of the Receipts and Expenditures of Public Monies upon Warrants from the Superintendent of Finance, from the 1st of January, 1782, to the 1st of January 1783.* Philadelphia: Register's Office, 1783.

Murat, Inès. *Colbert.* Translated by Robert Francis Cook and Jeannie Van Asselt. Charlottesville: University Press of Virginia, 1984.

Musson, A. E., and Eric Robinson. *Science and Technology in the Industrial Revolution.* Manchester, UK: Manchester University Press, 1969.

The Necessary Discourse. 1622.

Necker, Jacques. *Compte rendu au roi.* Paris: Imprimerie du Cabinet du Roi, 1781.

———. *De l'administration des finances de la France.* 1784.

———. *Nouveaux éclaircissemens par M. Necker.* Paris: Hôtel de Thou, 1788.

———. *Sur le Compte Rendu au Roi en 1781. Nouveaux éclaircissemens par M. Necker.* Paris: Hôtel de Thou, 1788.

Nicholson, John. *Accounts of Pennsylvania.* Philadelphia: Comptroller-General's Office, 1785.

Nikitin, Marc. "The Birth of a Modern Public Sector Accounting System in France and Britain and the Influence of Count Mollien." *Accounting History* 6, no. 1 (2001): 75–101.

North, Roger. *Gentleman Accomptant*. London: E. Curll, 1714.

Ogle, Vanessa. *Contesting Time: The Global Struggle for Uniformity and Its Unintended Consequences, 1870s–1940s*. Cambridge, MA: Harvard University Press, forthcoming.

Oldroyd, David. "The Role of Accounting in Public Expenditure and Monetary Policy in the First Century AD Roman Empire." *Accounting Historians Journal* 22, no. 2 (December 1995): 117–129.

Origo, Iris. *The Merchant of Prato: Daily Life in a Medieval Italian City*. London: Penguin Books, 1992.

Pâris La Montagne, Claude. *Traitté des Administrations des Recettes et des Dépenses du Royaume*. 1733. Archives Nationales, 1005, 2.

Parker, Geoffrey. *The Grand Strategy of Philip II*. New Haven, CT: Yale University Press, 1998.

Parks, Tim. *Medici Money: Banking, Metaphysics and Art in Fifteenth-Century Florence*. New York: W. W. Norton, 2006.

Parrott, David. *Richelieu's Army: War, Government and Society in France 1624–1642*. Cambridge: Cambridge University Press, 2001.

Paul, Helen. "Limiting the Witch-Hunt: Recovering from the South Sea Bubble." *Past, Present and Policy Conference* 3–4 (2011): 1–12.

Pearce, Edward. *The Great Man: Sir Robert Walpole: Scoundrel, Genius and Britain's First Prime Minister*. London: Jonathan Cape, 2007.

Peden, William. "Thomas Jefferson: The Man as Reflected in His Account Books." *Virginia Quarterly Review* 64, no. 4 (1988): 686–694.

Pepys, Samuel. *Diary of Samuel Pepys*. www.pepysdiary.com.

Peragallo, Edward. *Origin and Evolution of Double Entry Bookkeeping: A Study of Italian Practice from the Fourteenth Century*. New York: American Institute, 1938.

Perrot, Jean-Claude. "Nouveautés: L'économie politique et ses livres." In *L'Histoire de l'édition française*, edited by Roger Chartier and Henri-Jean Martin. Vol. 2, 298–328. Paris: Fayard/Promodis, 1984.

———. *Une histoire intellectuelle de l'économie politique XVIIe–XVIIIe siècle*. Paris: Éditions de l'EHESS, 1992.

Pico della Mirandola, Giovanni. *On the Dignity of Man*. Translated by Charles Glenn Wallis, Paul J. W. Miller, and Douglas Carmichael. Indianapolis, IN: Hackett, 1998.

Plato. *The Republic*. Book 7. Translated by Benjamin Jowett. Oxford: Oxford University Press, 1892.

Pliny the Elder. *Natural History*. Translated by H. Rackham. Cambridge, MA: Loeb Classical Library, 1942.

Plumb, J. H. *Sir Robert Walpole: The Making of a Statesman*. 2 vols. Boston: Houghton Mifflin, 1956.

Pocock, J. G. A. *The Machiavellian Moment: Florentine Political Thought and the Atlantic Republican Tradition*. Princeton, NJ: Princeton University Press, 1975.

Pollard, Sidney. *The Genesis of Modern Management: A Study of the Industrial Revolution in Great Britain*. London: Edward Arnold, 1965.

Pontalis, Antonin Lefèvre. *Vingt années de république parlementaire au dix-septième siècle. Jan de Witt, Grand Pensionnaire de Hollande*. 2 vols. Paris: E. Plon, Nourrit, 1884.

Poole, Stafford. *Juan de Ovando: Governing the Spanish Empire in the Reign of Philip II*. Norman: University of Oklahoma Press, 2004.

Poovey, Mary. *A History of the Modern Fact: Problems of Knowledge in the Sciences of Wealth and Society*. Chicago: University of Chicago Press, 1998.

Popkin, Jeremy. "Pamphlet Journalism at the End of the Old Regime." *Eighteenth-Century Studies* 22, no. 3 (1989): 351–367.

Porter, Theodore M. *Trust in Numbers: The Pursuit of Objectivity in Science and Public Life*. Princeton, NJ: Princeton University Press, 1995.

Previts, Gary John, and Barbara Dubis Merino. *A History of Accountancy in the United States*. Columbus: Ohio State University Press, 1998.

Price, Munro. *Preserving the Monarchy: The Comte de Vergennes 1784–1787*. Cambridge: Cambridge University Press, 1995.

Price, Richard. *Two Tracts on Civil Liberty, the War with America, and the Debts and Finances of the Kingdom with a General Introduction and Supplement*. London: T. Cadell, 1778.

Quattrone, Paolo. "Accounting for God: Accounting and Accountability Practices in the Society of Jesus (Italy, XVI–XVII centuries)." *Accounting Organizations and Society* 29, no. 7 (2004): 647–683.

Rakove, Jack. *Original Meanings: Politics and Ideas in the Making of the Constitution*. New York: Vintage Books, 1997.

———. *Revolutionaries: A New History of the Invention of America*. New York: Houghton Mifflin Harcourt, 2010.

Rappleye, Charles. *Robert Morris: Financier of the American Revolution*. New York: Simon and Schuster, 2010.

Reales Ordenancas y Pragmáticas 1527–1567. Valladolid, Spain: Editorial Lex Nova, 1987.

Reinert, Sophus. *Translating Empire: Emulation and the Origins of Political Economy*. Cambridge, MA: Harvard University Press, 2011.

Richardson, Samuel. *Pamela; or, Virtue Rewarded*. London: Riverton and Osborn, 1741.

Ripley, William Z. "Stop, Look, Listen! The Shareholder's Right to Adequate Information," *Atlantic Monthly*, January 1, 1926.

Robertson, Jeffrey, and Warwick Funnell. "The Dutch East India Company and Accounting for Social Capital at the Dawn of Modern Capitalism 1602–1623." *Accounting Organizations and Society* 37, no. 5 (2012): 342–360.

Roseveare, Henry. *The Treasury, 1660–1870: The Foundations of Control.* London: Allen and Unwin, 1973.

Rothkrug, Lionel. *Opposition to Louis XIV: The Political and Social Origins of the French Enlightenment.* Princeton, NJ: Princeton University Press, 1965.

Rowen, Herbert H. *John de Witt. Grand Pensionary of Holland 1625–1672.* Princeton, NJ: Princeton University Press, 1978.

Rowland, Ingrid D. *The Culture of the High Renaissance: Ancients and Moderns in Sixteenth-Century Rome.* Cambridge: Cambridge University Press, 1998.

Rubenstein, Nicolai. *The Government of Florence Under the Medici 1434–1494.* Oxford: Oxford University Press, 1998.

Santini, Pietro. "Frammenti di un libro di banchieri fiorentini scritto in volgare nel 1211." *Giornale storico della litteratura italiana* 10 (1887): 161–177.

Sarjeant, Thomas. *An Introduction to the Counting House.* Philadelphia: Dobson, 1789.

Savary, Jacques. *Le parfait Pégociant.* Paris, 1675.

Say, Jean-Baptiste. *Traité d'économie politique ou simple exposition de la manière dont se forment, se distribuent et se composent les richesses.* Paris: Crapalet, 1803.

Schaffern, Robert W. *The Penitent's Treasury: Indulgences in Latin Christendom, 1175–1375.* Scranton, PA: University of Scranton Press, 2007.

Schama, Simon. *The Embarrassment of Riches: An Interpretation of Dutch Culture in the Golden Age.* 2nd ed. New York: Vintage, 1997.

Schiff, Stacy. *A Great Improvisation: Franklin, France, and the Birth of America.* New York: Henry Holt, 2005.

Schoderbek, Michael P. "Robert Morris and Reporting for the Treasury Under the U.S. Continental Congress." *Accounting Historians Journal* 26, no. 2 (1999): 1–34.

Schumpeter, Joseph A. *History of Economic Analysis.* Edited by Elizabeth Boody Schumpeter. New York: Oxford University Press, 1954.

Seaward, Paul. "Parliament and the Idea of Political Accountability in Early Modern Britain." In *Realities of Representation: State Building in Early Modern Europe and European America,* edited by Maija Jansson, 45–62. New York: Palgrave Macmillan, 2007.

Sebregondi, Ludovica, and Tim Parks, eds. *Money and Beauty: Bankers, Botticelli and the Bonfire of the Vanities.* Florence: Giunti Editore, 2011.

Sévigné, Marie de Rabutin-Chantal. *Lettres de Mme de Sévigné.* Paris: Firmin Didot, 1846.

Shovlin, John. *The Political Economy of Virtue: Luxury, Patriotism, and the Origins of the French Revolution.* Ithaca, NY: Cornell University Press, 2006.

Skinner, Quentin. *The Foundations of Modern Political Thought*. 2 vols. Cambridge: Cambridge University Press, 1978.

Smallwood, Stephanie E. *Saltwater Slavery: A Middle Passage from Africa to American Diaspora*. Cambridge, MA: Harvard University Press, 2008.

Smith, Adam. *An Inquiry into the Nature and Causes of the Wealth of Nations*. Amherst, NY: Prometheus Books, 1991.

Smith, Woodruff D. "The Function of Commercial Centers in the Modernization of European Capitalism: Amsterdam as an Information Exchange in the Seventeenth Century." *Journal of Economic History* 44, no. 4 (1984): 985–1005.

Smyth, Adam. *Autobiography in Early Modern Britain*. Cambridge: Cambridge University Press, 2010.

Snell, Charles. *Accompts for landed-men: or; a plain and easie form which they may observe, in keeping accompts of their estates*. London: Thomas Baker, 1711.

Soll, Jacob. "Accounting for Government: Holland and the Rise of Political Economy in Seventeenth Century Europe." *Journal of Interdisciplinary History* 40, no. 2 (2009): 215–238.

———. *The Information Master: Jean-Baptiste Colbert's Secret State Information System*. Ann Arbor: University of Michigan Press, 2009.

Sombart, Werner. *Der Moderne Kapitalismus*. 6th ed. Leipzig, 1924.

Sonenscher, Michael. *Before the Deluge: Public Debt, Inequality, and the Intellectual Origins of the French Revolution*. Princeton, NJ: Princeton University Press, 2007.

Sorkin, Andrew Ross. "Realities Behind Prosecuting Big Banks." *New York Times*, March 11, 2013.

Soulavie, Jean-Louis. *Mémoires historiques et politiques du règne de Louis XIV*. 6 vols. Paris: Treuttel et Würtz, 1801.

Stallybrass, Peter, Roger Chartier, J. Franklin Mowrey, and Heather Wolfe. "Hamlet's Tables and the Technologies of Writing in Renaissance England." *Shakespeare Quarterly* 55, no. 4 (2004): 379–419.

Stevens, Mark. *The Big Six: The Selling Out of America's Accounting Firms*. New York: Simon and Schuster, 1991.

Stevin, Simon. *Livre de Compte de Prince à la manière de l'Italie*. Leiden: J. Paedts Jacobsz, 1608.

———. *Vorstelicke Bouckhouding op de Italiaensche wyse*. Leiden: Ian Bouwensz, 1607.

Stourm, René. *Les finances de l'Ancien Régime et de la Révolution. Origins du système actuel*. 2 vols. New York: Burt Franklin, 1968.

Suetonius. *The Twelve Caesars*. Translated by Robert Graves. Harmondsworth, UK: Penguin Books, 1982.

Sullivan, Ceri. *The Rhetoric of Credit: Merchants in Early Modern Writing*. Madison, WI: Associated University Presses, 2002.

Taibbi, Matt. "The People vs. Goldman Sachs," *Rolling Stone*, May 11, 2011.

Ten Have, O. "Simon Stevin of Bruges." In *Studies in the History of Accounting*, edited by A. C. Littleton and B. S. Yamey, 236–246. New York: Arno Press, 1978.

Thomas, Keith. "Numeracy in Early Modern England." *Transactions of the Royal Historical Society* 37 (1987): 103–132.

Thoreau, Henry David. *Walden or Life in the Woods*. Mansfield Centre, CT: Martino, 2009.

Toffler, Barbara Ley. *Final Accounting: Ambition, Greed and the Fall of Arthur Andersen*. New York: Crown, 2003.

Torrance, John. "Social Class and Bureaucratic Innovation: The Commissioners for Examining the Public Accounts 1780–1787." *Past and Present* 78 (1978): 56–81.

Tracy, James D. *A Financial Revolution in the Habsburg Netherlands: Renten and Renteniers in the County of Holland, 1515–1565*. Berkeley: University of California Press, 1985.

A Translation of the Charter of the Dutch East India Company (Verenigde Oostindische Compagnie, or VOC). Translated by Peter Reynders. Canberra: Map Division of the Australasian Hydrographic Society, 2009.

Trenchard, John. *An Examination and Explanation of the South Sea Company's Scheme for Taking in the Publick Debts. Shewing, That it is Not Encouraging to Those Who Shall Become Proprietors of the Company, at Any Advanced Price. And That it is Against the Interest of Those Proprietors Who Shall Remain with Their Stock Till They are Paid Off by the Government, That the Company Should Make Annually Great Dividend Than Their Profits Will Warrant. With Some National Considerations and Useful Observations*. London, 1720.

Trenchard, John, and Thomas Gordon. *Cato's Letter's, or, Essays on Liberty, Civil and Religious, and Other Important Subjects*. Edited and annotated by Ronald Hamowy. 2 vols. Indianapolis, IN: Liberty Fund, 1995.

Twain, Mark. Letter to *The San Francisco Alta California*, May 26, 1867.

Ungar, Miles. *Magnifico: The Brilliant Life and Violent Times of Lorenzo de' Medici*. New York: Simon and Schuster, 2008.

U.S. Congress. *Securities Act of 1933*. Washington, DC, 1933. www.sec.gov /about/laws/sa33.pdf.

U.S. District Court. *Securities and Exchange Commission v. David F. Myers*. New York and Washington, DC, 2002. www.sec.gov/litigation/complaints /comp17753.htm.

Vasari, Giorgio. *The Lives of the Artists*. Translated by Julia Conaway Bonadella and Peter Bonadella. Oxford: Oxford University Press, 1991.

Vickerey, Amanda. "His and Hers: Gender, Consumption and Household Accounting in Eighteenth-Century England." *Past and Present* 1 (2006): S12–S38.

Villain, Jean. *Mazarin, homme d'argent*. Paris: Club du Livre d'Histoire, 1956.

Vine, Angus. "Francis Bacon's Composition Books." *Transactions of the Cambridge Bibliographical Society* 14, no. 1 (2008): 1–31.

Wagenaar, Lodewijk J. "Les mécanismes de la prospérité." In *Amsterdam XVIIe siècle. Marchands et philosophes: les bénéfices de la tolerance*, edited by Henri Méchoulan. Paris: Editions Autrement, 1993.

Walpole, Robert. *A State of the Five and Thirty Millions mention'd in the Report of a Committee of the House of Commons.* London: E. Baldwin, 1712.

Warburg, Aby. "Francesco Sassetti's Last Injunctions to His Sons." In *The Renewal of Pagan Antiquity: Contributions to the Cultural History of the European Renaissance*, translated by David Britt, 222–264. Los Angeles: Getty Research Institute, 1999.

Washington, George. Facsimile of the *Accounts of G. Washington with the United States, Commencing June 1775, and Ending June 1783, Comprehending a Space of 8 Years.* Washington, DC: Treasury Department, 1833. http://memory.loc.gov/ammem/gwhtml/gwseries5.html.

Watt, James. *James Watt to his father, 21 July 1755.* James Watt Papers, MS 4/11, letters to father, 1754–74, Birmingham City Library.

Weber, Max. *General Economic History.* Translated by Frank Hyneman Knight. New York: Free Press, 1950.

———. *The Protestant Ethic and the Spirit of Capitalism.* Translated by Talcott Parsons. New York: Charles Scribner's Sons, 1958.

———. *The Theory of Social and Economic Organizations.* Translated and edited by A. M. Henderson and Talcott Parsons. New York: Free Press, 1947.

Wedgwood, Josiah. *Correspondence of Josiah Wedgwood.* Edited by Katherine Eufemia Farrer. 3 vols. Cambridge: Cambridge University Press, 2010.

White, Eugene Nelson. "The French Revolution and the Politics of Government Finance, 1770–1815." *Journal of Economic History* 55, no. 2 (1995): 227–255.

Willoughby, William F., Westel W. Willoughby, and Samuel McCune Lindsay. *The System of Financial Administration of Great Britain: A Report.* New York: D. Appleton, 1917.

Witt, Ronald. "What Did Giovanni Read and Write? Literacy in Early Renaissance Florence." *I Tatti Studies* 6 (1995): 83–114.

Woloch, Isser. *The New Régime: Transformations of the French Civic Order, 1789–1820s.* New York: W. W. Norton, 1994.

Yamey, Basil S. *Art and Accounting.* New Haven, CT: Yale University Press, 1989.

———. "Fifteenth and Sixteenth Century Manuscripts on the Art of Bookkeeping." *Journal of Accounting Research* 5, no. 1 (1967): 51–76.

———. "Scientific Bookkeeping and the Rise of Capitalism." *Economic History Review* 1, no. 2–3 (1949): 99–113.

Ympyn De Christoffels, Yan. *Nieuwe instructie ende bewijs der looffelijcker consten des Rekenboecks. Ghedruckt . . . in . . . Antwerpen: Ten versoecke ende aenlegghene van Anna Swinters, der weduwen wylen Jan Ympyns . . . duer Gillis Copyns van Diest.* Antwerp, 1543.

Zandvliet, Kees. *Maurits Prins van Oranje [Exhibition catalogue Rijksmuseum].* Amsterdam: Rijksmuseum Amsterdam/Waanders Uitgevers Zwolle, 2000.

Zeff, Stephen A. "The SEC Rules Historical Cost Accounting: 1934 to the 1970s." *Accounting and Business Research* 37 (2007): S1–S14.

INDEX